D0512627

THE CHANGING SOCIAL STRUCTURE
OF ENGLAND AND WALES

INTERNATIONAL LIBRARY OF SOCIOLOGY

Founded by Karl Mannheim
Editor: John Rex, University of Warwick

A Catalogue of the books available in the INTERNATIONAL LIBRARY OF SOCIOLOGY and other series of Social Science books published by Routledge & Kegan Paul will be found at the end of this volume.

THE
CHANGING
SOCIAL STRUCTURE
OF ENGLAND
AND WALES
1871–1961

by
David C. Marsh

ROUTLEDGE & KEGAN PAUL

LONDON AND HENLEY

First published 1958

*This revised edition was published in 1965
by Routledge & Kegan Paul Limited
39 Store Street
London. WC1E 7DD and
Broadway House, Newtown Road
Henley-on-Thames
Oxon. RG9 1EN*

*Reprinted in 1967 and 1971
First published as a paperback in 1977*

*Printed in Great Britain by
Cox and Wyman Limited
London, Fakenham and Reading*

*ISBN 0 7100 3373 7 (c)
ISBN 0 7100 8464 1 (p)*

CONTENTS

Acknowledgements   *page* xi

Preface   xiii

Introduction   1

I   The patterns of population growth in England and
     Wales   5

II   The sex, age and marital distribution of the
     population   19

III The family   40

IV   Regional variations in the composition and
     distribution of the population   59

V   The industrial and occupational distribution of the
     population   111

VI   Occupational and other associations   165

VII Social classes and educational opportunities   195

VIII The changing patterns of social problems   223

Conclusion   262

Index   271

LIST OF TABLES

                                                                 page

1 The population of England and Wales in selected Census
   years   6
2 Population increase in England and Wales in selected
   30-year periods   7
3 Natural increase in England and Wales, 1871–1961   11
4 England and Wales, natural increase per thousand of
   population in selected periods   11
5 Net gain or loss by migration in England and Wales,
   1871–1961   13
6 The movement of population in England and Wales;
   natural increase and net gain or loss by migration, 1871–
   1961   13
7 Sex ratios in England and Wales at selected Censuses –
   females per thousand males by age-groups   20
8 The age distribution of the population of England and
   Wales at the Censuses of 1871, 1901, 1931, 1961   24
9 The young, the working age and the elderly per hundred
   of the total population of England and Wales in 1871,
   1901, 1931, 1951 and 1961   25
10 The proportion of males and females aged 65 and over in
   each quinquennial age-group in England and Wales at
   the Censuses of 1871, 1901, 1951 and 1961   29
11 Marital distribution of the population of England and
   Wales at the Censuses of 1871, 1901, 1921, 1931 and 1961   34
12 Proportions of the population of England and Wales
   single, married, widowed and divorced at the Censuses of
   1871, 1901, 1921, 1931 and 1961   34
13 Percentage distribution of the widowed population of
   England and Wales by age-groups at the Censuses of 1871,
   1931 and 1961   38
14 Widowed persons aged 65 and over per cent of the population aged 65 and over at the Censuses of 1871, 1931,
   1951 and 1961, England and Wales   39
15 Changes in the distribution of families by size, England
   and Wales and Great Britain   43

List of Tables

page

16 Married women aged under 50 at the Census of 1951, size of family (live-born children) by duration of marriage and age-group, England and Wales   43

17 Percentage distribution of private households in England and Wales by social class, size and dependent children in 1951   51

18 Primary Family Unit households in England and Wales at the Census of 1951   52

19 Population growth and sex distribution in England and in Wales as shown by the Censuses of 1871, 1901, 1931, 1951 and 1961   60

20 Age and marital distribution of the populations of England and Wales at the Censuses of 1871, 1901, 1931, 1951 and 1961   61

21 Density of population in England and Wales at the Censuses of 1871, 1931, 1951 and 1961   64

22 Density of town populations in England and Wales as recorded by the Census of 1901   69

23 Numbers of towns in England and Wales with population over 50,000 in 1871, 1901, 1931, 1951 and 1961   71

24 Population changes in selected towns, 1901–61, due allowance having been made for boundary changes   73

25 The size of county populations in England and Wales, 1901–51   80

26 Size of counties in England and Wales by area in statute acres (land and inland water) 1951   82

27 Percentage increase and decrease of population in the counties of England and Wales in the intercensal periods 1901–31, 1911–31 and 1931–51   83

28 Percentage of enumerated persons born within the county of enumeration at the Censuses of 1901, 1931 and 1951   90

29 Selected counties – distribution of population according to county and country of birth, 1931 and 1951   93

30 The size of county populations in England and Wales at the census of 1951 and 1961   96

31 Percentage increase and decrease of population in the counties of England and Wales 1901–31 and 1931–61   98

32 Population growth in the conurbations of England, 1871–1961   106

33 Urban and rural populations of England and Wales, 1901, 1931, 1939, 1951 and 1961   108

List of Tables

page

34 Occupations of males and females aged 10 years and over in England and Wales at the Censuses of 1881 and 1901   118

35 The occupations of males and females aged 14 and over at the Census of 1931 and aged 15 and over in 1951 – England and Wales   135

36 Distribution of occupied persons by age-groups in England and Wales at the Censuses of 1901, 1931 and 1951   149

37 Occupational groups in which 20 per cent or more of the occupied persons were aged 55 years and over at the Censuses of 1901, 1931 and 1951, England and Wales   150

38 Industrial status of the occupied population of England and Wales at the Censuses of 1921, 1931 and 1951   153

39 The Occupations of males and females in England and Wales at the Census of 1961   156

40 Distribution of occupied persons by age-groups in England and Wales, 1951 and 1961   161

41 Employment status of the economically active population of England and Wales at the Censuses of 1951 and 1961   163

42 Number of Trade Unions and membership (at the end of each year) in 1896, 1906, 1920, 1930, 1941, 1951 and 1961 in the United Kingdom   168

43 Co-operative Retail Societies, number of societies, of members and sales in 1901, 1921, 1931, 1951 and 1961, Great Britain   177

44 Political representation in the House of Commons as a result of the General Elections of 1906, 1923, 1935, 1945, 1951, 1955, 1959 and 1961.   182

45 Buildings certified to the Registrar-General as meeting-places for religious worship in England and Wales, 1921, 1950 and 1962   188

46 Social class distribution of occupied and retired males in England and Wales at the Censuses of 1931, 1951 and 1961   198

47 Social class and socio-economic distribution of private households in England and Wales classified according to the social class of the head of the household at the Census of 1951   200

48 Destination of school-leavers aged 14 and over in England and Wales during the year ended 31st July, 1952 and aged 15 and over, 1960–61   214

49 University students in Great Britain, 1921–62   218

50 Deaths in England and Wales from certain causes in 1837 and in 1937   229

List of Tables

page

51 Indictable offences known to the police in England and
Wales, 1900–61   242

52 The most common offences against property with violence
known to the police in England and Wales, 1900–61   244

53 The most common offences against the person known to
the police in England and Wales, 1900–61   247

54 Indictable offences and offenders in England and Wales
in selected years   250

55 Percentage of persons found guilty of indictable offences
in England and Wales by age and sex, 1938, 1951 and
1961   250

56 Persons found guilty of non-indictable offences in England
and Wales, 1938–61, by age and sex   252

57 Number of persons found guilty of non-indictable offences
in England and Wales in 1938, 1951 and 1961 by type of
offence   254

58 Number of young persons found guilty of indictable
offences in England and Wales – all Courts – in 1938,
1948, 1951 and 1961   258

59 Boys and girls found guilty per hundred thousand by sex
and age group, 1938, 1951 and 1961   258

ACKNOWLEDGEMENTS

I AM indebted to the following for permission to quote from the books and reports as shown:

The Controller of Her Majesty's Stationery Office in respect of the Reports of the Censuses of Great Britain; the Statistical Reviews of the Registrar-General and other reports of the General Register Office; the *Annual Abstract of Statistics*; *Britain: an Official Hand-book*; the *Handbook of Industrial Relations*; the Annual Reports of the Ministries of Education, Health, Labour and National Service, Pensions and National Insurance; the *Criminal Statistics*; Reports of the Children's Department of the Home Office; the Reports of the Commissioners of Inland Revenue, and of the University Grants Committee; and of other Government publications acknowledged in the text.

The Reader's Digest Association Ltd., for *The Communication of Ideas* by T. Cauter and J. S. Downham.

C. A. Watts and Co. Ltd., for *Social Change in S. West Wales* by T. Brennan, E. W. Cooney and H. Pollins.

Jonathan Cape for *The Future of Socialism* by C. A. R. Crosland. The Oxford University Press for *Survey of the Social Structure of England and Wales* by A. Carr-Saunders and D. Caradog Jones.

I am extremely grateful to Mr. John Boreham, the Chief Statistician at the General Register Office and his colleagues who have unfailingly and most courteously answered the many questions I have raised with them concerning Census data.

PREFACE

THE first edition of this book, published in 1958, was so well received and appeared to meet the needs of so many students that I have been encouraged to bring it up to date. That is to say to extend the period covered from 1871 to 1961 without altering fundamentally the topics dealt with in the first edition. The only major alteration is that I have excluded the chapter on the distribution of wealth partly because it was in any case far from satisfactory and there are now a number of specialized studies of this subject available.

The main object of this book, therefore, as it was in the first edition, is to introduce the student and the general reader to the maze of social statistics, which in recent years have become available, concerning the social structure of England and Wales. The emphasis throughout is on applied or descriptive statistics and a knowledge of statistical techniques on the part of the reader is not assumed, therefore those (and they seem to be many) who have an instinctive dislike of mathematics need not be deterred from following the attempt which has been made to analyse the changing social structure with the aid of social statistics.

Statistical data can now be obtained from a great variety of sources, but it is the diversity and wide range of possible sources which all too often prevent the student and the well-informed citizen from making the attempt to add to their knowledge of the changing social structure. Most of us know that a Census of population is regularly taken in this country, but how many of us are aware of the wealth of information which is to be found in the official reports of the Census? Most of us know that nowadays there are a large number of Central Government Departments which are concerned with regulating factors of social and economic policy, but how many of us know that they publish annual reports containing valuable information relevant for a better understanding of the social structure, and above all how many of us have the time or inclination to read them, and if we do can we be sure of interpreting the data accurately?

It is, in part, as a guide to some of the relevant sources and as

Preface

an aid to the interpretation of the available information that this book is directed, and in effect I have tried to set up a series of signposts which indicate the present state of our knowledge (or more commonly our lack of knowledge) of the changing social structure.

One person cannot hope to examine, analyse and report on such a vast field of inquiry and produce a definitive study; no claim to completeness is made, but I have tried to select those aspects which seem to me to have undergone significant changes in modern times, and to illustrate the problems involved in measuring changes over time. I have deliberately emphasized throughout the book the difficulties and problems which confront anyone who attempts to measure such features of the social structure as I have selected, not because I want to create the impression that such tasks are especially onerous (as indeed they are), but because it seems to me essential that far more attention should be given to the development of methods of measuring social phenomena than is apparent at present.

Wherever practicable I have presented a great deal of the statistical data in (which I hope are) easily understood tables, but in compressing a mass of data into a comparatively simple table I may well have made errors of omission and/or commission and I would be grateful to any reader who detects obvious errors and informs me.

In making this study I have had of necessity to examine a very large quantity of official reports, journals, pamphlets and other books, and those which I am conscious of having quoted from, referred to or been influenced by in any way I have listed separately; if, however, there is anyone to whom I have not made acknowledgement I do so now with grateful thanks and an apology.

There are numerous colleagues and friends who in the course of discussion (often on matters unrelated to the topics in this book) have contributed advice from which I have benefited and to them I give my thanks. To my wife whose comments have been most helpful I am especially indebted and to Mrs. M. King who typed so efficiently the manuscript in her very limited spare time I am extremely grateful. Any errors, omissions or imperfections are, of course, mine alone.

DAVID C. MARSH

Nottingham, July, 1965.

INTRODUCTION

'THE social structure' is a phrase which may be, and often is, defined in a variety of different ways, but in this study it is confined to those aspects of social life associated with the composition, distribution and divisions of the population which are capable of quantitative measurement. This restrictive interpretation can be justified because the pattern of population growth and the manner in which individuals divide, or are divided, into families, educational, occupational, religious, political and other associations or groups constitute a major part of the social structure of any complex society. In England and Wales significant changes appear to have occurred in recent years in many of these factors and it is with the measurable changes that this book is concerned.

England and Wales have been chosen rather than Great Britain or the United Kingdom because Scotland and Northern Ireland are distinct entities whose social structures may well be quite different from those of England and Wales. A valid case could be argued for separate treatment of Wales, but, until 1954, it was unusual for official statistics (on which this study largely relies) to be made available in which Wales could be identified apart from England.[1] On some aspects (see particularly Chapter IV) Wales is treated as a separate entity, but there are others on which it is not possible even to consider England and Wales together because data is available only for the United Kingdom or Great Britain. Where references are perforce made to the United Kingdom and/or Great Britain then these extensions of the field of study are clearly indicated.

The social structure is continually changing but the rate of

[1] The first issue of a digest of Welsh statistics was made in 1954 and covered the years 1938 and 1945 to 1953 in relation to most of the information provided. Therefifter it is intended to publish annually statistics relating to Wales and Monmouthshire in conjunction with the *Annual Report of Government Action in Wales and Monmouthshire*, see *Digest of Welsh Statistics*, No. 1, H.M.S.O., 1954.

Introduction

change in the last quarter of the nineteenth and the first half of the twentieth centuries was, probably, faster than at any other period in modern times, and it is since 1871 that social statistics of the kind required to provide forms of measurement of changes have been most fully developed. For these and other reasons the years 1871 to 1961 inclusive have been used as the broad limits for this study, but too much emphasis should not be laid on precise periods of time. Social change is a continuous process and there are variations not only from decade to decade but from year to year and even within a year. Starting-points are often impossible to determine and the end of many changes which may well have begun long before 1871 still cannot be foreseen. Nevertheless a period of time must be accepted and in the main an attempt has been made to analyse the changes which have occurred between 1871 and 1961.

There are some features for which reliable information over periods of time is not available, there are others where useful data can be found only for the very recent past. Inevitably, therefore, some sectors of the social structure are examined only for the changes which occurred between 1921 or 1931 and 1961 whilst others are considered for the full ninety years. Where it is thought to be useful to provide some indication of data relating to years before 1871 or after 1961 for purposes of comparison or to ensure completeness these have been included. On all the aspects treated in this book an attempt has been made to ensure that wherever practicable the years 1931–61 are examined in some detail.

The limitation of this study to a specified period has the danger that it may be regarded as a social history of modern England and Wales. I am not a professional historian therefore it has not been my intention that this book should in any way make a contribution to our knowledge of modern history, on the other hand I believe that an understanding of the past is essential to an understanding of the present and that it would be extremely difficult to recognize the existing features of our social structure without an adequate background knowledge of our historical development.

The sources of data available on England and Wales are now more plentiful than ever before in recorded history, and are to be found in the main in the official publications of the Registrar-

Introduction

General (who first assumed control of the Census, which provides so much of the essential data on the social structure, in 1841), the Central Statistical Office (established in 1940) and other Central Government Departments and recognized national organizations. The plethora of sources does not necessarily mean that all the information which is required for complete understanding is readily available, and there is the disadvantage that all too often information on one subject is provided in such diverse ways that it is difficult to believe that it does in fact deal with the same subject. It is perhaps, inevitable that each source should provide data in its own way and for the period which those responsible for the compilation deem to be appropriate, but the confusion and inadequacy of knowledge which follows are not conducive to a better understanding of the facts. It is, in part, for this reason that an attempt has been made to bring together information from a variety of sources in order to provide a guide to the main features of the changes in modern times. Wherever possible references are given to the diversity of sources and comments are offered on their interpretation, but it must be admitted that there are still many aspects about which we know all too little.

No more could be attempted in this book than the setting up of signposts which give some indication of the changes which have occurred in (what appear to me to be) some of the fundamental features of our social structure; the instruments used to establish those signposts are social statistics, but they give no more than the bare outline of the scene and it is their interpretation and analysis which fills in the details. The interpretation and analysis of facts and figures relating to one's fellows must inevitably involve subjective judgements, but as far as it is humanly possible an attempt has been made to avoid personal prejudices and preferences so that the facts (limited though they may be on occasion) may speak for themselves. That does not mean that this book is confined to the recording of a collection of facts from figures; what I have tried to do is to present the relevant data available from a variety of statistical sources in a coherent form and above all to encourage criticism of the adequacy of the existing sources. We must know what data is available, how it is collected, what it purports to describe, and the limits of its applicability before we can assess its limitations, and that is the way in which the data relating to the social structure has been examined in this study.

The measurement of social facts and phenomena is by no means an exact science and all too often 'facts' (or more commonly what are assumed to be facts) are accepted at their face value, or inflated (or deflated as the case may be) to suit the purposes of those who use them. It is, unfortunately, very easy to collect information, clothe it with an air of respectability and certainty by labelling it 'statistical', and use it as a means to justify particular ends, and in the realm of human affairs it is not uncommon for unwarranted generalizations to be made from limited statistical data. I have attempted to provide such facts as are available in an objective form and to show the necessity for considering each facet of the social structure not in isolation but in the perspective of the whole. If this book becomes a useful work of reference it will fulfil one of the aims of its author and if it stimulates a more critical appreciation of the inadequate state of our knowledge of the changing social structure of England and Wales it will have achieved its main purpose.

CHAPTER I

THE PATTERNS OF POPULATION GROWTH IN ENGLAND AND WALES

THE development of the social structure of any country depends to a considerable extent on changes in the rate and manner of population growth and certainly in England and Wales, since the beginning of the nineteenth century, fluctuations in the patterns of growth have played a vital part. Our knowledge of the change in the size, composition and distribution of the population at any one point in time is by no means exact, but, we can at least see the way in which there have been broad changes in the patterns of growth from the regular censuses of population.

The first official Census of population in England and Wales was taken in 1801 and thereafter, apart from 1941, an official count of the population has been made in the first year of every decade.[1] The censuses up to 1871 were by no means as accurate or as comprehensive as those which have been taken in the twentieth century yet they are obviously the only reasonably accurate sources of information available on the over-all growth of population. From the censuses it is apparent that there was a greater growth in the nineteenth than in the twentieth century, as shown in Table 1.

The total population revealed by the Census is not necessarily the absolute total number of persons who belong to England and Wales in any one year. The Census covers the 'home'

---

[1] For a brief account of the method of Census taking and of the changes in its scope in modern times see *Census Reports of Great Britain 1801–1931*, Guides to Official Sources, No. 2, H.M.S.O. The need for a smaller interval between censuses has now been recognised and in 1966 a census is to be taken on a sample of the population.

population, that is living persons actually in this country at the precise moment (usually one minute to midnight) of the Census day, and therefore it provides no more than a 'snapshot' at

TABLE I

The population of England and Wales in selected Census years

Year	Pop. in thousands		1851–1901	1901–51	1861–1911	1911–1961
1801	8,893	Absolute				
1831	13,897	increase				
1851	17,928	(000's)	14,600	11,230	16,004	10,035
1861	20,066					
1871	22,712	Percentage	%	%	%	%
1891	29,003	increase	81	34	80	28
1901	32,528					
1911	36,070					
1921	37,887					
1931	39,952					
1951	43,758					
1961	46,105					

that one point in time.[1] Estimates of the size of the population at other times are now regularly compiled and published, but to determine the pattern of growth with a reasonable degree of accuracy we must rely on successive censuses, and from these it is apparent that there have been significant changes in the rate of growth in modern times.

Changes in the rate of growth of the population of Great Britain in the nineteenth and first half of the twentieth centuries were the subject of intensive investigation by the Royal Commission on Population,[2] whose members examined in particular the factors which contributed to the marked reduction in the rate of growth in the twentieth century. It is, of course, the slowing down of the rate of increase which has been the most significant feature of the changing pattern in modern times and the extent of the change is clearly indicated by an examination of the average rate of increase per cent per annum of total population since 1831. In England and Wales the average rate of increase per cent per annum of total population between 1831 and 1861 was 1·48 per cent, whereas between 1931 and

[1] See succeeding chapters, particularly Chapter IV, for comments on the difficulties of ensuring accuracy in the Census.

[2] See the *Report of the Royal Commission on Population*, Cmd. 7695, H.M.S.O., June 1949.

1961 it had dropped to 0·51 per cent. This striking reduction in the twentieth century is remarkable in that throughout the nineteenth century the average rate had been maintained at well over 1 per cent per annum and it was not until the end of the First World War that it fell significantly. However, that is not to say that the rate of population growth dropped dramatically in or about 1920. It was, of course, a gradual process which began in the last quarter of the nineteenth century and gathered momentum in the period following the 1914–18 war, and this change is illustrated in Table 2.

TABLE 2

Population increase in England and Wales in selected 30-year periods

Years	Total population gain (000's)	Average increase per annum %
1831–61	6,169	1·48
1871–1901	9,816	1·46
1901–31	7,424	0·76
1931–61	6,153	0·51

Despite the marked fall in the rate of increase substantial additions were made to the total population in every period with the result that it was in 1961 more than twice as large as it was in 1861. Nevertheless the changes in the rate of growth have a particular significance in the social structure and consequently it is essential to consider the factors which contributed to this changing pattern.

The population of a particular country grows as a result of the operation of two factors, natural increase and the balance of migration. Natural increase depends on the relationship between births and deaths, the balance of migration is determined by the difference between immigration into and emigration out of a country, and in England and Wales in the past 100 years it is clear that natural increase has been a more powerful factor in population growth than has the balance of migration.[1]

[1] In Wales alone (as distinct from England and Wales) the balance of migration has played a significant part in the pattern of population growth. See Chapter IV.

The Patterns of Population Growth in England and Wales

Throughout the nineteenth century the birth-rate, that is the ratio of total live births to the total population in a year, remained at a relatively high level of, for example, never less than 30 live births per thousand of total population and often (even in the last quarter of the century) it was as high as 35.[1] In terms of total number of births there were usually about 800,000 to 900,000 babies born every year between 1875 and 1900. In the twentieth century the birth-rate declined sharply from an annual average of 28·2 live births per thousand of total population in 1901–05 to 22·4 in 1921, 15·8 in 1931, 15·5 in 1951 and 15 in 1955. The fall in the total number of births was not, however, so striking because the total population in the twentieth century was larger than that of the late nineteenth century with the result that the total number of babies born fell from just over 900,000 per annum at the turn of the century to about 600,000 in the early 1930's. From 1930 onwards the number of births remained fairly constant at this lower level until the abnormal conditions of life arising out of the Second World War were reflected in a further fall in birth-rates. Towards the end of the war and the immediate post-war years there was a dramatic spurt in birth-rates which reached a peak in 1947, when the birth-rate rose to 20·5 and 881,000 babies were born in that year. Thereafter until 1956 the rate declined to a level just above that of the 1930's, whilst the total number of babies born remained at about 670,000 per annum.

Since 1956 birth-rates have followed an upward trend rising from 15·6 in that year to 17·4 in 1961, and the total numbers of babies born have increased from about 700,000 in 1956 to just over 800,000 in 1961. The total number of births is, therefore, in 1961 approaching that of the late nineteenth century even though the birth-rate is still less than half of what it used to be, and this upward trend in the number of births constitutes a major departure from the pattern followed in the previous fifty years.

The vast majority of live births in England and Wales have been, and still are, legitimate and the addition made to the total population by illegitimate births is relatively small. There has been a consistent fall (except in times of war) in the annual

---

[1] These are, of course, crude birth-rates which though commonly quoted are by no means very satisfactory for measuring precisely population growth, but they are adequate for general outline purposes.

number of illegitimate births from an annual average of about 45,000 in 1870–2 to about 33,000 in 1951. From 1951 the numbers fell slightly to 31,000 in 1955, then they began to rise and in 1961 there were 47,000 illegitimate births. There is, however, a surprising constancy in the ratio of illegitimate to total births except in times of war. Since the last quarter of the nineteenth century and up to 1959 about 4 to 5 per cent of all births in England and Wales have been illegitimate apart from the years 1918, 1943, 1944, 1945 and 1946, when illegitimate births accounted for 6·2 per cent, 6·4 per cent, 7·3 per cent, 9·3 per cent and 6·6 per cent respectively of total live births. In 1960 and 1961, however, the ratio increased to 5·4 per cent and 5·9 per cent respectively so that the long-established pattern of the recent past may now be changing. Obviously therefore in normal conditions it is legitimate births which have made the greater contribution to total population growth in England and Wales, but since total births have declined it is essential to examine how the population continued to grow despite the decline in births.[1] This involves an examination of the other factor which contributes to natural increase—deaths.

A crude death-rate is the ratio of total deaths to total population in a year and even though it is in many ways unsatisfactory for comparative purposes it is sufficiently useful to indicate the dramatic change which has taken place in mortality in modern times. From the last quarter of the nineteenth century until about 1920 death-rates fell steadily, for example, the annual average death-rate per thousand of the population in England and Wales in 1871–5 was 22, in 1881–5 it was 19·4, in 1901–05 it was 16·1 and in 1921 the death-rate was 12·4. Thus by 1921 the death-rate had fallen nearly 50 per cent in a period of fifty years, but since the 1920's there has been relatively little improvement and the over-all rate has continued at about 12 per thousand.[2]

There are, of course, marked differences in the death-rates of

[1] Some of the factors which contributed to the decline in births are considered in Chapter II and III.

[2] Death-rates have been declining since the end of the eighteenth century and it was primarily the continuous fall in death-rates rather than any dramatic increase in birth-rates which brought about the rapid increase in population in the first half of the nineteenth century. For comments on the changes in the causes of death see Chapter VIII.

males and females and in age-groups. In general the rates for males are higher than those for females though the downward trend has been equally applicable to both sexes. The most significant reductions in death-rates, however, have taken place among the younger age-groups of the population. In children aged under five years the annual number of deaths in England and Wales has fallen from about 205,000 in 1871 to about 24,000 in 1951 and about 20,000 in 1961 and the fall in the rate of infant mortality, i.e. the ratio of deaths of infants under one year of age to total live births is particularly striking. For example, between 1841 and 1850 the annual average number of deaths of infants under one year of age per thousand live births was 153, and it continued at about this figure for the remainder of the century, but in the twentieth century there was a drama-tic reduction to an annual average of 72 per thousand between 1921–30. So that in just under 100 years the rate of infant mortality had been more than halved, yet since 1930 progress in preventing infant mortality has continued to such an extent that by 1931 the rate had dropped to 66, by 1951 to 29·7 and in 1961 it was 21·6.

It is possible that mortality rates will continue to improve though the experience of the past thirty years suggests that among the older age-groups in the population the chances of any substantial reductions in mortality are not very great. There are, however, reasonable prospects of reducing still further in-fant mortality since there are some countries in the world which have succeeded in achieving a rate as low as less than 20 per thousand live births and clearly any additional reductions would make a valuable contribution to population growth. What is abundantly clear is that the dramatic improvement in infant mortality in the twentieth century afforded some compensation for the declining birth-rate, and coupled with the substantial fall in mortality of females in the reproductive age-groups had a marked effect on the rate of natural increase of the population. The factors which contributed to these reductions in mortality were numerous and varied, but obviously the development of public health services, progress in medical knowledge, rising standards of living and the extension of social services were important in combating the epidemics of infectious diseases which had been such powerful killers in earlier centuries.

The Patterns of Population Growth in England and Wales

In view of the fact that it was among the younger age-groups that the greatest improvements in mortality occurred the reproductive potential of the nation was considerably strengthened in the twentieth century, but, because of the decline in fertility (i.e. the actual number of babies born to women) the amount and rate of natural increase declined steadily in the first quarter and dramatically in the second quarter of the century as shown in Tables 3 and 4.

TABLE 3

Natural increase in England and Wales 1871–1961

Period	Total pop. at beginning of period (000's)	Births	Deaths	Excess of births over deaths (000's)
		in period (000's)		
1871–91	22,712	17,498	10,443	7,055
1891–1911	29,003	18,447	10,809	7,638
1911–31	36,070	15,209	10,537*	4,672
1931–51	39,952	13,299	10,248*	3,051
1951–61	43,758	7,138	5,180	1,958
1871–1901	22,712	26,655	16,006	10,649
1931–1961	39,952	20,420	15,407*	5,013

* Includes deaths of non-civilians and merchant seamen who died outside England and Wales amounting to 577,000 between 1911–31 and 240,000 between 1931–51.

TABLE 4

England and Wales, natural increase per thousand of population in selected periods. (Annual average or calendar years)

Period	Births	Deaths	Natural increase per thousand of population
	per thousand of population		
1871–75	35·5	22·0	13·5
1901–05	28·2	16·0	12·2
1921	22·4	12·1	10·3
1931	15·8	12·3	3·5
1951	15·5	12·5	3·0
1961	17·6	12·0	5·6

Tables 3 and 4 require little comment except to emphasize the fact that even though the population in 1961 was more than double that of 1871 the number of births in each twenty-year period up to 1951 fell sharply, but the number of deaths remained relatively constant. Indeed, if the deaths resulting from wars were excluded then the total number of deaths in each twenty-year period since 1871 has declined slightly despite the increase in total population, which is a striking commentary on the great improvement in mortality. The decade 1951–61, however, shows a pattern of growth different from that of any decade since 1911–1921 in that the total number of births was larger and the number of deaths remained stable, hence the annual rate of natural increase was faster than in most years since 1921.[1]

The course of births and deaths, and hence of natural increase, is affected by a variety of factors, especially changes in the sex and age composition of the population,[2] but it is interesting to reflect that had the late nineteenth-century rates of natural increase continued up to the present time then we would have had by the 1960's a population at least twice as large as that which now exists. In many ways this would have created a difficult situation since we are in any case a country with a density of population (about 790 persons per square mile in England and Wales in 1961), which is among the highest in the world.[3] On the other hand, it is conceivable that had population continued to grow at the nineteenth-century rate a greater number of people would have emigrated from this country and the balance of migration would, therefore, have been very different from that experienced in modern times.

The balance of migration is by no means easy to calculate since persons may leave the country with the intention of taking up permanent residence elsewhere yet return within a short time, and immigrants arriving in this country as intended permanent residents may equally depart again after a short stay.[4] However, there has been an improvement in the keeping of migration records in recent years with the result that it is possible now to show with greater accuracy the net gain or loss from migration and hence the addition to or subtraction from total population. From 1871–1931 England and Wales (and the

[1] Decennial periods were not shown in Tables 3 and 4 because there was no Census in 1941.

[2] See Chapters II and III.

[3] For example only the Netherlands in Europe has a higher density of population, 893 persons per square mile (in 1958). Compare other countries such as Belgium 769 (in 1958), Japan 642, India 313, China 156, U.S.A. 49 and Australia 3.

[4] Residence for twelve months or more is usually regarded as permanent.

The Patterns of Population Growth in England and Wales

United Kingdom as a whole) experienced a continual net loss by migration, but from 1931–61 the balance of migration was inward for England and Wales (though not for Scotland and Northern Ireland). The extent of gain and loss from migration is shown in Table 5.

TABLE 5

Net gain (+) or loss (−) by migration in England and Wales, 1871–1961

	Net gain (+) or loss (−) in 000's				
	1871–91	1891–1911	1911–31	1931–51	1951–61
England and Wales	− 765	− 570	− 790	+ 755	+ 389

In the sixty years after 1871 England and Wales lost on the balance of migration well over 2 million people, the majority of whom were males in the younger age-groups, yet the population continued to grow because of the high fertility in the nineteenth century, though migration on this scale must have had an effect on the sex composition of the population and hence on the reproductive capacity of the nation. When, however, the rate of natural increase had reached its lowest levels the balance of migration was reversed and consequently the net gain from migration after 1931 offset to some extent the decline in natural increase. Over the whole period from 1871–1961 migration has in fact played a relatively minor role as compared with natural increase in determining the pattern of population growth in England and Wales, as shown in Table 6.

The reasons for the inward migration from 1931 are varied. For example, in the 1930's there was an influx of political

TABLE 6

The movement of population in England and Wales; natural increase and net gain or loss by migration, 1871–1961. (000's).

	1871–91	1891–1911	1911–31	1931–51	1951–61	1871–1961
Actual increase	6,290	7,068	3,882	3,806	2,347	23,360
Natural increase ..	7,055	7,638	4,672	3,051	1,958	24,378
Balance of migration (+ or −)	− 765	− 570	− 790	+ 755	+ 389	− 1,018

refugees from Europe; a number of erstwhile emigrants to the U.S.A. and the Dominions returned because of the depression in world trade; and there was a flow of immigrants from Eire. During the war (1939–46) the inward migration continued, but after the war (particularly in 1946 and 1947) there was a considerable outward flow of, for example, wives and children of Commonwealth and United States servicemen (100,000 in 1946) and, of course, there were the emigration schemes to Australia, Canada, New Zealand and South Africa which attracted large numbers of people from England and Wales. In 1946 and 1947 there was, therefore, a net loss by migration, but in 1948 the outward flow was offset by, for example, the demobilization of the Polish and other Allied armed forces in this country, some 80,000 of whom chose to remain and by the arrival of displaced persons and European voluntary workers. There was, too, a movement of population from Scotland, Northern Ireland and Eire to England and Wales, so that in the period 1945–50 though the balance of migration fluctuated from year to year, there was ultimately a small net gain. From 1950–54 the balance of migration was outward, but from 1956 the number of immigrants has exceeded the number of emigrants and from 1958–61 there was a heavy inward migration. For example it has been suggested that in 1960 and 1961 the balance of migration was inward to the extent that 194,000 more people came to this country than left it and that of the new-comers 116,000 were West Indians. Whatever the exact figures are the Government was clearly perturbed by the increasing inward migration and hence in 1962 the Commonwealth Immigration Act was passed to restrict the free entry of Commonwealth and Eire citizens to this country.

Although natural increase has played a greater part in determining the pattern of population growth in England and Wales in modern times the effects of movement into and out of the country must not be minimized; the outward flow of migrants in the nineteenth century obviously had some effect on the sex composition of the population and may have contributed to the relatively large numbers of unmarried women in the early part of the twentieth century, whilst the inward flow since 1931 has helped to increase the proportion of men to women in recent years. How far natural increase was affected by the balance of migration is difficult to determine, but it is possible that had fewer men emigrated then the decline in natural increase might have been less marked than it was. On the other hand, the population of some of the Commonwealth countries and of North America would have been affected had there been less emigration from this country, and certainly British influence in countries beyond the seas would have been considerably lessened. It may well be that the importance of the balance of migration in the past hundred years is to be found not in its effects on our own population, but in the spread of British influence abroad which in turn has influenced the social structure of this country.

The pattern of population growth in England and Wales during and after the nineteenth century is by no means unique; in most European countries and in North America population grew rapidly in the nineteenth century and then the rate of growth slackened appreciably in the twentieth century. In some areas, notably in Australasia and North America the rate of growth in the early nineteenth century was due more to immigration than to natural increase, but once they were firmly settled the rate of natural increase became the determining factor in the growth of population. As in Britain, so, too, in other European countries the rate of natural increase was affected in the twentieth century by declining birth- and death-rates, which reached their lowest levels in the 1930's. Since then they have experienced slight improvements in birth-rates whilst death-rates have remained stable, but whether this slight upward trend in natural increase indicates a real and continuing change in, for example, fertility cannot be determined until the families established since the 1940's have completed their fertility cycle.

World population is, however, growing rapidly as a result of declining death-rates and stationary or rising birth-rates. In the economically developed countries the rate of growth is broadly similar to that in Britain, but in the economically less-developed countries (which already have vast populations) death-rates are falling and as yet there is no apparent decline in fertility.[1]

---

[1] For up-to-date information on birth- and death-rates throughout the world see the *Demographic Year Book* published by the United Nations Department of Social Affairs.

It is, therefore, these latter countries which are contributing most to the rapid growth of world population and they have in effect taken over the role which belonged to the more economically advanced countries in the nineteenth century. Then it was the populations of Europe and North America which were increasing rapidly while the population of Asia increased more slowly and that of Africa hardly increased at all, now the rate of growth in Asia and Africa is believed to be much faster than anywhere else with the result that the balance of world population is changing rapidly and fears are being expressed about the pressure of population on natural resources, particularly food supplies.

Population increase or decline has been the subject of alarm and anxiety for centuries past, even the pattern of growth of the relatively small population of England and Wales has been the subject of acute controversy at various times in the past 150 years. At the end of the eighteenth century the Rev. T. R. Malthus published, anonymously, an 'Essay on the Principle of Population', in which he expressed fears concerning the rapid growth of population and the dangers of over-population.[1] On the other hand, there were those who welcomed the rapid growth in the late eighteenth and early nineteenth centuries because it increased the supply of labour and hence stimulated industrial development. Towards the end of the nineteenth century there emerged another kind of criticism of too rapid population growth, which was concerned not so much with the dangers of over-population as with the misery and poverty suffered by the poorer sections of the population in which large families were all too common.

Obviously a rapid rate of growth of population creates difficulties for society and for certain of its members, and it was undoubtedly true that among the poorer families the existence of large numbers of children was a factor which contributed substantially to the degree of poverty in which they existed. In the late nineteenth century children were becoming a liability rather than an asset because of, for example, social legislation which prohibited the employment of children and the gradual introduction of compulsory education which prevented a child from contributing to the family income. Measures of this kind

[1] See D. V. Glass (ed.): *Introduction to Malthus* (Watts & Co., 1953).

placed the parents of a large number of children at a disadvantage in the economic system, and therefore the obvious solution to this population problem was to encourage family limitation by means of birth control.

Public discussion on the aims and methods of family limitation was stimulated by the celebrated Bradlaugh-Besant trial in 1877 when Charles Bradlaugh and Annie Besant were prosecuted for publishing in Britain an American pamphlet on birth control. The publicity given to this trial undoubtedly contributed to a more widespread acceptance of the idea that parents could and should limit the size of their families, and there is clear evidence to show that in the twentieth century the decline in fertility and in family size is due primarily to deliberate limitation of family size by means of methods of birth control.

The decline in the birth-rate in the twentieth century resulted in yet another wave of opinion concerning the pattern of population growth. By the 1930's alarmist views were being expressed about the dangers of depopulation and the gloomier prophets were predicting that by the middle of the century the number of people in England and Wales would be very much smaller than it has in fact become. Optimism and pessimism have been the dominating factors in moulding the opinions of population forecasters in this country and certainly in the past 150 years we have alternated between moods of fear of over-population and under-population. In the 1950's we appeared to have achieved a more balanced view concerning past and future population growth and this is due primarily to the excellent report of the Royal Commission on Population.

The appointment of the Royal Commission on Population in June, 1944, 'to examine the facts relating to the present population trends in Great Britain; to investigate the causes of these trends and to consider their probable consequences; to consider what measures, if any, should be taken in the national interest to influence the future trend of population and to make recommendations', was evidence of the continuing interest in the changes which had occurred (and were likely to take place) in our rate and manner of growth of population. The Commission sat for nearly five years and the Report, published in 1949, has (for the present at least) allayed the extreme fears of rapid depopulation in the near future. For the next ten years the changing pattern of over-all population growth in England and Wales appeared to excite very little public discussion, the more common topic was world population growth.[1] One feature of our own population structure was, however, the subject of most animated discussion in the 1950's and that was the change in age distribution.[2] By 1961 even this particular topic was no longer as widely discussed as it had been, and the main trends of discussion on our own population seemed to be centred around the inflow of immigrants and the difficulties of ensuring an adequate supply of houses for the growing population, schools for the increasing number of children and higher education for the teenagers in the middle 1960's.

A movement in the balance of age-groups in the population over time is both a cause and a result of the changing pattern of population growth, but it is by no means the only feature of our social structure which has undergone a radical transformation in the past century. Our whole way of life has been changed and certainly the composition and distribution of the population of England and Wales is very different today from what it was even sixty years ago. The variation in the patterns of growth have obviously played a part in the process of change, but modifications in other parts of the social structure are as (and perhaps even more) significant as those which have occurred in the over-all growth of population.

[1] The total population of the world is still not known precisely, but for a balanced view of the problem of world population and resources see *World Population and Resources*, a report by P.E.P., 1955.

[2] See Chapter II.

THE SEX, AGE AND MARITAL DISTRIBUTION OF THE POPULATION

IT would be unusual to find a country in which the population was so evenly balanced that the total number of males and females was equal, and each age-group was so constituted that it would exactly replace that which preceded it. In England and Wales, since records were first maintained, there has always been a marked disparity in the distribution of the sexes and in the size of the various age-groups. These disparities are both a cause and a result of the changing pattern of population growth and they have undoubtedly contributed to significant changes in our social system.

SEX DISTRIBUTION

Since adequate records were first maintained there has always been an excess of females in the population of England and Wales,[1] despite the fact that more boys have been born than girls. In any year since 1870 for every 1,000 females born there have been between 1,036 and 1,062 male births, yet in the total population, in every Census from 1871 onwards, females have outnumbered males to the extent shown in Table 7, and the highest ratio ever recorded was in 1921 when for every 1,000 males there were 1,096 females.[2]

The main factors which resulted in the predominance of

[1] Though not in Wales alone. See Chapter IV.

[2] The sex-ratio at the Census is, of course, affected by the absence of members of either sex from the country at the time when the Census is taken, and in recent years with young men abroad on military service the male population is understated.

females were the higher death-rates of males and the greater number of male emigrants in the past. The abnormal situation in 1921, was, of course, due primarily to the large number of male deaths in the 1914–18 war, but even in normal times the higher death-rates of males more than offset the initial advantage of a greater number of male births. However, the surplus of women in the population as a whole obscures the fundamental fact that the predominance of women is not uniformly spread over all age-groups and that the excess is most marked in the older age-groups (see Table 7).

TABLE 7

Sex Ratios in England and Wales at selected Censuses – females per thousand males by age-groups

Year	Age-groups							
	All ages	0–14	15–19	20–39	40–59	60–64	65–74	75 and over
1871 ..	1,054	996	1,001	1,100	1,078	1,111	1,154	1,288
1901 ..	1,068	1,003	1,019	1,107	1,079	1,141	1,251	1,415
1931 ..	1,088	980	1,008	1,103	1,139	1,130	1,244	1,581
1951 ..	1,081	953	1,025	1,034	1,096	1,282	1,375	1,609
1961 ..	1,066	951	973	976	1,048	1,242	1,482	1,890

The sex ratios in intercensal years vary considerably, but the over-all pattern of a population in which females outnumber males, particularly in the higher age-groups, has remained unchanged for at least the past century.[1] The female excess becomes most marked at about sixty years, though even in the reproductive age-groups (i.e. broadly from age 15–44 years) there has usually been a surplus of women, and this was particularly marked in the early 1920's. For example, in the age-group 15–44 the number of females per 1,000 males was 1,099 in 1871, 1,144 in 1901, 1,141 in 1921, 1,091 in 1931 and 1,032 in 1951. Since 1951, however, the trend towards an excess of males in the reproductive age-groups has become pronounced and at the Census of 1961 for every 1,000 males in the age-group 15–44 there were only 995 females. Thus the predominance of

[1] For numbers of males and females by age-groups in England and Wales from 1871–1961 see Table 8, page 24.

male births is being maintained into adulthood, and for the first time for over a hundred years there are more males than females in the reproductive age-groups.

Only once in any Census since 1870 has there been an excess of females in the age-group 0–14 and that was in 1901. The factors responsible for this situation may have been a slightly smaller than usual excess of male births in the previous twenty years and a greater decline in infant mortality among females. Now that infant mortality has reached such low levels for both sexes the male predominance among the under 15-year-olds in the population has become more marked, and if mortality and birth patterns remain as at present then the excess of males will continue up to and through the reproductive age-groups.

A change in the ratio of males to females in the reproductive age-groups could have a marked effect on the pattern of population growth in the future, and it will almost certainly bring about changes in the relationship between the sexes. Already the number of marriages has increased as compared with earlier years and one wonders what will be the effect on the social structure of two few women being chased by too many men. This will be a new experience for the males in this country, who up to the present have been in the fortunate position of having more than one woman to choose from when considering marriage.

Just as there are variations in the sex ratios among the different age-groups, so, too, are there geographical variations in sex distribution. In recent years the excess of females has been greater in England than in Wales, and since the 1920's in both England and Wales the proportion of females to males has usually been higher in urban than rural areas and the larger the town the greater is the excess of females. The predominance of females in towns may merely be a reflection of the greater variety of avenues of employment for women in urban as compared with rural areas which results in female migration from the country to the towns, but with the tendency for large towns to extend their boundaries and 'overspill' their populations into neighbouring areas the distinctions between urban and rural are less real today than they were in the past.[1]

[1] See Chapter IV for comments on the difficulties of measuring urban and rural populations.

The Sex, Age and Marital Distribution of the Population

The results of any future variations in sex ratios are not easily predictable, but any marked change in the balance of the sexes in, for example, the working age-groups could bring about changes in the economic system. It was, perhaps, fortunate that there were women available to replace men in traditionally male jobs during the wars of 1914 and 1939; women now have a greater variety of employments than ever before, but should the sex ratios change so that males exceed females in the working age-groups we may yet see males in conflict with females over traditionally female jobs. Changes have already occurred in the distribution of male and female occupations[1] which are in part the result of changes in sex ratios, and the gradual acceptance of the demand for 'equal pay for men and women' (which has already been conceded in the Civil Service) may be a reflection of the increasing influence of the female in our economic system. The status of women has been radically altered in the past fifty years and this undoubtedly gives greater significance to the sex ratio today than it had in the past.

The predominance of the female in the population as a whole is unlikely to change significantly in the near future, since it is improbable that there will be any startling change in male mortality. All official projections of population up to the end of the present century show an excess of females in the population as a whole, and particularly in the higher age-groups. It would appear, therefore, that we shall continue to be, as we have been for at least the past century, a population in which females outnumber males, but it would be unwise to assume that the female excess will have the same effects in the future as it had in the past. The relative scarcity of younger women could well result in patterns of behaviour and relationships very different from those which now prevail.

AGE DISTRIBUTION

In the years 1946–56 the changing age structure of the population became as serious a topic of discussion as the decline of the birth-rate was in the 1930's, and alarmist views were frequently expressed about our 'ageing population'. Yet the change in the balance of age-groups did not occur overnight. It was a gradual

[1] See Chapter V.

process extending over the previous half-century, which gained momentum in the period after the First World War and then reached its peak. The feature of the change in age structure which aroused most comment was the increase in the number and proportion of elderly persons in the population as a whole, but any discussion of old age is immediately made difficult by the problem of adequately definining the term 'old'.

The age at which a person ceases to be young or middle-aged in a society like ours still cannot satisfactorily be determined. For convenience we have, up to the present, accepted the age at which it is deemed a person should retire from gainful employment as the point at which a person enters the elderly age-group. At the beginning of the twentieth century 70 years was accepted as the qualifying age for the grant of a non-contributory old age pension under the Old Age Pensions Act, 1908. In 1925, however, the Widows', Orphans and Old Age Contributory Pensions Act reduced the qualifying age for a contributory old age pension to 65 for men and women, and then in 1940 the qualifying age for women was reduced to 60 years. It has by now become customary to accept 65 for men and 60 for women as the ages at which an old age pension may be claimed, and to a considerable extent these represent the normal ages for retirement from gainful employment because of old age. Yet there is no real justification for accepting that every man at 65 is old, and certainly it is difficult to justify the lower age limit for women in view of the fact they normally outlive men. The reasons advanced in Parliament in 1940 that as wives are on the average four years younger than their husbands a lower age limit is necessary so that they may qualify for a pension at the same time as their husbands, and that a lower age limit is justified for single women, are hardly valid grounds for determining the point of entry into old age in general.

Recent surveys of the elderly have shown that there are wide differences in the physical and mental capacities of men aged 65 and over and women aged 60 and over,[1] but for retirement

---

[1] See, for example, *Old People – a Report of a Survey Committee on the Problems of Ageing and the Care of Old People* published by the Nuffield Foundation in 1947; J. W. Sheldon: *The Social Medicine of Old Age* (Oxford University Press, 1948); and *Over Seventy* published by the Sir Halley Stewart Trust and the National Corporation for the Care of Old People in 1954, which also gives a list of other old age surveys.

TABLE 8

The age distribution of the population of England and Wales at the Censuses of 1871, 1901, 1931 and 1961

Population in thousands

Age group	Sex	1871	Total	Age group % of total pop.	1901	Total	Age group % of total pop.	1931	Total	Age group % of total pop.	1961	Total	Age group % of total pop.
0–14 yrs.	M.	4,108	8,203	36·0	5,265	10,545	32·4	4,808	9,520	23·8	5,424	10,584	22·9
	F.	4,094			5,280			4,712			5,160		
15–19 yrs.	M.	1,085	2,181	9·7	1,608	3,247	10·0	1,710	3,435	8·6	1,622	3,201	6·9
	F.	1,096			1,639			1,725			1,579		
20–39 yrs.	M.	3,182	6,686	29·4	4,993	10,522	32·3	6,044	12,709	31·8	5,998	11,950	25·9
	F.	3,504			5,529			6,665			5,952		
40–59 yrs.	M.	1,899	3,946	17·4	2,791	5,805	17·8	4,520	9,668	24·2	6,061	12,414	26·9
	F.	2,047			3,014			5,148			6,353		
60–64 yrs.	M.	295	623	2·7	410	890	2·7	778	1,657	4·1	1,096	2,458	5·3
	F.	328			480			879			1,362		
65–74 yrs.	M.	355	765	3·4	478	1,076	3·3	954	2,141	5·4	1,419	3,521	7·6
	F.	410			598			1,187			2,102		
75 yrs. and over	M.	135	309	1·4	183	442	1·4	318	821	2·0	684	1,976	4·4
	F.	174			259			503			1,292		
All ages	M.	11,059	22,712	100	15,729	32,528	100	19,133	39,952	100	22,304	46,105	100
	F.	11,653			16,799			20,819			23,801		

(N.B. – Rounding off to the nearest digit results in a slight discrepancy between the sum of the constituent items and the totals.)

and pension purposes an agreed age is necessary to mark off the elderly from the rest of the population. It may well be that 65 years for both men and women is an appropriate age to denote the lower limit of the elderly age-group, and if we accept this basis then we can see (from Table 8)[1] the changes which have taken place in the number and proportion of the elderly in modern times, and, too, the variations in the balance of age-groups in the population of England and Wales.

If we accept the conventional divisions of the population into the young aged 0–14 years, the working group aged 15–64 years, and the elderly aged 65 and over, then it is apparent that there have been dominant 'shifts' in these three groups since 1871. In 1871 the young accounted for 36 per cent of the total population and then declined to 32·4 per cent, 23·8 per cent, and 22·9 per cent in 1901, 1931 and 1961 respectively. On the other hand, the elderly formed a relatively small and constant proportion of the population in 1871 and 1901 and then gradually increased to 7·4 per cent in 1931 and 12·0 per cent in 1961. So that whereas the young varied slightly in number and significantly as a proportion of the total population in the twentieth century the elderly increased substantially both in number and as a proportion of the population as a whole. This radical change in the balance of age-groups is illustrated more clearly in Table 9, where the three major groups are expressed in round numbers in terms of every 100 persons in the total population.

TABLE 9

The young, the working age and the elderly per hundred of the total population of England and Wales in 1871, 1901, 1931, 1951 and 1961.

Year	The young 0–14	The working age 15–64	The elderly 65 and over	All ages
1871	36	59	5	100
1901	32	63	5	100
1931	24	69	7	100
1951	22	67	11	100
1961	23	65	12	100

[1] Page 24.

These changes in age distribution are the result of the variations in birth and death patterns (and to a lesser extent the balance of migration) in the past; the decline in births contributing to the fall in the proportion of the young and the decline in mortality has contributed substantially to the increases in the proportion of those of working age and to a smaller extent of the elderly. One result of these changes in births and mortality is that whereas in the nineteenth century any one age-group was considerably larger than the next older group, in the first half of the twentieth century the differences between them were not so substantial. For example, in 1871, the 0–19 age-group contained just over 10 million young people compared with just over 6½ million in the 20–39 age-group; by 1931 these two groups were almost equal in numbers and so, too, were they in 1951. By 1961, however, due mainly to a continuing high level of births and relatively constant mortality since the early 1950's, the 0–19 age-group is now much larger than the 20–39 group, but unlike the nineteenth century the 20–39 age-group is still not as large as the 40–59 age-group. This fundamental change which will in part determine the future pattern of population growth and age structure has, in the years 1945–60, aroused less discussion than the effect on the economy of the country of the increase in the number of the elderly.

The emphasis on the growing numbers of the elderly was due primarily to the burdens which retirement pensions and other forms of social provision for the old imposed on the national economy. This problem of making adequate financial and other services available to old persons through a system of social security was examined in detail and given especial prominence in the Beveridge report on *Social Insurance and Allied Services* (Cmd. 6404, 1942). Estimates of the future age structure of the population of Great Britain up to 1971 were prepared for the Beveridge Committee and these showed that the population of pensionable age (65 for men and 60 for women) would, by 1971, outnumber the population aged under 15 and account for 20·8 per cent of the total population. These projections of future population have since been revised, but the difficulties of providing adequate pensions for an ever-growing pensionable population were believed to be acute and the problems of the aged were the subject of many committees of inquiry. The most recent investigation was carried out by the 'Committee on the Economic and Financial Problems of the Provision for Old Age' under the chairmanship of Sir Thomas Phillips, whose report (Cmd. 9333, Dec. 1954) placed the change in age structure in its proper perspective.

The Phillips Committee, having the advantage of the report of the Royal Commission on Population and the results of the 1951 Census on which to base its estimates of future age distribution, suggested that though the proportion of old people would continue to increase 'we are already half-way – and perhaps more than half-way – between the proportion normal in the latter half of the nineteenth century and the eventual proportion to which we have to look forward'. The rate of increase in the elderly sector of the population is, therefore, likely to be less rapid in the next twenty years than it has been for the past two decades.

In view of the development of retirement and pension schemes in the twentieth century it is understandable that attention should have been directed to the increase in the proportion of the elderly, but the emphasis placed on the elderly sector of the population has tended to obscure the real changes which have taken place in the balance of age-groups. In the nineteenth century we were essentially a young population, but as a result of changes in births, mortality and the balance of migration we have become, gradually, a nation in which the young and old are more evenly balanced. It may well be that we are, in the second half of the twentieth century, a better balanced population than we were in the past and even the ratio of dependents to producers has not changed as radically as is so often suggested. If we accept as the dependent groups those aged 0–14, and 65 years and over, then in 1871 they accounted for about 41 per cent, and in 1951 and 1961 about 33 and 35 per cent of the total population. On the other hand, the working age-group increased its proportion from 59 per cent in 1871 to 67 per cent of the population in 1951 and 65 per cent in 1961. Therefore the producing group has increased appreciably whilst the dependent group has declined. In fact, for every one dependent in 1871 there were less than one and a half producers, whereas in 1951 there were more than two producers for every one dependent. There are, however, valid objections to comparisons of this kind because by no means all persons in the age-group 15–64 are producers, nor equally are all aged 65 and over dependents, and furthermore social policy in the twentieth century has in effect created dependents out of persons who in the nineteenth century would have been producers. Yet the fact remains that the working age population and the labour force has increased,[1] though the shift in age balance obviously has had repercussions on the economic and social system.

The impact on the social structure of the changes in age balance is to a considerable extent affected by social policy. For example, the size of the dependent group is determined in part by society's attitude towards the care and upbringing of children and indeed by the age at which it is deemed that a person ceases to be a child. If the school-leaving age were raised to 18 then the dependent section would automatically be increased, equally retirement schemes remove from the working population persons who might not otherwise become dependent. In the twentieth century we have artificially increased the size of the dependent groups through, for example, compulsory education to a later age than in the past and by retirement schemes, so that social policy has accentuated the 'natural' changes in age balance. However, we must be clear about the way in which the age structure has changed before we condemn or praise the part which social policy has played in defining the limits of the three major age-groups.

It seems to be commonly assumed that the so-called ageing of the population is due to an increased expectation of life at all ages, but in the main the dramatic increases in expectation of life have occurred at birth and in the younger age-groups. At the other end of the age scale the expectation of life for a man aged 65 in 1961 would not be much greater than it would have been for a man at that age a hundred years earlier. For older women, however, there has been an increase and since 1951 there has been a slight shift in the composition of the elderly population. Between 1871 and 1951 there was very little variation in the proportions of the elderly population in each age-group (see Table 10), but between 1951 and 1961

[1] See Chapter V for changes in the size and distribution of the working population.

there was a marked tendency for the proportions in the higher age-groups to be larger than they were in the past.

TABLE 10

The proportion of males and females aged 65 and over in each quinquennial age-group in England and Wales at the Censuses of 1871, 1901, 1951 and 1961

Age-group	Age-group per cent of males and females aged 65 and over							
	1871		1901		1951		1961	
	M.	F.	M.	F.	M.	F.	M.	F.
65–69..	43	40	42	40	40	37	39	34
70–74..	30	30	30	29	30	29	29	28
75–79..	17	17	17	18	19	19	18	20
80–84..	8	9	8	9	8	10	10	12
85 and over	2	4	3	4	3	5	4	6
	100	100	100	100	100	100	100	100

The great increase in expectation of life has taken place in the young population, and this was clearly shown in the report of the Phillips Committee, where it was stated that in Great Britain (and the pattern would be very similar for England and Wales) 'of 100 boys born in 1901, only 36 seemed likely to survive to the age of 65 at the rates of mortality then prevailing . . . of 100 boys born in 1951, 65 were likely at current rates of mortality to reach 65.' The result is that in the middle of the twentieth century we are a predominantly middle-aged rather than an old population, and according to the latest estimates of future age structure it is unlikely that any radical change in age balance will occur until at least the end of the century. In a memorandum prepared by the Government Actuary for the Phillips Committee it is suggested that by 1979 the balance of age-groups will be as follows:

	Per cent of total population of Great Britain in each age-group in 1979
Age-group	
0–14	20
15–44	40
45–64	25
65 and over	15
	100

The Sex, Age and Marital Distribution of the Population

If this forecast proves to be accurate then we have by now passed through the stage of rapid increase in the proportion of elderly persons in the population as a whole and are entering upon a phase of relative stability in the balance of age-groups at least for the foreseeable future. The changing age structure cannot, however, be considered in isolation, it is (and will be) affected by changes in the sex ratios, in mortality, in marital distribution and it will influence (as well as being affected by) changes in social policy. The gradual change-over from a predominantly young to a middle-aged population is an experience which we have shared with other economically developed countries, we are not unique, though the shifts in age balance may well have different effects in countries having a similar pattern of change. In our own case the effects on our economy may be far-reaching.

In the nineteenth century we had an ever-growing supply of youthful labour continally coming forward to replace (and more than replace) the older workers; the labour force was young and adaptable – an obvious asset in the development of industrialization; restrictions on the employment of labour were few and consequently we had a continually expanding, youthful and virile labour force. In the first half of the twentieth century the supply of young persons for the labour force was barely sufficient to replace the next higher age-group and the working population as a whole had a higher proportion of older workers than it had in the past. This change alone would be sufficient to affect our economy, but other factors, such as restrictions on the employment of young persons at one end of the age scale and compulsory retirement schemes at the other; changes in the nature and types of employment and in working conditions; new conceptions of standards of living for all and the like combine to accentuate the effects of changes in the age structure.[1] Since 1951 the continued relatively high birth-rate is tending to alter the pattern which prevailed in the previous thirty years in that the proportion of young people is increasing slowly, but so too is the proportion of the elderly. It must be emphasized, however, that the repercussions on the economic and social

[1] For an excellent discussion of the implications of the change in age distribution in relation to the standards of living see the *Report of the Royal Commission on Population*.

system arising out of the changes in age distribution are not the result simply of the increase in the proportion of the elderly. In the twentieth century ideas and opinions concerning the roles of the young and the elderly have changed appreciably and to over-emphasize the growing proportion of the elderly tends to distort what is after all merely a part of the natural process of population growth. It may well be that we have not, as yet, considered sufficiently what part elderly people should play in our society, but there is, surely, no justification for assuming that the elderly are necessarily a 'problem group', and no reason at all for alarm over the fact that more people are now surviving the hazards of early life and living through to old age.

The changing patterns of sex and age distribution are reflected in a variety of ways in the social system as a whole, and they are, too, determinants of so much of the social structure. For example, the marital distribution in a society based on monogamy depends to a considerable extent on the sex and age composition of the population, and the marital distribution in turn determines in part the pattern of population growth. There is no single factor which can be isolated and accepted as the starting-point of social change. Changes occur because of the inter-play of a variety of factors and forces acting and reacting on each other, and a minor change in one direction may set in train a whole series of chain-reactions, which in the course of time may alter the social structure as a whole. A modest change in sex ratios or in age balance may transform a society, and certainly fluctuations in the proportions of the population who are married, widowed, divorced or single (which in turn are affected by and at the same time contribute to changes in sex and age distribution) may result in different patterns of social relationships in a relatively short period of time. In England and Wales in modern times there have been marked changes in age (and to a lesser extent in sex) distribution which have been accompanied by changes in the marital distribution and these have a particular significance in the development of the social structure.

31

The Sex, Age and Marital Distribution of the Population

The marital status of a population depends not only on the relative numbers of males and females but on the social institutions, of which marriage is the most important, which have been established and accepted by the society to which that population belongs. Even within Great Britain there are differences between the legal requirements for marriage in Scotland and England and Wales which could (though in practice they probably do not) markedly affect the marital distribution of the population, and throughout the world there are wide differences in marriage customs and conventions which obviously create difficulties in the making of comparisons of marital distribution. In England and Wales, however, there has been little alteration in the legal requirements for marriage in modern times with the result that it is possible to compare the marital distribution with a reasonable degree of accuracy.

The main restrictions on marriage in England and Wales are age, no person may marry who is below the age of 16 years;[1] the prohibited degrees of consanguinity which place restrictions on the marriage of blood relations and since the Marriage Act, 1949, there is a slight difference between the prohibited degrees allowed under secular as against non-secular law, particularly in respect of the marriage of a man to his deceased wife's sister; and the place in which a marriage may be legally effected. Since 1871, however, there has been so little change in the legal requirements relating to first marriages that conditions then and in the 1960's are broadly comparable. On the other hand, there have been significant changes in the law relating to divorce which could affect comparisons of marital distribution in earlier periods with those of the twentieth century, but even now the divorced consitute only a relatively small proportion of the married population.

Before 1857 a legal divorce was beyond the reach of the great majority of the population and even in the late nineteenth century it was a costly and difficult process. In that period the married population was, therefore, probably composed almost

[1] Before the Age of Marriage Act, 1929, a lawful marriage could be contracted by girls aged 12 and over. It was this Act which made 16 years the minimum age at which males and females could marry.

entirely of persons who had been married once only and of widowed who had re-married, whereas in the twentieth century the extension of the grounds on which divorce may be granted has made it possible for larger numbers of the married population to have been married more than once. Furthermore a new type of marital condition has been added to the usual categories of single, married and widowed, namely the divorced.

It is difficult to obtain information about the size of the divorced group in the nineteenth and early twentieth centuries because it was not until 1921 that divorced persons were asked to state this fact on the Census return, hitherto they had been shown in the Census results as widowed. Detailed comparisons of the marital states of the population before and after 1921 are, therefore, not possible but a broad picture can be drawn which is sufficiently useful to indicate the major changes which have taken place.

Tables 11 and 12 show the marital distribution of the population at selected censuses and it is apparent that since 1871 the single have declined appreciably and the married have increased substantially as a proportion of the total population of England and Wales. Whilst the total population in 1961 was slightly more than double that of 1871 the number of married persons in 1961 was nearly three times greater than that of 1871; the number of widowed persons had increased at a rate slightly faster than that of the total population and the number of single persons in 1961 was only about 50 per cent more than that of 1871. Since 1921, however, the most spectacular increase is to be found in the number of divorced persons, yet even in 1961 they constitute a relatively small proportion of the total population.[1]

The fact that there were, at every Census, more married females than married males seems incongruous, the discrepancy is due mainly to the absence of husbands from this country at the one point in time when the Census is taken. The difference is particularly marked in the younger married population, for example, at the Census of 1961 in the age-group 15–19 there were 103,536 married females but only 17,040 married males, and in the age-group 20–24 there were 833,643 married females and only 443,938 married males. On the other hand, among the

[1] Divorced persons who have re-married are, of course, shown as married so that the Census does not show the total of all persons who have been divorced.

elderly married population there were more males than females, for example, in the age-group 65 and over there were 1,477,679 married males and 1,163,091 married females. These differences are in part accounted for by the fact that husbands tend to be older than their wives and by absence of either spouse from home at the date of the Census.

The reasons for these changes in marital distribution are

TABLE 11

Marital distribution of the population of England and Wales at the Censuses of 1871, 1901, 1921, 1931 and 1961

Marital status	Males					Per cent of all Males				
	Numbers (000's)									
	1871	1901	1921	1931	1961	1871	1901	1921	1931	1961
Single ..	6,777	9,567	9,949	9,911	9,738	61·3	60·8	55·0	51·8	43·7
Married ..	3,883	5,611	7,475	8,490	11,813	35·1	35·7	41·4	44·4	52·9
Widowed ..	} 398	} 550	643	719	658	} 3·6	} 3·5	3·56	3·74	3·0
Divorced ..			8	13	94			0·04	0·06	0·4
	11,058	15,728	18,075	19,133	22,304	100	100	100	100	100
	Females					Per cent of all Females				
Single ..	6,826	9,835	10,591	10,414	9,242	58·6	58·6	53·5	50·0	38·9
Married ..	3,949	5,718	7,590	8,604	11,860	33·9	34·0	38·3	41·3	49·8
Widowed ..	} 879	} 1,246	1,622	1,782	2,528	} 7·5	} 7·4	8·16	8·6	10·6
Divorced ..			8	19	170			0·04	0·09	0·7
	11,654	16,799	19,811	20,819	23,800	100	100	100	100	100

TABLE 12

Proportions of the population of England and Wales single, married, widowed and divorced at the Censuses of 1871, 1901, 1921, 1931 and 1961

Marital status	Per cent				
	1871	1901	1921	1931	1961
Single	59·9	59·7	54·3	50·87	41·17
Married	34·5	34·8	39·7	42·79	51·35
Widowed	} 5·6	} 5·5	5·96	6·26	6·90
Divorced			0·04	0·08	0·58
	100	100	100	100	100

complex and varied, but there is obviously an association between the variations in marital distribution and the changes in sex and age distribution. In an older population we should expect a larger proportion to be married, and a more evenly balanced sex distribution ought equally to lead to more marriages. The number of marriages in England and Wales has grown substantially in the past ninety years (though not at a rate greater than the growth of population), for example, the annual number of marriages was on the average about 191,000 between 1870–2, and between 1930–2 it was 311,400; in 1951 there were 360,624 and in 1961, 347,752 marriages. The main change in the pattern of marriage, however, has been in the age at which persons marry. The general trend in the twentieth century is for couples to marry at earlier ages than they did in the nineteenth century, and since 1931 the proportion of young people between the ages of 16 and 25 who are (or have been) married has increased substantially.[1]

The downward trend in age at marriage is probably a reflection of changes in the attitude towards marriage and in economic conditions. In the twentieth century the wedding is no longer followed automatically (within the appropriate time) by the birth of a child nor is it considered necessary that the bride should retire from gainful employment. It is becoming increasingly common for young couples to continue in gainful employment and for the wife to remain a wage earner until a child is conceived. Marriage has become to a considerable extent and for a large proportion of the population a method of setting up a joint home without necessarily increasing the size of the family by the addition of children. Presumably the greater availability and use of methods of birth control has made possible this changed conception of the purpose of marriage, but it may well be that the emancipation of women and their different status in present-day society as compared with even Victorian times has helped to bring about the mid-twentieth-century type of married couple. The fact remains, however, that marriage is still extremely popular and that a larger proportion of the population is married.

[1] See the Registrar-General's *Statistical Review of England and Wales, 1946–1950* for detailed commentaries, and the annual Registrar-General's *Statistical Review for England and Wales, Part II, Tables–Population.*

The Sex, Age and Maritial Distribution of the Population

The absolute increase in the number of married persons and the extension of the grounds on which divorce may be granted has been accompanied by a marked increase in the number of divorced persons in the population. The extent to which divorce has now become a feature of social life may be gauged by the increase in the number of petitions filed annually for dissolution or nullity of marriage.[1] In the last quarter of the nineteenth century the number of petitions filed for dissolution and nullity in England and Wales did not exceed an annual average of 700, after the First World War the annual average rose to nearly 3,000 for the years 1921–5, and then to between 4,000 and 5,000 annually from 1926 to 1935. During the Second World War there was a sharp increase to an annual average of 16,000 petitions for the years 1941–5, but this number was to grow yet again in the period immediately following the war. Between 1946 and 1950 the annual average rose to 38,901 and in the peak year, 1947, there were 47,041 petitions for dissolution and 1,460 for nullity in England and Wales. Between 1953 and 1960 the number of petitions remained relatively stable at between 26,000 and 30,000 petitions for dissolution and nullity per annum. Since 1961 there has been a tendency for them to rise again to over 31,000 per annum, for example, in 1961 they numbered 31,905 and in 1962 there were 34,625 petitions filed.[2]

The appointment of a Royal Commission on Marriage and Divorce in 1945 is evidence of public interest in and concern for the growing prevalence of marital problems in our society.[3] The Report of the Commission, published in 1954, is by no means conclusive in its recommendations, and on the fundamental question of whether divorce ought, as at present, to be limited to those cases in which a matrimonial offence has been proved the members of the Commission were almost equally divided. As a result the proposal that the grounds for divorce ought to be extended so as to include 'the doctrine of breakdown

[1] The number of petitions filed for dissolution is far greater than the number filed for nullity.

[2] Petitions filed is a better measure of the desire to terminate marriages than decrees granted, though in fact the vast majority of petitions filed in recent years have resulted in decrees.

[3] See O. R. McGregor: *Divorce in England* (Heinemann, 1957) for a study of the changes in the attitude towards divorces between 1857 and 1957 and for comments on the reports of the various Royal Commissions.

36

of marriage to a limited extent' also receives approval and disapproval equally from the members of the Commission. It may well be that the Report is an accurate reflection of the ambivalent attitude which has grown up in this country towards divorce, despite the fact that it is now a recognized and significant feature of our matrimonial system.

Whether 'marriage breakdown' today is so much greater than it was in the last century cannot easily be determined, and certainly cannot be proved by divorce statistics. Had the grounds for and the process of obtaining a divorce been similar in the nineteenth century to those which exist today the increase in the incidence of divorce may not have been so spectacular, but we shall never know the extent of marital disharmony in the past, all we do know is that in the twentieth century far more marriages are terminated by divorce than ever before.

It is among persons who marry young that divorces are most common, the Registrar-General estimates that on the basis of recent trends 'about 1 in 4 of the women marrying now at ages 16–18, 1 in 10 of those marrying at ages 19–22, and 1 in 16 of those marrying at ages 23–27 will have been divorced by the twentieth anniversary of their marriage' (Registrar-General's *Statistical Review of England and Wales for 1946–50 – Text Civil, 1954*). This estimate may, or may not, be substantiated. However, of all the dissolutions and annulments of marriage made absolute in 1962 nearly one third were for persons under 30 years of age and in view of the fact that in this century the percentage of marriages terminated by divorce has risen from less than one-half per cent before the First World War to about 7 per cent in the 1950's it is unlikely that divorce will become less prevalent in the near future.

The effects of divorce on marital distribution are not such as constantly to reduce the number of families in the population because the majority of divorced persons re-marry. The Registrar-General has calculated that over 60 per cent of all divorcees in recent years have re-married, so that the married population in, for example, 1961 must include a larger proportion of persons married more than once (assuming that re-marriage after widowhood has remained constant) than in the past.

Divorce has undoubtedly become a significant feature of our

The Sex, Age and Marital Distribution of the Population

matrimonial system and is an outstanding example of one aspect of the changing social structure, but it affects less people and is certainly a less common method of breaking up a family than widowhood. On the other hand divorce is in general more prevalent among the younger married population and could, therefore, have serious implications for future population growth, whereas widowhood is largely confined to the older age-groups and particularly to women over the reproductive ages.

The incidence of widowhood has changed relatively little in the population as a whole in modern times; its outstanding feature is that widowed females greatly outnumber widowed males. At every Census since 1870 there have been at least two widowed females for every one widowed male (see Table 11), and this is a reflection of the higher mortality among males particularly in the middle and elderly age-groups. The changing age structure has accentuated the tendency towards a predominance of the widowed in the higher age-groups and changes have occurred in the age composition of the widowed population since the last quarter of the nineteenth century (see Table 13).

TABLE 13

Percentage distribution of the widowed population of England and Wales by age-groups at the Censuses of 1871, 1931 and 1961

Age-group	Widowed males			Widowed females			Age-group per cent of all widows		
	1871	1931	1961	1871	1931	1961	1871	1931	1961
	%	%	%	%	%	%	%	%	%
15–44 ..	18	10	3	19	11	3	19	10	3
45–64 ..	40	38	27	43	42	30	42	40	30
65 and over ..	42	52	70	38	47	67	39	50	67
	100	100	100	100	100	100	100	100	100

The change in age distribution of the widowed is further evidence of the improvements in mortality at younger ages, and the increase in the proportion of widows in the elderly population is indicative of this change.

The widowed population has changed least in modern times,

38

TABLE 14

Widowed persons aged 65 and over per cent of the population aged 65 and over at the Censuses of 1871, 1931, 1951 and 1961, England and Wales.

Year	Widowed males aged 65 and over per cent of all males aged 65 and over	Widowed females aged 65 and over per cent of all females aged 65 and over	Widowed males and females
1871	34	56	46
1931	30	50	42
1951	25	49	39
1961	22	49	37

though the problems arising out of the death of a husband have been recognized in the twentieth century as meriting special assistance from the State. The widowed mother today is undoubtedly assisted more generously than the widow of the nineteenth century and the fact that families are smaller now than in the past may to some extent have limited the effects of the death of a spouse, yet at any one time a not inconsiderable proportion of the population is affected by widowhood and with the increase in the married population it is likely that little change will occur in its incidence in the near future.

The changes which have taken place in the marital distribution of the population of England and Wales since 1871 have been substantial and significant, but they have not been followed by the results which could have been expected. Earlier marriages, a larger proportion of the population married than ever before, decreasing mortality rates and a relatively stable balance of migration should have increased the rate of population growth whereas it has in fact declined, and the reason is that couples marrying in the twentieth century have had (and are having) fewer children than their ancestors. We must, therefore, examine the changes in family size in order to assess the effects of the variations in sex, age and marital distribution on the pattern of population growth and the social structure as a whole.

CHAPTER III

THE FAMILY

IN our society a family comes into being by the marriage of two persons of the opposite sex, therefore the number of families in existence depends on the rate of marriage which in turn will be determined by the sex and age distribution of the population, the conventional attitudes towards marriage and a variety of other factors which may well vary from time to time. Whether the marriage of two persons who then proceed to live together is sufficient to establish a family in the commonly accepted sense of the term is open to question because it seems to be generally accepted that a family comprises the mating pair and their offspring. The restriction of the term family only to those marriages which result in the birth of a child or children cannot very strongly be defended since a number of marriages in the past (and most certainly in the present) did not produce children even though the intention of the marital pair may well have been to 'raise a family'.

In ancient times the term family was used to describe the whole household so as to include not only the mating pair and their offspring (if any) but slaves and domestics belonging to the household as well, and even in modern times it is commonly used to denote a group of persons linked together by ancestry. The husband and wife are obviously the nucleus of the family in our society and we cannot be concerned with the intricate problems of definition since our main interest is to examine the changes which have occurred in the number of children produced by marriage and hence the size of the family in this limited sense.[1]

[1] For a detailed discussion of the nature and types of families in a number of societies see N. W. Bell and E. F. Vogel: *A Modern Introduction to the Family* (Routledge, 1961).

The Family

The measurement of family size is by no means easy even in England and Wales where regular censuses have been taken for the past 160 years. If, for example, we want to distinguish childless couples from those with one, two or more children, then the best and most accurate method of doing so would be to count and record each family in detail, but the official Census has encountered innumerable difficulties in so doing with any great degree of accuracy. This problem of accurate measurement of family size was considered at length by the Royal Commission on Population and as a result of the efforts of its members and of recent changes in the form of questions asked at the Census and in analysing the results it is possible at least to obtain an idea of the changes which have taken place in the way in which marriages produce (or do not produce) children, and hence of the family as a biological unit.

At the Census of 1911 a special inquiry was instituted among married couples who were asked to state their date of marriage and the number of children born to them, and from this Fertility Census the Royal Commission on Population estimated that mid-Victorian couples in England and Wales produced on average between five and six children for every marriage of completed fertility (i.e. a marriage in which the wife has passed the limit of child-bearing age). The average includes of course childless marriages and gives no indication of the distribution of family size, but it is sufficiently valuable to serve as a guide to the broad pattern of family size in the middle of the nineteenth century (see Table 15).

When the Royal Commission attempted to determine family size in the 1940's they found that there was no up-to-date information available and consequently they asked for facilities to be granted for the taking of a special census of families. In 1946 this Family Census was taken among a 10 per cent sample of all women in the population of Great Britain who were or had been married.[1] Every woman in the sample was asked to provide information concerning the date of her birth, marriage (and where applicable termination of marriage), the dates of

---

[1] The complete account of the Family Census was published in *Papers of the Royal Commission on Population*, Vol. VI, 'The Trend and Pattern of Fertility in Great Britain', H.M.S.O., 1954.

birth of every live-born child and the occupation of her husband. From the results of this Census it was estimated that since the middle of the nineteenth century family size had declined appreciably. Exact comparisons were not possible because, for example, the 1946 Census covered a sample of the population of Great Britain, whereas the 1911 data referred to England and Wales though the pattern in the latter would probably be very similar to that in the former. Accepting this reservation it was found that among couples married in 1900–09 'the average number of children born was two less than in mid-Victorian families' and that couples married in 1925–29 had one child less per couple than those married in 1900–9.[1] In broad terms couples marrying in 1925–9 had an average of just over two children compared with the five to six children produced by mid-Victorian parents.

It was (and is) abundantly clear that the number of live children born per marriage declined appreciably from the middle of the nineteenth century. Even the crude birth and marriage rates and the absolute number of births and marriages were a positive indication of the change, but until the Royal Commission reported there was no precise indication of the extent to which family size had shrunk. Using information derived from the Fertility Census, 1911 for England and Wales and the Family Census, 1946 for Great Britain, Table 15 (reproduced from the Report of the Royal Commission) shows the change which the Commission estimates had occurred in family size.

The contrast between the results of marriages taking place about 1860 and 1925 is striking; in the twentieth century families of four or more children constituted a minority (20 per cent) of all families, whereas in the nineteenth century they were the majority (72 per cent); the proportion of childless couples had nearly doubled, but the proportion of marriages producing ten children or more had fallen to negligible proportions. Victorian couples were obviously more prolific than their descendents and were well distributed over all sizes of family whereas modern marriages have tended to produce at most two children.

The Census of 1951 confirmed the trend towards a small

[1] See the *Report of the Royal Commission on Population*, Chapter 3, Sects. 58–73.

TABLE 15

Changes in the distribution of families by size,
England and Wales and Great Britain.

Number of children born	Marriages taking place about 1860 (England and Wales)	Marriages taking place about 1925 (Great Britain)
	%	%
0	9	17
1	5	25
2	6	25
3	8	14
4	9	8
5	10	5
6	10	3
7	10	2
8	9	1
9	8	0·6
10	6	0·4
Over 10	10	0·3

TABLE 16

Married women aged under 50 at the Census of 1951, size of
family (live-born children) by duration of marriage and age-group,
England and Wales

Number of live-born children	All married women aged 15–49; all durations of marriage	Married woman aged 20–25 and married for 5 years	Married woman aged 30–35 and married for 10–14 years	Married woman aged 45–49 and married for 25 years and over
	%	%	%	%
0	21·8	10·6	7·8	8·6
1	30·5	36·3	26·3	19·8
2	26·1	37·0	34·9	24·2
3	11·7	13·0	18·7	16·8
4	5·0	2·8	7·3	11·6
5–6	3·3	0·3	4·1	11·5
7–9	1·3	—	0·9	5·7
10 and over	0·3	—	—	1·8
	100·0	100·0	100·0	100·0
Total women	7,104,500	32,200	553,300	342,400
Total children	11,993,400	52,300	1,165,000	998,700

43

number of children per married woman and the prevalence of the small family of children. At this Census each married woman under the age of 50 was asked to provide, for example, particulars of live-born children born in marriage, and from the One Per Cent Sample[1] results it is clear that of all married women aged 15–49 in England and Wales in 1951 less than 10 per cent had borne four or more live-born children. The pattern of children per married woman at the Census is shown in Table 16. The majority of married women in England and Wales who were under the age of 50 in 1951 had borne one or two live-born children, but only a small proportion had more than three. Even the women who were (or were very nearly) at the end of their reproductive lives in 1951 and had been married for twenty-five years or more followed the general pattern.

The over-all pattern conceals the variations in the child-bearing experience of married women and three factors in particular appear to affect the number of children born in marriage, viz, the age of the woman at marriage, the occupation of the husband, and the area in which the woman lives. The younger the woman at marriage the greater the number of children she bears, for example, of those women who were aged 45–49 in 1951 and had been married for 25 years or more those who married at under age 20 had an average of 3·7 children, but those who were between 30 and 35 years of age at marriage and the marriage duration was 15–19 years had an average of just over one child, and of course the later the age of marriage the greater the proportion of childless married women. Women married younger into the households of manual workers than to those in professional occupations and certainly the wives of unskilled, semi-skilled and agricultural workers had more children than those of 'higher professional' and clerical workers.[2] Married women in rural areas were more prolific than those who lived in towns, and London (perhaps because of its high proportion of clerical workers who seem to be very infertile) was much

---

[1] The One Per Cent Sample technique was first used at the Census of 1951 in order to present results quickly, but the information given is nevertheless very full, especially on fertility. See *Census 1951–One Per Cent Sample Tables, Great Britain*, Parts 1 and 2, H.M.S.O.

[2] For comments on occupational classifications and their validity see Chapter V.

less fertile than any other region.[1] Yet despite marked variations of this kind the fact remains that married women produced fewer children than they did fifty years before, and certainly much less than the mid-Victorian wives.

Whether there has been any radical change in the fertility of women since 1951 cannot as yet be ascertained. The data from the 1961 Census had not been processed by July 1965 but when the Fertility Tables become available it will be possible to see whether there has been any change. Studies made by the Registrar-General in the intercensal years do not suggest that there has been any reversal of the trend towards the small family and it is unlikely that the Census of 1961 will show any dramatic variation in pattern from that of 1951. For example, in the Registrar-General's *Statistical Review of England and Wales, Part III, Commentary*, for the Year 1962, it is shown that though marriage rates have remained high, and the average age of marriage is falling from 23·8 years for a spinster marrying a bachelor in 1946–50 to 22·4 years in 1961, 'there has as yet been no indication of any substantial increase in average completed family size. The average size of family for the 1946 marriages (now of 17 years' duration) looks like being 2·2 children; the 1950 marriages look like being 2·3. The critical issue is whether the shorter birth spacing means more babies or the same number of babies in a shorter time . . . a levelling off of average family size at 2·4 seems probable'. If this view is confirmed by the 1961 Census then obviously we have remained a nation of small families.

The decline in family size is unmistakable, but the reduction has not been uniform among all social groups. Just as there are wide differences between the birth-rates of the various social groups and in geographical regions so too are there fluctuations in family size. The variation is particularly marked between the so-called 'social classes' based on the occupation of the husband.[2] In the latter part of the nineteenth century the decline in family size was especially rapid in the professional and employing

---

[1] For comments on the difficulties involved in classifying the population on the basis of geographical areas see Chapter IV. Full details of the child-bearing experiences of married women of different ages at the Census are given in the *One Per Cent Sample Tables*.

[2] See Chapter VII for comments on the meaning and measurement of social class.

classes, though the differences in average family size throughout the population were not particularly great.[1] Indeed Queen Victoria with her large family was fairly representative of the 'upper and middle and lower orders' of English society. In the early years of the twentieth century the fall in size of family among the professional and employing classes continued and the gap between the average size of family in the 'upper' and 'lower' social classes became wider. After the First World War the trend towards smaller families spread to all social classes and by the middle of the twentieth century we have become a nation of small families.

The main factor responsible for this reduction in family size is undoubtedly the more widespread practice of family limitation. There is very little evidence to support the view that there has been any dramatic change in the reproductive capacity of women, or that the frequency of sexual intercourse between married persons is much lower now than in the past, but there is on the other hand evidence supporting the argument that the majority of married persons nowadays practice some form of birth control in order to limit the size of their families.[2] This does not mean that birth control is a modern invention or that effective methods have been devised only in recent years. What has happened is that birth control, i.e. 'all deliberate practices which have the effect of permitting sexual intercourse to take place while suppressing or reducing the risk of conception'[3] has become more widely accepted and practised. But methods of family limitation are the means and not the cause of the reduction in family size, therefore the reasons why there should have been this marked reduction in modern times must be sought elsewhere.

A variety of forces must have contributed to the change which has occurred in the desire of married couples to have children and in their acceptance of methods of deliberate family limita-

[1] See J. A. Banks: *Prosperity and Parenthood* (Routledge, 1954) for an interesting analysis of the factors contributing to the decline in fertility in the middle classes.

[2] See the *Report of the Royal Commission on Population*, Chapter 4 and *Papers of the Royal Commission on Population*, Vol. 1, 'Family Limitation and its Influence on Human Fertility during the Past Fifty Years' by E. Lewis-Fanning. See too some recent reports of the Family Planning Association.

[3] *Report of the Royal Commission on Population.*

tion. The Royal Commission suggested that the social and economic revolutions which gathered momentum in the nineteenth century; the decline in economic importance and the changes in the functions of the family in modern times; the emancipation of women and their revolt against the injurious effects of excessive child-bearing; and the growing prestige of science and the loosening of the taboos surrounding the functions of sex were, *inter alia*, contributory factors in bringing about this most significant change.[1] Coupled with forces of this kind there were the controversial discussions in the early nineteenth century of the dangers of over-population following the publication in 1798 of the *Essay on Population* by the Rev. T. R. Malthus, and towards the end of the century public discussion of birth control and the spread of birth control propaganda were stimulated by the Bradlaugh–Besant trial of 1877. All these factors created, as it were, a climate of opinion which favoured the development of the small family system, and transformed the British family from being typically large to one which is now predominantly small.

Even though we know that the modern family is small we still do not know precisely the change which has taken place in the number and relative size of families in England and Wales. It may be assumed that in the past there was a smallish number of large families and that in the present there is a large number of small families, but direct evidence to prove the extent to which this change has occurred is exceedingly difficult to obtain. In every Census prior to 1911 the only possible way of estimating the number of families was to accept the Census classification of 'separate occupiers' of dwellings as being equal to the number of families, which was of course by no means true. Since 1911, however, an attempt has been made to identify 'private families', but by definition these include single persons living alone and certain categories of lodgers which again make it difficult to distinguish precisely the number of separate families in existence. Yet despite all these problems of definition, classification and identification one fact stands out in the Census results, and that is the vast majority of persons in England and Wales have lived and continue to live as members of private

[1] See Chapter 4 of the *Report of the Royal Commission* for a brief but valuable discussion of the causes of family limitation.

households. At every Census during and after 1911 less than 5 per cent of the population have been found to live in institutions such as hotels, schools, hospitals and the like.

In the latter half of the nineteenth century the total number of 'separate occupiers' in England and Wales rose from just over 5 million in 1871 to just over 7 million in 1901, and these may have been the total number of families in existence, though we can be certain only of the fact that these were the numbers of units of occupation. In 1911 when the attempt was made to identify private families it was found that there were nearly 8 million including, of course, single persons living alone and visitors, lodgers and others who happened to be in the household at the date of the Census. By 1921 the number of private families had grown to 8¾ million and in 1931 there were just over 10 million. In 1931 just over 688,000 private families consisted of one person only but it was not possible to distinguish the private family of, say, husband, wife and near relatives from the household containing the family and outsiders. The Census, therefore, did not give an accurate picture of the family situation in this country, though it would be safe to assume that the number of families increased at a rate greater than the rate of increase of total population between 1871 and 1931.[1]

At the Census of 1951 a more determined effort was made to distinguish the various types of family in the population as a whole 'in response to expressed requests of sociologists and others for a knowledge of the numbers and types of combinations of individuals who, by virtue of family ties or affections on the one hand, or as a result of economic constraints and other reasons on the other, are voluntarily living together at the present time, in the sense of sharing the same living-rooms or eating at the same table'.[2] Persons sharing a common habitation may or may not be members of the same family, and they may or may not form one household, but in the 1951 Census a distinction was drawn between Primary Family Unit households, i.e. households consisting of the head of the household; spouse of head; all the children of the head or spouse whatever their age except such

[1] See the *Housing Report* and *Tables* of the Census of England and Wales 1931, for an interesting account of the attempts made by the Census authorities to determine the number of families.

[2] *Census 1951 – One Per Cent Sample Tables, Great Britain,* Part 2.

as were married, or if widowed or divorced were accompanied by children of their own, and other children under age 16 such as brother or sister of head or spouse, and children apparently without any parent and children of resident domestic servants; near relatives of head or spouse and resident domestic servants; and Composite households, i.e. a Primary Family Unit and any other persons. This refinement of household data gave a clearer picture of the composition of households than was hitherto provided by the Census, but it was still only a broad picture because even the Primary Family Unit included persons who may not be members of a family, and no details were available of husbands and wives not enumerated together. Nevertheless it was a better means of estimating family patterns in the middle of the twentieth century.

In 1951 there were in England and Wales just over 13 million private households (compared with just over 10 million in 1931) and they were distributed by size as follows:

Number of persons in household	Number of households (millions)		Per cent of all households	
	1951	1931	1951	1931
1	1·4	0·7	10·7	6·7
2	3·6	2·2	27·7	21·9
3	3·3	2·5	25·3	24·1
4	2·5	2·0	19·0	19·4
5	1·2	1·3	9·6	12·4
6	0·6	0·7	4·3	7·3
7	0·2	0·4	1·9	4·1
8 or more	0·2	0·4	1·5	4·1
All sizes	13·0	10·2	100	100

The majority of the 1951 households (nearly 10 million) had as head a married person most of whom (just over 6½ million) were aged 40 years or more, nearly half (approximately 6 million) contained one earner, nearly 3½ million had two earners and just over 1½ million had three earners. There were, therefore, nearly 2 million households without any earners, and of these the great majority probably contained retired persons. It is likely that this broad pattern of households corresponded to the family pattern of this country, and if it did then it confirms the view that we had become a nation of small families. Furthermore it is apparent that between 1931 and 1951 there was a redistribution of households by size, the small households had become numerically and proportionately more common whilst the larger declined both in number and as a proportion of all households. In 1931 the three-person household was the most common type, but by 1951 it had been replaced by the two-person household, and between 1931 and 1951 the number of one-person households increased by 100 per cent whilst seven or more person households were halved.

An examination of the number of children under the age of 16 in private households shows that in 1951 nearly 7½ million (approximately 57 per cent) contained no children, just over 2¾ million had one child, 1¾ million had two children and just over 1 million had three or more children. Many of the households which had no children in 1951 may have had some in the past or may have some in the future, but there is no reason to assume that the pattern on Census day was any different from that on any other day in or around 1951, and the really significant fact is that nearly 60 per cent of all households in England and Wales in 1951 contained no children under the age of 16.

This broad pattern for the country as a whole was applicable to most social classes; there was in other words, more uniformity in the household composition of the various social classes in 1951 than there was (in all probability) at the beginning of the century. If we accept the Registrar-General's division of the population into five social classes based on occupation, viz. Class 1 professional occupations, Class 2 intermediate occupations, Class 3 skilled occupations, Class 4 partly skilled occupations, and Class 5 unskilled, then in 1951 there was relatively little difference between the size of household in each class.[1] Table 17 shows the distribution of households by size and social class.

Table 17 should be interpreted very broadly because there are objections to this method of grouping the population, and these percentages were derived from the One Per Cent Sample of the 13 million households of which nearly 2 million could not be classified. Yet the table is sufficiently useful to portray the uniformity of household composition and it does show that all social classes had small numbers of children and that no one

[1] See Chapter VII for comments on this method of measuring social class.

The Family

TABLE 17

Percentage distribution of private households in England and Wales by social class, size and dependent children in 1951

Number of persons in household	Social class of household					
	1	2	3	4	5	All social classes
1	5	8	6	8	8	6·8
2–3	58	57	55	50	50	53·9
4–5	31	29	32	32	30	30·9
6–7	5	5	6	8	9	6·7
8 or more	1	1	1	2	3	1·7
	100	100	100	100	100	100
Children under 16 in household						
0	55	60	51	52	55	55·3
1	22	21	24	23	21	23·1
2	16	13	16	15	13	15·1
3–4	6	5	8	9	9	7·4
5 or more	(less than 1)	(less than 1)	1	1	2	1·1
	100	100	100	100	100	100
All sizes of households ..	3	19	50	16	12	100

class was far removed from the average for all classes. The main exceptions were Classes 4 and 5 in which households of six or more people, including three or more children, were slightly more prevalent.

A similar pattern of small size was to be found among the Primary Family Units in 1951, and of the 13 million households in England and Wales 11·2 million were Primary Family Units and 1·8 were Composite households at the census. The sizes and distribution of P.F.U. households (revealed by the One Per Cent Sample of the 1951 Census) are given in Table 18.

Composite households differed from P.F.U. households in that they had a higher proportion of one person (32 per cent), a smaller proportion of five or more persons (7·4 per cent) and a larger proportion of households with no children (59 per cent), but they were nevertheless predominantly small households.

The more elaborate household data provided in the Census of 1951 which enabled us to distinguish private households by marital condition, age (in broad groups) and sex of the head; by size, numbers of earners, children (even adopted children where shown separately for P.F.U. households in Great Britain),[1] near relatives, visitors and domestic servants, were undoubtedly valuable, yet they did not show the exact relationship between persons living together which is essential for accurate measurement of the family. All we can say is that in all probability our pattern of family composition and distribution corresponded to that of the P.F.U. households.

TABLE 18

Primary Family Unit households in England and Wales at the Census of 1951

Number of persons per P.F.U. household	Number of households (millions)	Per cent	Designated children in each P.F.U. household	Number of households (millions)	Per cent
1	1·47	13·1	0	4·72	42·0
2	3·51	31·2	1	3·14	28·0
3	2·88	25·7	2	2·05	18·3
4	1·98	17·6	3	0·80	7·1
5	0·83	7·4	4–5	0·42	3·7
6–7	0·45	4·0	6–8	0·09	0·8
8–9	0·09	0·8	9 or more	0·01	0·1
10 or more	0·02	0·2			
All sizes	11·23	100		11·23	100

N.B. – 'Designated children' includes children of any age with the exception of such as were married, or if widowed or divorced were accompanied by children of their own and certain other categories of children under age 16.

The 1961 Census continued to distinguish the private from the non-private households though the Primary Family Unit was no longer identified. However much more detailed information was obtained in 1961 about, for example, the types of tenure of household dwellings i.e. whether owner-occupier, rented from a Local Authority or employer and so on, and of persons in non-private households.[2] It is apparent that as in the past the great majority of persons live in private households. The definition of a private household for the Census of 1961 was as follows: 'a household comprises one person living alone or a

[1] Of the 12·5 million P.F.U. households in Great Britain some 51,000 contained adopted children and about 30,000 had adopted and other children.

[2] See *Census 1961 – Housing Tables*, Parts 1, 2 and 3, and for details of non-private households see the *Age, Marital Condition and General Tables*.

group of persons living together, partaking of meals prepared together and benefiting from a common housekeeping. A person or persons living but not boarding with a household in a house, flat, etc. should be treated as a separate household. But a person living with a household who usually has at least one main meal a day provided by that household while in residence is part of that household (Breakfast counts as a meal for this purpose)'. (*Census 1961 – Housing Tables, Part I*). In 1961 just over 96 per cent of the population of England and Wales were enumerated in private households which had increased in number from about 13 million in 1951 to just over 14½ million in 1961. So that whereas the total increase of population between 1951 and 1961 was just over 5 per cent the number of private households increased by about 12 per cent. Again the trend towards the smaller household (or family?) continued and just over two-thirds of all persons lived in households of three persons or less, as shown below:

Number of Persons in Household	Number of Households (millions)		Per Cent of all Households	
	1961	1951	1961	1951
1	1·97	1·40	13·4	10·7
2	4·38	3·63	29·9	27·7
3	3·35	3·31	22·9	25·3
4	2·68	2·49	18·3	19·0
5	1·29	1·26	8·8	9·6
6	0·56	0·57	3·8	4·3
7	0·23	0·26	1·6	1·9
8 or more	0·18	0·20	1·3	1·5
All sizes	14·64	13·12	100	100

The outstanding feature of household patterns in England and Wales in modern times is the relatively large proportion of 'one-person' households. In 1951 nearly one in ten of all private, one in nine of all P.F.U. and one in three of all Composite households contained one person only. We cannot measure with complete accuracy the extent to which 'one-person' households have become more common in the population as a whole, but if we accept for purposes of comparison that the 'private household' as defined for the Census of 1951 was broadly similar to the 'private families' of earlier censuses then the proportion of 'one person' has quite definitely increased. In 1911 'one-person' families accounted for 5·3 per cent of all private families,

6·0 per cent in 1921, 6·7 per cent in 1931, 10·7 per cent (of all private households) in 1951 and 13·4 per cent in 1961. The 'one-person' household is not necessarily synonymous with one person living alone in a house; it includes a person occupying a part of a house, or a flat, or an apartment and even the 'bed-sitting-room', and though no direct statistical evidence is available it is probable that the majority of such households are confined to young men and women working away from home and elderly widowed persons.

Of the members of households there is one at least about whom we can be positive of change in modern times, and he (or she) is the resident domestic servant. In 1931 nearly 5 per cent of all the households in England and Wales employed a 'resident domestic', by 1951 about 1 per cent of all households had resident servants, and the extent of change can be gauged from the fact that in 1931 there were 706,800 persons in resident domestic service, whereas in 1951 there were only 178,000. The proportion of households with three or more resident domestic servants fell from 0·4 per cent (i.e. about 41,000 households) in 1931 to 0·02 per cent (i.e. about 3,000 households) in 1951. At the Census of 1961 the 10 per cent sample of the population who were required to provide full information gave details of households containing domestic servants, and the trend so firmly established between 1931 and 1951 has been maintained. In 1961 only 0·6 per cent of all households in England and Wales had domestic servants and the proportion having three or more was so small that it would be unwise to calculate it on a percentage basis. In terms of absolute numbers whereas there were about 3,000 households with domestic servants in 1951 by 1961 there were only about 1,790, and of course the total numbers of domestic servants was reduced from about 178,000 in 1951 to about 103,000 in 1961. To some extent the 'resident' may have been replaced by the 'daily help', but the mid-twentieth-century English household is, compared with the nineteenth century, relatively servantless.[1]

[1] When Seebohm Rowntree made his first social survey of York in 1899 he believed that 29 per cent of the population kept a resident domestic servant, and he used 'the keeping or not keeping of domestic servants ... as marking the division between the working classes and those of a higher social scale' (*Poverty: A Study of Town Life*, S. Rowntree). Could this mean that about one-third of the households in York kept servants, and if so, was York typical of England?

The Family

The virtual elimination of the resident domestic servant, the decrease in the number of children and the reduction in the size of households in general, are positive indicators of the changes which have taken place in social conditions in modern times. The family, obviously, has not been immune to the economic and social revolutions of the past century and a half and many of its functions have been seriously modified. It has no longer the definite economic function, which it possessed even in the early nineteenth century, when its members produced jointly their means of subsistence, and many other functions which hitherto belonged to the family have been taken away or curtailed by, in particular, recent developments in social policy. For example, the family had a 'protective' function which embraced the physical care of all members in time of need, and though it is still the duty of parents to protect their children a great part of the care and protection which in the past would have had to be provided by members of the family, or not at all, is now given by social service agencies. The replacement of family care by 'social care' is well illustrated in the history of the Poor Law. In the early seventeenth-century Poor Law statutes the duty of providing assistance to individuals was placed firmly on the family, and even in the 1930's the determination of the amount of financial help to be given by the State to the unemployed was based very largely on the resources of the family, but under the National Assistance Act, 1948, the assessment of the needs of an applicant bear no relation to the resources of the family. It is now possible for an aged parent of limited means to be cared for by the State even though he (or she) may have wealthy sons or daughters, and this clearly represents a marked change in the development of social policy towards what would have been in the past purely 'family obligations'.[1]

Changes in economic and social conditions, scientific advances and the growth in the body of knowledge generally in modern times have all played a part in bringing about the twentieth-century type of family, but the modification or even removal of functions previously reserved to it does not mean that it is

---

[1] Recent surveys of the elderly have shown that there is very little neglect of aged parents by their children or other relatives, and it would be difficult to substantiate the argument (which is commonly put forward) that elderly persons are now being cast aside by members of their families.

fundamentally different now from what it was in the past. It is still the means through which the race survives and it provides in most (though not all) cases the best method of rearing children and of personality formation of the young, above all it retains an 'affectional' function in that it provides the greatest opportunity for the development of affectionate relationships between individuals.

Modern marriages probably encourage a greater degree of genuine affection between husband and wife than ever before because of the changes in the status of married women. Before 1882 a married woman possessed few legal rights, in effect she and her property (in the absence of a marriage settlement) were the property of her husband. Gradually she acquired the right to possess her own property, to make her own contracts and in general she has by now become an equal legal partner with her husband in marriage. There are, of course, legal obligations which a wife can be required to fulfil in her relationship with her husband, but equally the husband has obligations to his wife and in general marriage, in the eyes of the law, is now looked upon as a partnership of equals rather than, as in the past, an association of unequals in which all power was vested in the husband.[1]

This relatively new status of married women has undoubtedly been accompanied by changes in the marital relationship and it is probable that the reduction in family size is to a considerable degree a reflection of this change. The Royal Commission on Population argued that the emancipation of women and the movement towards equality of the sexes tended 'to weaken the traditional dominance of the husband, to raise the woman's status in marriage, with interests outside the home as well as inside, and to emphasize the wife's role as a companion to her husband as well as a producer of children. Unrestricted childbearing, which involved hardship and danger to women, became increasingly incompatible with the rising status of women and the development of a more considerate attitude of husbands to wives' (the *Report of the Royal Commission*). The readjustment of the relationship of husbands to wives began effectively in the

---

[1] For a comprehensive account of the law relating to the family in England and Wales see P. R. H. Webb and H. K. Bevan: *Source Book of Family Law* (Butterworths, 1964).

latter half of the nineteenth century, gathered momentum during the First World War, when women were encouraged to engage in activities outside the home to a greater extent than ever before, and has continued up to the present time. Further readjustments may well take place in marital relationships, and if the tendency for young married women to remain in gainful employment becomes even more pronounced it is unlikely that there will be any increase in family size.

The attainment of a higher material standard of living from a joint income, which could not possibly be achieved on the income of the husband alone, would be jeopardized by the birth of even one child, and the loss of income incurred by the withdrawal of the wife from gainful employment would not be offset by the various 'economic measures in favour of the family' which have been developed to ease the burdens of 'the family man'.[1] They would certainly not compensate a young mother for her withdrawal from the social activities which are now enjoyed by a larger proportion of the population than ever before.

Control over the size of the family has by now become firmly accepted as a normal feature of married life and 'this fundamental – and momentous – adjustment to modern life'[2] is obviously the most striking change in the history of the family in this country. It has been suggested that the prevalence of the small-family system is evidence of a deterioration in our national character, of growing selfishness on the part of married persons, and that it is detrimental to the national interest. Indeed, one critic has argued that 'the declining birth-rate, the decay of parental control, the increase in juvenile delinquency, and the growing prevalence of divorce are ominous indications of a widespread revolt against the restraints, sacrifices and duties of family life',[3] yet marriage, which brings the family into being, is as popular as ever and even those who have been unsuccessful

[1] For an excellent survey of measures used in twenty-four different countries to aid the family see *Economic Measures in Favour of the Family*, a report of the United Nations Department of Social Affairs, 1952.

[2] Royal Commission on Population.

[3] The Right Rev. E. J. Hagan in an essay on 'The Spiritual Foundations of the Family' in Sir James Marchant (ed.): *Rebuilding Family Life in the Post-War World* (Odhams, 1945). But for a spirited defence of the modern family see Ronald Fletcher: *The Family and Marriage* (Penguin Books, 1962).

in one marriage tend to try again. The family in England and Wales in the middle of the twentieth century is obviously very different from that of the past: it is noticeably smaller in size, it has lost some of its functions, it has in short changed but not necessarily for the worse.

CHAPTER IV

REGIONAL VARIATIONS IN THE COMPOSITION AND DISTRIBUTION OF THE POPULATION

THE population of England and Wales occupies a relatively small area of habitable land, yet it has succeeded in achieving a remarkable degree of variety in the manner in which it distributes itself over geographical areas and more particularly in the patterns of life within the various regions. Even that most obvious division of the population into those who live in England and those who live in Wales (who may not, of course, be respectively English and Welsh) provides interesting examples of variations in distribution, composition and manner of growth. For example, between 1871 and 1961 the population of England increased by about 104 per cent, whereas the population of Wales (including Monmouthshire)[1] increased by about 87 per cent; on the other hand, whilst England during that period continuously increased its population (though of course the rate of increase declined appreciably after 1911), Wales in one intercensal period, 1921–31, actually had a decrease of population of 2·4 per cent, and even during the years 1931–51 the percentage increase of population was much greater in England (approximately 10 per cent) than it was in Wales (approximately 0·2 per cent). Between 1951 and 1961 the total increase for England was just over 5 per cent whereas for Wales it was only just over 1½ per cent. Some of the important differences in the manner of growth and the composition of the population of England and Wales are shown in Tables 19 and 20.

[1] Throughout this chapter Wales includes Monmouthshire unless otherwise stated.

TABLE 19

Population growth and sex distribution in England and in Wales as shown by the Censuses of 1871, 1901, 1931, 1951 and 1961

Population in 000's

	1871 M.	1871 F.	1901 M.	1901 F.	1931 M.	1931 F.	1951 M.	1951 F.	1961 M.	1961 F.
England ..	10,353	10,946	14,718	15,798	17,839	19,519	19,746	21,413	21,012	22,448
Wales ..	706	707	1,011	1,001	1,294	1,300	1,270	1,329	1,292	1,352

Total population in 000's in selected Census years and percentage increase in 30-year periods

	Years 1871	1901	Inc. %	Years 1901	1931	Inc. %	Years 1931	1961	Inc. %
England ..	21,299	30,516	43·3	30,516	37,358	28·4	37,358	43,461	16·0
Wales ..	1,413	2,012	42·4	2,012	2,594	28·9	2,594	2,644	1·9

Ratio of Females per 1,000 males

	1871	1901	1931	1961
England	1,057	1,072	1,094	1,068
Wales	1,001	981	1,004	1,046

TABLE 20

Age and marital distribution of the populations of England and Wales at the Censuses of 1871, 1901, 1931, 1951 and 1961

Per Cent

	1871		1901		1931		1951		1961	
	E.	W.	E.	W.	E.	W.	E.	W.	E.	W.
Age-groups										
0–14 ..	36·1	36·8	32·3	34·0	23·6	26·6	22·1	22·8	22·9	23·4
15–39 ..	39·1	37·9	42·4	41·7	40·5	39·3	35·0	34·7	32·9	32·2
40–64 ..	20·1	20·0	20·6	19·7	28·4	27·3	31·8	31·7	32·3	32·4
65 and over ..	4·7	5·3	4·7	4·6	7·5	6·8	11·1	10·8	11·9	12·0
All ages	100	100	100	100	100	100	100	100	100	100
Single			59·6	60·7	50·7	52·9	42·0	43·2	41·1	41·7
Married			34·9	33·9	42·9	41·1	50·6	49·2	51·4	50·3
Widowed and Divorced ..			5·5	5·4	6·4	6·0	7·4	7·6	7·5	8·0

61

Variations in the Composition of the Population

In the late nineteenth century the manner of growth of population in England and in Wales was broadly similar. In both countries it was still relatively rapid as a result of fairly high birth-rates and more particularly falling death-rates. In the twentieth century, however, there have been marked differences and the outstanding feature is the rapid decline in the rate of growth in Wales since 1921. The declining rate and more particularly the decrease in the total population of Wales from (approximately) 2,656,000 in 1921 to 2,594,000 in 1931 was obviously not due solely to 'natural' causes. The total number of births fell appreciably in Wales but so did they in England, while death-rates in both countries were broadly similar, therefore the major factor contributing to the decline in Wales was emigration. As a result of depression conditions large numbers of people moved from Wales to England, hence helping to offset the decline in natural increase in England and accentuating the decline of population growth in Wales. Since 1931 the decline in the rate of growth in Wales has been arrested but compared with England the rate of increase has been small, thus whereas England increased its total population by 16 per cent in the period 1931–61, in Wales the percentage increase was only 1·7 per cent.

In addition to this exceptional variation in population growth in recent years there are other demographic differences between the peoples who live (or have lived) in Wales and those in England. There is, as shown in Table 19, a marked disparity in the distribution of the sexes. Whereas England since 1871 has always had more females than males the excess in Wales has always been smaller and indeed, in 1901 there were in Wales more males than females. As there has been virtually no difference in the ratio of male to female births or deaths in both countries the variation in sex ratios can be accounted for almost wholly by economic factors. Industrialization in Wales created demands for male labour and opportunities for female employment were limited. It seems likely, therefore, that in the late nineteenth and the early twentieth centuries young women left Wales to find employment in England (hence helping to accentuate the excess of women in England) while inward migration to Wales brought in male labour in response to the demands of industry (hence accentuating the surplus of males

62

Variations in the Composition of the Population

in Wales). In the 1940's, however, new light industries requiring female labour began to be established in Wales and the need to emigrate became less strong, so that by 1961 the differences in sex ratios had become less marked and Wales like England now has more females than males.

The differences in the marital and age distributions of both populations are not particularly striking; in general Wales has consistently maintained a slightly higher proportion of children, and a slightly lower proportion of youngish, middle-aged and elderly persons; a slightly higher proportion of single and a slightly lower proportion of married persons. The trend towards marriage at an earlier age has not been quite as strong in Wales as it has in England, and though birth-rates have declined appreciably in both countries since the 1870's, Wales has consistently maintained a slightly higher crude birth-rate and a higher rate of births per thousand women aged 15–44, but since the beginning of the twentieth century, when infant mortality rates in England and Wales as a whole began to decline sharply, Wales has continuously had a higher infant mortality rate than England.[1] On the other hand, Wales in the twentieth century (though not in the last quarter of the nineteenth century) regularly had, in relation to total live births, a smaller percentage of illegitimate births, but this 'moral superiority' of Wales could easily be offset if it could be shown that in Wales there is a higher proportion of pre-maritally conceived births.[2] In general, however, there is more similarity than dissimilarity in the births, marriages and deaths history of England and of Wales in the past ninety years, but in the pattern of population growth as a

[1] For example the infant mortality rates in selected years were:

	1900–02 (Annual average)	1930–32 (Annual average)	1951	1961
England ..	145	63	30	21·5
Wales ..	150	70	36	24

[2] In the Registrar-General's *Statistical Review of England and Wales for 1946–50* a study of pre-maritally conceived legitimate maternities, i.e. births occurring within 8½ months of marriage, and of illegitimate maternities shows that in the years 1946–50 in England and Wales 12·6 per cent (as compared with 14·6 per cent in 1938) of all maternities (i.e. pregnancies which have terminated in the birth of one or more live or stillborn children) were either illegitimate or pre-maritally conceived. Of the total maternities (497,199) conceived out of wedlock in England and Wales in 1946–50 approximately 299,000 were pre-maritally conceived and approximately 218,000 were illegitimate. Unfortunately there is no separation of the statistical evidence for Wales.

whole a marked disparity has arisen since the 1920's because of the loss of population by emigration from Wales.

The variation in the pattern of over-all growth is in part responsible for the dissimilarity in the density of population in relation to land area. Since records were first adequately maintained England has had a much higher density of population per square mile than Wales, and some examples of the changes in density in modern times are shown in Table 21.

TABLE 21

*Density of population in England and Wales at the Censuses of
1871, 1931, 1951 and 1961*

	Persons per square mile			
	1871	1931	1951	1961
England	432	742	818	863
Wales	178	324	324	329
England and Wales ..	389	685	750	790

The over-all densities in England and in Wales conceal the very wide divergencies within each country. Just as Wales differs from England so, too, are there distinctive areas within each country differing from each other, but, whereas the political, administrative and geographical boundaries between England and Wales are clear-cut and have remained stable for a long time past, there is no simple and universally acceptable method of dividing each country into separate areas. In the censuses taken in the first half of the nineteenth century the principal areas for which populations were shown separately were ancient counties, hundreds, ancient parishes, tythings, chapelries, townships and boroughs. From 1851 to 1881 a variety of new divisions, such as parliamentary counties and boroughs, dioceses, ecclesiastical districts and parishes and Poor Law Unions were distinguished, and then as a result of the creation of new administrative areas following the passing of the Local Government Acts of 1888 and 1894, even greater varieties of areas were added, such as urban districts, rural districts, administrative counties and county boroughs.[1] The effect

[1] See *Census Reports of Great Britain 1801–1931*, Guides to Official Sources, No. 2, for a summary of the changes in areas of population.

of all these changes was primarily to create confusion and to make comparisons from one Census to the next a hazardous operation. Even now extreme care is necessary when examining earlier Census reports because boundary changes continued to be made, as, for example, in 1929, when the Local Government Act modified the boundaries of certain kinds of administrative areas. There is, in fact, no completely satisfactory method of dividing the country into distinct areas which would be suitable for all purposes, but the Census authorities have been particularly careful to note boundary and other changes in order to ensure as far as possible comparability.

At the Census of 1921 a new system of geographical divisions was introduced, but in 1931 they were replaced by geographical regions, and these with only slight modifications remained in force in 1961. By today, therefore, standardized geographical regions are distinguished in addition to the political and administrative areas under the control of county, county borough, municipal borough, urban district and rural district councils, and of course due consideration is given to the growth of towns and the modern conurbation. But even these refinements have not eliminated all the difficulties involved in making comparisons over periods of years of distinct areas of population, because, apart from the obvious problems created by boundary changes, there are difficulties which are inherent in the Census, for example, the size of the resident population may be inflated or deflated according to the date on which the Census is taken. Normally the decennial Census has been taken in late March or early April, but, for example, in 1921 there had to be a postponement from the date originally chosen, April 24th to June 19th, and quite clearly the resident populations of some areas, such as holiday resorts, were greater on this latter date than they would have been on that originally chosen. There is, of course, a continual movement of population throughout the year and some areas (such as towns with universities and large public schools) have a regular ebb and flow which would make an enumeration of the 'normal' resident population difficult at any time. It is essential therefore that factors such as these should be borne in mind when making comparisons of areas of population over periods of time.

65

Variations in the Composition of the Population

Despite the difficulties involved in measuring satisfactorily the changes in population of living areas it is apparent that the trend towards living in 'towns' had been firmly established by the end of the nineteenth century.[1] In previous centuries there was only one very large town in England and Wales – London. Even at the beginning of the eighteenth century there were, apart from London, very few towns with a population of over 20,000 and only two, Bristol and Norwich, with a population of over 30,000.[2] By 1871, however, excluding London, there was one town with a population of over 400,000 (Liverpool), two with over 300,000 (Birmingham and Manchester), two (Leeds and Sheffield) with over 200,000, eight (Bradford, Bristol, Hull, Newcastle-on-Tyne, Portsmouth, Salford, Stoke-on-Trent and Sunderland) with over 100,000 and another twenty-three towns each with a population of over 50,000 but less than 100,000 (see Table 23). Wales had only three areas whose populations were included in this special group of what was to be called in later Census reports 'London and the Great Towns' and they were Cardiff, Swansea and Merthyr Tydfil whose separate populations numbered more than 50,000 but less than 100,000.[3]

Many of these 'great towns' even in 1871 were already beginning to sprawl outwards and absorb into town life the peoples who lived in hamlets, villages and small towns and at the same time the growth of population was more varied in the urban

[1] The term 'town' cannot satisfactorily be defined for all purposes and it is used in this context to denote a considerable collection of inhabited dwellings comprising a common living area where boundaries are definable and in which the inhabitants would probably have a sense of 'belonging'. The definable boundaries are generally those established for the purposes of local government.

[2] London has been for centuries unique in its size of population and certainly by 1871 it had already established itself as an area of extremely high density of population. In 1871, for example, London, i.e. the area 'within the radial lines of the Metropolitan Police District, drawn from 12 to 15 miles around Charing Cross . . . had a population in intimate fusion and close relation' of 3,883,902 (*Census 1871 – Preliminary Report*).

[3] Cardiff, Swansea and Merthyr as recorded in this Census were districts rather than towns and many of the persons enumerated in outlying areas would probably not have considered themselves as citizens of these three towns.

66

than in the rural areas.[1] The rapid growth of town populations was of course not unconnected with the economic developments of the eighteenth and nineteenth centuries and certainly there is strong evidence for the view that the growth of town populations was affected by industrialization. For example, in the period 1861–71 the populations of some of the Yorkshire towns such as Huddersfield, Halifax, Bradford, Leeds, Sheffield and Hull increased more rapidly than did those of most of the towns in Lancashire which in part was due to the relative decline of the cotton industry in this period and the resurgence of the Yorkshire woollen industry. Most of the ancient towns of England, with the exception of London, were already showing signs of relative decline in growth by the middle of the nineteenth century whereas the newer industrial and commercial towns were expanding rapidly not only in their numbers of people but in area as well. Yet even in 1871 the majority (approximately 64 per cent) of persons in England and Wales lived in towns, villages or hamlets of less than 50,000 population, but the trend towards town living had been firmly established and was to be strengthened in succeeding years.

By 1901 the number of places included in the group 'London and the Great Towns' had increased considerably compared with 1871 (see Table 23). Whereas in 1871 the total number of towns having a population of over 50,000 was thirty-seven (including London) in 1901 there were seventy-five (including London) in England and Wales.[2] All the towns included in the list in 1871 except Bath retained their places in 1901 and therefore thirty-nine additional towns had grown to over 50,000

[1] See pages 105–110 for a discussion of urban and rural population distribution. For an extremely interesting account of the movement of population from City Centres (such as those of Manchester and Liverpool) to areas on the fringes which then became part of the 'great town' see the introduction by the Registrar-General to the *Census 1871 – Preliminary Report.*

[2] 'The towns' listed in 1871 were Cities and Boroughs having defined Municipal or Parliamentary limits. By 1901 the local government boundaries, following the Local Government Acts of 1888 and 1894, were much more clearly defined and correspond more closely than those of 1871 to the present-day boundaries. But between 1911 and 1921 further boundary changes were to affect in particular the very large towns such as Birmingham and Liverpool and therefore in the Census Reports after 1901 adjustments have been made to the original 1901 enumerations in order to provide a greater measure of comparability with the present-day boundaries. The results of allowing for these boundary changes are shown in Table 23.

population in the thirty years from 1871 to 1901. Nearly all the 'great towns' of 1871 had increased their population, some dramatically, in the last thirty years of the nineteenth century, and of the new 'great towns' in 1901 nearly all were in the 50,000 to 100,000 population group. In 1901, therefore, excluding London (i.e. the City of London and the 28 Metropolitan Boroughs which had a population of approximately 4,536,000) there were three towns (Liverpool, Manchester and Birmingham[1]) which had populations of between 500,000 and 800,000, three (Leeds, Sheffield and Bristol) with between 300,000 and 500,000; seven with between 200,000 and 300,000; nineteen with between 100,000 and 200,000; and forty-two towns with over 50,000 and less than 100,000 population.[2]

In general it was the towns which in 1871 had populations of between 50,000 and 200,000 which grew fastest in the period 1871–1901 (for example, Leicester and Nottingham increased by well over 100 per cent, and Hull and Bradford increased by over 90 per cent), while the very large towns (Liverpool, Manchester and Birmingham) grew less rapidly (if we ignore the enlargement of their areas) recording increases of between 40 and 50 per cent, and the very small towns of under 10,000 and London at the other end of the scale increased least. The connection between industrial development and the size of towns is made abundantly clear in this period by the growth of towns such as Manchester, Birmingham, Leeds, Sheffield, Bradford, Bolton, Derby, Leicester, Nottingham, Northampton, Coventry and Wolverhampton which were intimately concerned with the manufacturing industries.

The enumerated population living in London and the seventy-four great towns in 1901 was approximately 14,507,000

---

[1] In the Census report for 1901 Birmingham and Liverpool are shown as having populations of 522,204 and 684,958 respectively, but in later Census reports their 1901 populations are shown as 759,063 and 711,276. These latter figures refer to the enlarged areas of Birmingham and Liverpool which came into being in the period 1911–21 when, for example, in Birmingham places such as Aston Manor, King's Norton and Northfield were absorbed which in 1901 were listed as separate towns. If the enlarged Birmingham is accepted for 1901 then Birmingham had a greater population than Liverpool, and Manchester, Birmingham and Liverpool should be shown as having populations of over 700,000 and less than 800,000 as in 1901, Col. *b*. in Table 23.

[2] For a complete list of these towns and comments on their growth see the *Census 1901 – General Report.*

(15,458,000 in the enlarged boundaries) or nearly 45 per cent (47·5 per cent) of the total population of England and Wales. More than half the total population therefore lived in small towns, villages or hamlets of less than 50,000 people but in the thirty years following 1871 the 'great towns' population as a proportion of the total population had increased from about 36 per cent to 45 per cent. This continual expansion of town populations though it was accompanied in many cases by an extension of town boundaries resulted in an extremely high density of population in these areas, as shown in Table 22.

TABLE 22

Density of town populations in England and Wales as recorded by the Census of 1901

Population of town areas	Persons per square mile
Over 700,000*	38,795
250,000 and under 700,000 ..	18,435
100,000 ,, ,, 250,000 ..	13,524
50,000 ,, ,, 100,000 ..	9,138
England and Wales	558

* London.

These high densities gave rise to innumerable problems not the least being that of overcrowding of persons in dwellings which in turn were overcrowded in relatively small areas of land, but at the turn of the century the rate of population growth was slowing down and in the first thirty years of the twentieth century towns of over 50,000 population grew less rapidly in number and most of them at a slower individual rate than in the last three decades of the nineteenth century.

Between 1901 and 1931 there were many boundary changes which make comparisons between the late nineteenth and the twentieth century a difficult operation, but the Census authorities in all reports since 1911 have, as far as possible, made allowances for these changes so that comparisons of the rate of growth of towns in the twentieth century are less liable to serious error. By 1931 the number of towns having a population of over 50,000 had grown to 113 as compared with 79 in 1901, so that whereas in the last thirty years of the nineteenth century the number of 'great towns' increased by more than 100 per cent, in the first thirty years of the twentieth century the rate of increase was less than 50 per cent. The greatest increase from 1901–31 (as in 1871–1901) was in the number of towns with a population of between 50,000 and 200,000, but in the great towns as a whole population grew less rapidly than in the previous thirty years, so that by 1931 the proportion of the population of England and Wales living in London and the Great Towns was approximately 51 per cent as compared with 47 per cent in 1901 (see Table 23). Some towns, notably London (see Table 24) actually declined in the first three decades of this century but with one or two other minor exceptions all the towns with over 50,000 population in 1901 continued to grow. Of the towns which entered the list of the 'great towns' for the first time in 1931 some had grown remarkably rapidly, for example, Dagenham whose population grew from about 8,000 in 1911 to 89,362 in 1931 and which in the intercensal period 1921–31 increased by 879·1 per cent. At the same time we see the beginnings of the expansion of other towns around the London area, such as Harrow, Hendon, Wembley, Hornchurch, Romford and Hayes which nearly (and in some cases more than) doubled their population from 1921–31 and were to become still larger in the period 1931–51.

The dramatic change in economic conditions after the First World War had its effects on the growth of towns; those whose fortunes had been linked with coal, cotton, wool, iron and steel had grown rapidly up to the war years and then experienced a much less rapid rate of growth in the period 1921–31. For example, Manchester, Sheffield, Leeds, Bradford, Stoke, Oldham, Preston, Gateshead, Newcastle-on-Tyne, Swansea and Cardiff all increased by less than 5 per cent, and towns like Salford, Bolton, Blackburn, Rochdale, Wigan, Rhondda and Merthyr actually recorded decreases of population in this decade. In the years during and following the Second World War nearly all these towns while remaining in the 50,000 and over group recorded still further decreases of population so that even by 1951 they had not recovered from the depopulating effects of depression conditions.

The years 1931–51 were, of course, affected by depression

TABLE 23

Numbers of towns in England and Wales with population over 50,000 in 1871, 1901, 1931, 1951 and 1961.

	1871	1901 a	1901 b	1931	1951	1961
Number of towns with population over 50,000	37	75	79	113	157	184
Population of 1 million and under 5 million	1 (London)	1 (London)	1 (London)	2 (London) (Birmingham)	2 (London) (Birmingham)	2 (London) (Birmingham)
700,000 and under 1 million	—	—	2 (Birmingham) (Liverpool)	2 (Liverpool) (Manchester)	2 (Liverpool) (Manchester)	1 (Liverpool)
500,000 and under 700,000	—	3 (Liverpool) (Manchester) (Birmingham)	1 (Manchester)	1 (Sheffield)	2 (Sheffield) (Leeds)	2 (Manchester) (Leeds)
300,000 and under 500,000	3	3 (Leeds) (Sheffield) (Bristol)	3 (Sheffield) (Leeds) (Bristol)	3 (Leeds) (Bristol) (Hull)	2 (Bristol) (Nottingham)	5 (Sheffield) (Bristol) (Nottingham) (Coventry) (Kingston upon Hull)
200,000 and under 300,000	2	7	8	11	11	10
100,000 and under 200,000	8	19	23	32	47	47
50,000 and under 100,000	23	42	41	62	91	117
Total population in these towns (000's omitted)	8,293	14,507	15,458	20,242	23,029	24,561
Population of England and Wales (000's omitted)	22,712	32,528	32,528	39,952	43,758	46,105
Percentage of total population living in towns of 50,000 and over	36·5%	44·6%	47·5%	50·7%	52·6%	53·3%

a – Town boundaries corresponding more closely to those in 1871.   b – Town boundaries corresponding more closely to those after 1901.

conditions, the war, changes in the rate of natural increase, the balance of migration and other factors which had their repercussions on town growth, but by 1951 there were 157 'great towns', so that in this period the rate of increase in the number of 'great towns' was greater than it had been in the earlier years of the twentieth century. Once more the greatest increase was in those with a population of between 50,000 and 200,000, but the increase in the accumulation of population in the great towns as a whole was less rapid than the increase in the number of towns (see Tables 23 and 24). Nevertheless by 1951 approximately 53 per cent of the total population of England and Wales were living in London and the Great Towns compared with approximately 37 per cent in 1871.

In the period 1951–61 the problems of ever-increasing populations within static town boundaries were seen to be more serious than ever before. Even though the number of great towns was by 1961 nearly five times as great as that of 1871 the limits of expansion in the largest towns had been reached. Hence in this decade some of the large towns which had grown continuously up to 1951 began to lose population as shown in Table 24. The obvious examples are Birmingham and Ilford, and it is significant that only Coventry and Leeds continued to grow.

We have become quite clearly a nation in which over half the total population are large-town dwellers and the stage has already been reached in some of the largest towns when future additions to their existing populations will have to be housed outside the present town boundaries. In London and Birmingham, for example, discussions have been going on for some time about the building of 'over-spill' towns to house their excess citizens whose place of employment is within the town areas. In part these difficulties have arisen because these twentieth-century additions to the town populations are the result of immigration by persons born in other parts of the country. For example, in the period of 1931–51, the increase of 45 per cent in the population of Coventry was made up of 18·7 per cent excess of births over deaths and 26·3 per cent by the balance of migration. The one major exception to this general rule was Birmingham, whose 11 per cent increase was accounted for by 13 per cent excess of births over deaths and − 2 per cent by balance of migration. In those towns which showed a decline

TABLE 24

Population changes in selected towns, 1901–61, due allowance having been made for boundary changes

	Population (000's omitted)				Increase (+) or decrease (−) per cent in the intercensal period				
	1901	1931	1951	1961	1901–11	1911–21	1921–31	1931–51	1951–61
London	4,536	4,397	3,348	3,195	− 0·3	− 0·8	− 2·0	− 23·9	− 0·46
Birmingham ..	759	1,003	1,113	1,106	+ 10·7	+ 9·5	+ 8·7	+ 11·0	− 0·06
Liverpool ..	711	856	789	748	+ 5·9	+ 6·5	+ 6·3	− 7·9	− 0·56
Manchester ..	645	766	703	661	+ 10·8	+ 2·3	+ 4·2	− 8·3	− 0·61
Sheffield ..	411	518	513	494	+ 11·9	+ 6·8	+ 0·4	− 1·0	+ 0·37
Leeds	436	483	505	511	+ 4·1	+ 0·9	+ 4·2	+ 4·6	+ 0·09
Coventry ..	70	178	258	305	+ 52·0	+ 27·4	+ 16·5	+ 45·0	+ 1·67
Ilford	41	131	185	178	+ 89·6	+ 9·0	+ 53·8	+ 40·9	− 0·36
Southend-on-Sea	33	130	152	165	+ 116·5	+ 50·0	+ 14·2	+ 17·0	+ 0·83
Ealing	33	117	187	183	+ 85·3	+ 10·3	+ 29·3	+ 60·5	− 0·22
Hendon	22	116	156	152	+ 72·9	+ 43·7	+ 100·9	+ 34·8	− 0·28

in total population the main factor responsible was emigration either to outer suburbs or other towns as, for example, in the case of London where the decrease of 23·9 per cent was due to emigration — 27·8 per cent and natural increase + 3·9 per cent, and Liverpool with natural increase of 13 per cent and emigration — 20·9 per cent between 1931 and 1951. In the period 1951–61 changes have occurred again as a result of the growing pressure of population within limited town boundaries. Some of the fast-growing towns have now had to 'export' their populations to new areas, and what were smallish areas of population even in 1951 have become towns in their own right. Nearly all the large towns (i.e. of over 100,000 people) have shown a decrease or only a very slight increase of population. The main growth now is in the 'new' and smaller towns. There has been therefore a varied pattern of growth and decline in recent years but over all the trend towards living in towns has continued with the result that measures have had to be devised to deal with the problems of housing the ever-growing town populations.

One method of dealing with this situation was to create new towns and under the New Towns Act, 1946, attempts have been made to create living areas free from the congestion and other obvious defects of most of the 'great towns' already in existence.[1] By 1951 twelve new towns had been established as a result of this Act, but they were all small in that the largest had a population of less than 25,000 in 1951. However, in the next ten years they were to grow rapidly, for example, the twelve new towns established by 1951 increased their populations as follows: Aycliffe from 594 in 1951 to 12,101 in 1961; Bracknell from 5,143 to 20,380; Corby from 16,743 to 35,880; Crawley from 10,707 to 54,065; Cwmbran from 13,656 to 30,043, Harlow from 5,825 to 53,496; Hatfield from 9,256 to 20,504; Hemel Hempstead from 21,976 to 54,816; Peterlee from 298 to 13,792; Stevenage from 7,311 to 42,422; and Welwyn from 18,804 to 34,944. In total these new towns grew from 134,974 in 1951 to 426,150 in 1961, a remarkable rate of increase, yet they have not solved the problems of housing the population and more new

---

[1] This was of course by no means the first attempt to create properly planned living areas. The 'Garden City' movement for example had been well established in the nineteenth century.

towns are still required. In most respects the new differ markedly from the older towns in that they are being developed deliberately as residential areas whereas most of the latter have grown haphazardly in response to a variety of changing circumstances.[1]

The device of the 'new town' is by no means the only method at present being used to deal with the problem of the growth of town populations. Many large towns have undertaken, in recent years in particular, vast schemes for the housing and re-housing of their populations, and in some cases very large local authority housing estates have been built which are in themselves small towns. The pattern of town living will doubtless be changed by developments of this kind and in the course of time it may well be that what are now vast municipal housing estates will themselves become towns in their own right. It would seem to be inevitable that in a society with a continuously growing population, with ever-changing social and economic conditions and standards that the areas in which people live should also be subject to continual transformation. The towns of the nineteenth century grew rapidly and haphazardly, and in the industrial areas in particular they became in some cases nothing more than a kind of overcrowded barracks to house an army of industrial workers, but with the advances which have been made in means of communication, with the changes which have taken place in the social conscience and in social policy, and with the revival of interest in town planning we ought in future to see a very different pattern of development of towns from that witnessed in the nineteenth century.[2] We seem at last to have realized that even a town designed specifically to house 'an industrial army' for heavy industry purposes need not be an ugly and squalid collection of ill-designed houses, shops, churches, pubs and schools with no function or beauty and devoid of the essential elements which enable people not merely to exist but to live.[3]

[1] The growth of the new towns despite being planned have not solved all the problems of 'town life'. See J. H. Nicholson: *New Communities in Britain: Achievements and Problems* published by the National Council of Social Service in 1961.

[2] See the proposals to develop living areas on a regional basis, e.g. *The North East, a Programme for Regional Development and Growth*, Cmd. 2206, H.M.S.O., 1963 and *The South East Study – 1961–81*, H.M.S.O., 1964.

[3] Apart from the problems of housing we now have to face the growing problem of traffic congestion see *Traffic in Towns* (the Buchanan Report), H.M.S.O., 1963.

Variations in the Composition of the Population

The distribution of that section of the population which lives in towns and the growth of towns has been treated first because it would appear that the Englishman (and even the Welshman) still pays due regard to the rights of a citizen, and one suspects that most people when asked 'Where do you come from?' will give the name of their place of birth or if they have moved, their usual place of residence – their town. The town, be it large or small, to which one feels a sense of belonging clearly plays a part in moulding the lives of its inhabitants, just as the inhabitants have a part to play in forming the character of the town. But Englishmen (with the exception perhaps of the true Londoner) and Welshmen have in essence a dual loyalty in that in addition to their town they belong to a county.

THE COUNTIES – CHANGING PATTERNS OF GROWTH 1901–51

The county is one of the oldest divisions of the country for administrative and other purposes, but the areas of the ancient counties were altered by the Local Government Act, 1888, which created 'Administrative Counties' and 'County Boroughs'.[1] Of the sixty-two administrative counties (forty-nine in England and thirteen in Wales) created by this Act only fifteen were identical with the ancient or geographical counties then in existence, but in most of the others administrative county boundaries were broadly similar to those which had previously been accepted. There have been further slight alterations of administrative county boundaries but the Census authorities have made allowance for these changes and it is possible therefore to examine with a fair degree of accuracy the changes in the distribution of population in counties in the first half of the twentieth century. The administrative counties were not, however, in all cases identical with 'the County' to which a person would give his allegiance, for example, Yorkshire was divided into three administrative counties though obviously a person born in the East, West or North Riding of Yorkshire would lay claim to being a Yorkshireman; and a person who

[1] See the introduction to the *Census 1901 – General Report*, for a good brief description of the changes which had been made in the number and nature of areas into which England and Wales had been divided at different times.

76

claimed Sussex as his county would not be unduly perturbed by the fact that his administrative county was either Sussex East or Sussex West. Again the county boroughs were not strictly a part of administrative counties, but, surely a person who claimed to be a citizen of Leeds County Borough would also lay claim to being a Yorkshireman, and a citizen of Southend-on-Sea County Borough would surely admit that he was a 'man of Essex'. In order therefore to give a picture of the distribution of population in each county, using that term in the sense in which it is probably understood by most people as being the area to which they belong, it is necessary to merge some of the administrative counties and include the county boroughs with the administrative counties with which they are associated.[1] On this basis there were forty counties in England and thirteen in Wales.[2]

The fifty-three counties of England and Wales have for centuries exhibited wide variations in their economic and social development and indeed even in the character of their peoples. The ancient rivalries which sometimes in the past were occasionally fought out on the field of battle are perhaps now confined to the field of sport, but individual characteristics are still recognizable and county loyalties are often a means of bringing together groups of people for specific purposes. Each county and its people has special features which perhaps more than anything else contribute to the mosaic which is England and Wales, and even the spread of industrialization, of urbanization and the levelling effects of national services such as universal education have done no more than blur the distinctions which help to differentiate the Yorkshireman from the Lancastrian or the folk of Somerset from those of Norfolk.

The distribution of county populations is remarkably uneven, and there is certainly more variation in the size of population than there is in the area of each county (see Tables 25 and 26). In this century there has been relatively little change in the

---

[1] Some county boroughs straddle more than one county area but the Census reports place all county boroughs in direct association with one county only.

[2] That is the forty-nine administrative counties of England are reduced to forty by combining the three Ridings into Yorkshire; Lindsey, Holland and Kesteven into Lincolnshire; Southampton and the Isle of Wight into Hampshire; East and West Sussex and Suffolk into Sussex and Suffolk; and merging the Isle of Ely and the Soke of Peterborough into Cambridgeshire and Northamptonshire respectively.

proportional area of the country as a whole occupied by each county but on the other hand there have been significant changes in the way in which counties have shown an increase or decrease of population. The over-all distribution of counties by size of population from 1901–51 and their relative areas by acreage in 1951 are shown in Tables 25 and 26[1] from which it can be seen that in England there has been a considerable upward movement of counties (with the exception of London) from one population group to another whereas in Wales there has been a less pronounced movement. In England seventeen counties remained in the same population group for fifty years, seventeen moved up to the next higher group, four (Derbyshire, Hertfordshire, Nottinghamshire, and Surrey) moved up two groups higher, Middlesex moved three groups higher while London moved down one group, but in Wales no county moved up more than one group higher than that which it occupied in 1901 and seven remained in the same group throughout the period. All the counties in England which remained within the same group in fact increased their population though in some cases only slightly, whereas of seven Welsh counties remaining in their orignal groups three had smaller populations in 1951 than they had in 1901. In general, however, there was very little change in the population size of counties relatively to each other in either England or Wales, for example, the three smallest counties in England in 1901 (Rutland, approximately 20,000; Huntingdonshire, approximately 54,000 and Westmorland, approximately 64,000) were still the smallest in 1951 and the three largest in 1901 (Yorkshire, approximately 3·2 million, Lancashire, approximately 4·4 million and London, approximately 4·5 million) were still the three largest in 1951.

There appears to have been no positive correlation between county areas and population in England or Wales (see Tables 25 and 26) and this of course is one reason for the demands which have been made in recent years for a drastic revision of local government boundaries. Whereas population grew rapidly in some counties the land area available for housing and other needs hardly changed at all so that it is perhaps not surprising that two of the counties with the biggest populations in England were also two of the smallest in area, but any

[1] On pages 80–81.

revision of boundaries inevitably raises innumerable objections and rouses the strongest of parochial passions despite the obvious fact that the determination of county areas was made at a time when social and economic conditions were very different from what they are now. It is, of course, extremely difficult to forecast with any degree of accuracy the future size of a county population because unforeseeable factors may arise which attract or drive away persons over relatively short periods of time. In this century rapid changes in economic conditions, which could not necessarily have been foreseen even at the end of the nineteenth century, have influenced migration between counties and so helped to bring about a very varied pattern of growth and decline of population within counties. Some of these changes are made obvious in Table 25, but in order to illustrate more clearly the extent of increase or decrease in this century in the populations of the counties in England and Wales Table 27 has been constructed.

It is not possible to choose periods of equal length to cover the first half of the twentieth century in part because there was no Census in 1941 and therefore in Table 27 an attempt has been made to show the changes which occurred in the period extending just beyond the first quarter and just under the second quarter of this century and in two successive twenty-year periods. It is significant that only five counties in England and not one in Wales maintained their position in the same percentage group of increase over all three periods, whilst only one county in England and three in Wales consistently suffered a decrease of population in this fifty years. Even these consistent counties have shown marked variations annually and decennially, but for only nine to maintain their position in their original group is indicative of the great changes in the patterns of growth. This is emphasized, too, by the fact that even in the two successive twenty-year periods from 1911 there were only sixteen counties in England and three in Wales which remained in the same percentage group of increase whilst one county in England and four in Wales had a decrease in both periods.

In England whilst most of the counties continued to grow it is those around London which exhibited the most rapid rates of growth, for example, Middlesex, Surrey and Essex, whose populations increased between 1901 and 1931 by 106·8 per

79

TABLE 25

The size of county population in England and Wales, 1901-51

N.B. – Counties above the dotted line have remained in the same population group at each Census.

ENGLAND

Population	1901	1931	1951
Under 200,000	Herefords; Hunts; Rutland; Westmorland.	→ do. →	do.
	Beds; Bucks; Cambs; Oxon.		
200,000 and less than 400,000	Cornwall; Cumberland; Dorset, Salop; Wilts.	→ do. →	do.
	Berks; Herts; Northants; Suffolk; Worcs.	Beds; Berks; Bucks; Cambs; Northants.	Beds; Bucks; Cambs; Oxon.
400,000 and less than 600,000	Norfolk; Somerset	→ do. →	do.
	Derbs; Leics; Lincs; Notts.	Herts; Leics; Suffolk; Worcs.	Berks; Northants; Suffolk; Worcs.
600,000 and less than 800,000	Devon; Northumberland.	→ do. →	do.
	Glos; Mddx; Surrey; Sussex.	Derbys; Glos; Lincs; Notts; Sussex.	Herts; Leics; Lincs.
800,000 and less than 1 million	Cheshire; Hants; Kent.	—	Derbys; Glos; Notts; Sussex.
1 million and less than 2 million	Durham; Staffs; Warwicks.	→ do. →	do.
	Essex.	Cheshire; Essex; Hants; Kent; Mddx; Surrey.	Cheshire; Hants; Kent; Surrey.
2 million and less than 4 million	Yorks.	—	Essex; London; Middx.
4 million and less than 6 million	Lancs.	→ do. →	do.
	London.	London; Yorks.	Yorks.

Variations in the Composition of the Population

Population	1901	1931	1951
Under 50,000	Merionethshire; Radnorshire.	→ do. →	do.
	—	Anglesey; Montgomeryshire.	Montgomeryshire.
50,000 and less than 100,000	Brecon; Cardigan; Pembrokes.	→ do. →	do.
	Anglesey; Flintshire; Montgomeryshire.	—	Anglesey.
100,000 and less than 150,000	Caernarvonshire.	→ do. →	do.
	Carmarthenshire; Denbighshire.	Flintshire.	Flintshire.
150,000 and less than 250,000	—	Carmarthenshire; Denbighshire.	Carmarthenshire; Denbighshire.
250,000 and less than 750,000	Monmouthshire.	→ do. →	do.
750,000 and less than 1 million	Glamorgan.	—	—
1 million and less than 1,500,000	—	Glamorgan.	Glamorgan.

N.B. – The County areas are those in existence in 1951, therefore the 1901 and 1931 populations are for the areas as constituted in 1951. If the 1901 or 1931 boundaries had been maintained then the only counties whose grouping would have to be altered in the 1901 column of this Table are Derbyshire, Hampshire, Warwickshire and Worcestershire. However, readers who may wish to examine the Census reports for further detailed information concerning counties should ensure that they note carefully the boundaries used in the Census reports.

cent, 80·7 per cent and 61·9 per cent respectively. They were quite out of step with the country as a whole in which the total population increase between 1901 and 1931 was 22·4 per cent, and as there were only eighteen counties (i.e. all those in Table 27 in the groups 20 per cent and over in 1901–31, except Staffordshire and Yorkshire) which exceeded this national figure they absorbed an undue share of the national increase. The exceptional growth of the 'Home Counties' was in part a reflection of the movement of population for living purposes out of

TABLE 26

*Size of counties in England and Wales by
area in statute acres (land and inland water), 1951*

Acreage	English counties	Welsh counties
Less than 200,000 acres	London; Mddx; Rutland.	Anglesey; Flintshire.
200,000 and less than 400,000	Beds; Hunts.	Caernarvon; Monmouth; Pembrokes; Radnor.
400,000 and less than 600,000	Berks; Bucks; Cambs; Herefords; Leics; Notts; Oxon; Surrey; Westmorland; Worcs.	Brecon; Cardigan; Carmarthen; Denbigh; Glamorgan; Merioneth; Montgomery.
600,000 and less than 800,000	Cheshire; Derbys; Dorset; Durham; Herts; Northants; Staffs; Warwicks.	
800,000 and less than 1 million	Cornwall; Cumberland; Essex; Glos; Kent; Salop; Suffolk; Sussex; Wilts.	
1 million and less than 2 million	Devon; Hants; Lancs; Lincs; Norfolk; Northumberland; Somerset.	
2 million and less than 4 million.	Yorks.	

London to the bordering counties and of the growth of 'newer' industries in these areas attracting population from other parts of the country. In the same way the Midland Counties (Warwickshire and Nottinghamshire in particular) grew rapidly in this period, indicating a movement of population towards the industrial areas which were continuing to expand in the twentieth century. On the other hand, those counties which were concerned predominantly with agriculture or with the thriving nineteenth-century industries based on coal, cotton and wool grew much less rapidly and in some cases recorded decreases of population.

The period 1901–31 in effect marks the culminating stage in the pattern of growth which had existed from the middle of the nineteenth century, in which the counties of England were broadly divisible into four main groups based on their increase (or decrease) of population in the period 1861–1931, as follows:

TABLE 27

Percentage increase and decrease of population in the Counties of England and Wales in the intercensal periods 1901–31, 1911–31 and 1931–51. County areas as constituted in 1951. (Counties above the dotted line have remained in the same percentage group in the three periods and those in italics have remained in the same group in the periods 1911–31 and 1931–51).

ENGLAND

Percentage	1901–31	1911–31	1931–51
Increase Under 10 per cent.	Norfolk; Westmorland. .... Hunts; Northants; Salop; Somerset; Suffolk.	⟶ do. ⟶ .... *Devon*; Durham; Dorset; Glos; *Lancs*; Northants; *Northumb*; Somerset; Suffolk; Wilts.	do. .... Cornwall; Cumberland; *Devon*; *Lancs*; *Northumb*; Yorks.
10 and under 20 per cent.	Cambs. .... Devon; Dorset; Glos; Lancs; Oxon; Wilts; Worcs.	⟶ do. ⟶ .... Beds; Berks; *Ches*; *Derbys*; *Hants*; Hunts; Kent; *Leics*; *Lincs*; *Notts*; Oxon; *Staffs*; Sussex; Worcs; Yorks.	do. .... *Ches*; *Derbys*; Essex; Glos; *Hants*; Herefords; *Leics*; *Lincs*; Northants; *Notts*; Rutland; Salop; Somerset; *Staffs*; Suffolk.
20 and under 30 per cent.	Berks; Beds; Ches; Derbys; Durham; Kent; Leics; Lincs; Northumb; Staffs; Sussex; Yorks.	Bucks; Essex; Herts; *Warwicks*.	Berks; Dorset; Hunts; Kent; Sussex; *Warwicks*; Wilts; Worcs.
30 per cent and over.	Mddx; Surrey .... Bucks; Essex; Hants; Herts; Notts; Warwicks.	⟶ do. ⟶	do. .... Beds; Bucks; Herts; Oxon.
Decrease 1–25 per cent.	London. .... Cornwall; Cumberland; Herefords; Rutland.	⟶ do. ⟶ .... Cornwall; Cumberland; Hereford; Rutland; Salop.	do. .... Durham.

Variations in the Composition of the Population

WALES

Percentage	1901–31	1911–31	1931–51
Increase Under 10 per cent.	Brecon.	*Denbigh*; Glam; Monmouth; *Pembrokes*; Radnor.	Anglesey; Caernarvon; *Denbigh*; *Pembrokes*.
10 and under 20 per cent.	Denbigh.	Carmarthen.	—
20 and under 30 per cent.	—	*Flint*.	*Flint*.
30 per cent and over.	Carmarthen; Flint; Glam; Monmouth.	—	—
Decrease 0–10 per cent.	Cardigan; Montgomery; Merioneth.	⟶ do. ⟶	do.
	Anglesey; Caernarvon; Pembrokes; Radnor.	Anglesey; Caernarvon; *Brecon*.	*Brecon*; Carmarthen; Glam; Monmouth; Radnor.

Group 1. Counties which increased their population continuously and in some cases very considerably: Bedfordshire; Berkshire; Buckinghamshire; Cheshire; Derbyshire; Essex; Hampshire; Hertfordshire; Lincolnshire; Middlesex; Nottinghamshire; Surrey; Sussex, Warwickshire.

Group 2. Counties which grew continuously but whose rate of growth slackened in the twentieth century; Durham; Kent; Lancashire; Leicestershire; London; Northamptonshire; Northumberland; Staffordshire; Worcestershire; Yorkshire.

Group 3. Counties which grew slowly (and on occasion even declined): Cambridgeshire; Cumberland; Devonshire; Dorsetshire; Gloucestershire; Norfolk; Oxfordshire; Salop; Somerset; Suffolk; Westmorland; Wiltshire.

Group 4. Counties whose populations decreased: Cornwall; Herefordshire; Huntingdonshire; Rutland.

Variations in the Composition of the Population

The depression of the 1930's and the war of 1939–46 (with its destruction of houses, evacuation of population and later resettlement of ex-Service men and women) and modern technological developments contributed to still further variations in the pattern of growth of counties. Table 27 shows that in the two successive twenty-year periods from 1911 only sixteen counties in England remained relatively constant in their rate of increase and one continued to decrease so that twenty-three of the forty counties changed their pattern of growth. Eleven moved up into the next higher percentage group of increase, four accelerated their rate of increase by moving up two groups higher, five changed their pattern from that of a decrease in 1911–31 to an increase in the next twenty years, two (Yorkshire and Essex) experienced a slackening in their rate of increase by moving down one group and one (Durham) after having consistently increased its population from 1861–1931 recorded a decrease from 1931–51.

 If we extend the period 1861–1931 up to 1951 the four broad groups of counties shown above would remain unaltered since, despite the changes in pattern exhibited in the period 1931–51, none changed sufficiently radically to move out of the group they occupied in the period 1861–1931.

It would seem, therefore, that for ninety years there was a broad pattern of growth of counties in spite of marked variations within counties and that it consists of those which grew continuously and in most cases rapidly (Group 1), those which grew but whose rate of growth declined (in some cases appreciably) in the twentieth century (Group 2); those whose growth was steady but in most cases slow (Group 3), and those which suffered a decrease in population (Group 4). The reasons for this pattern are many, but undoubtedly economic changes have played an important part in bringing about the redistribution of populations between counties. As we shall see later, most of the rapidly-growing counties had a relatively high proportion of persons living in the county at the date of the Census who were born elsewhere and with the relative decline of some of the staple nineteenth-century industries and the demands for labour created by the 'newer' industries established in the twentieth century there was a tendency for persons to move away from the older industrial areas located predominantly in the north to the newer industrial areas of the Midlands and the South of England.

The effect of economic changes on county populations was even more striking in Wales, and Tables 25 and 27 indicate the differences between the patterns in Wales and those in England. In the late nineteenth century, although Wales increased its population by roughly the same percentage as England, the increase was much more unevenly distributed over counties, for example, between 1861 and 1901 no less than seven[1] of the thirteen counties in Wales actually suffered a decrease in population, four (Carmarthenshire; Denbighshire; Flintshire and Merioneth) showed moderate increases and two (Glamorganshire and Monmouthshire) increased appreciably. Glamorganshire and Monmouthshire increased to such an extent that they accounted for approximately 80 per cent of the total increase of population in Wales in this period, and there can be little doubt that the main reason for their rapid growth was that their coal and steel industries in particular attracted labour from other parts of the country.

In the first three decades of the twentieth century the population of Wales increased at a rate greater than that of England, but again the increase was unevenly distributed. Seven Welsh counties (in this period Breconshire increased and was replaced in the decrease group by Merionethshire) continued to lose population, two (Breconshire and Denbighshire) showed moderate increases and four (Carmarthenshire, Flintshire, Glamorganshire and Monmouthshire) increased appreciably. But in these thirty years there was a significant difference in the pattern of growth between 1901–11 and 1921–31 particularly, for those counties which recorded increases in the period as a whole. For example, Glamorganshire had percentage increases of 30·4 between 1901 and 1911, 11·8 between 1911 and 1921, and a decrease of 2·0 per cent between 1921 and 1931, and Monmouthshire in the first two decades recorded increases of 32·7 per cent and 13·9 per cent and then a decrease of 4·0 per cent between 1921 and 1931, whilst for the period 1901–31 Glamorganshire's increase was 42·3 per cent and Monmouth's 45·1 per cent. This change in pattern is illustrated by the fact

[1] Anglesey, Breconshire, Caernarvonshire, Cardiganshire, Montgomery, Pembrokeshire and Radnorshire.

that between 1901–11 eight Welsh counties increased their population whilst five had a modest decrease, but from 1921–31 no less than ten suffered a decrease and the remaining three (Carmarthenshire, Denbighshire and Flintshire) had only moderate increases. The decrease of population in this decade was in most cases appreciable, for example, Cardigan and Radnor had a percentage decrease of nearly 10 per cent, a rate of decrease experienced by only one English county (Rutland in 1911–21) in any of the first three decades of the twentieth century. This change over from an increase of 32·1 per cent in the population of Wales in the period 1901–21 to a decrease of 2·4 per cent in the years 1921–31 created alarm and aroused fears about depopulation in a relatively short time, and to some extent there was justification for these views because, unlike England in which a decline in population in some counties merely resulted in an increase of population in others, the movement of population from the Welsh counties was to a considerable degree a movement away from Wales. Predominantly, the decline in the Welsh counties was counter-balanced by a gain in some English counties, but the effects on Wales were serious from the point of view of future economic and social development.

The pattern of growth of the counties in Wales from 1861–1931 is, therefore, different from that of England, and broadly Welsh counties may be divided into three groups based on their increase or decrease of population in this period, as follows:

(1) Counties which increased their population almost continuously:
   Denbigh, Flintshire.

(2) Counties which increased their population but at a declining rate in the twentieth century:
   Caernarvon, Carmarthen, Glamorgan, Merioneth, Monmouth.

(3) Counties whose population decreased (though not necessarily continuously):
   Anglesey, Brecon, Cardigan, Montgomery, Pembrokes, Radnor.

In the period from 1931–51 there were further changes in the pattern of Welsh population growth. Total population increased slightly despite the fact that eight counties (see Table 27) recorded a decrease and only one (Flint) showed an appreciable increase. But the rate of decrease had moderated and the five counties recording increases were just able to outweigh the losses and so provide a net gain of population for the country as a whole. This was not a dramatic recovery and it would have been premature to assume that the downward trend in the population of most Welsh counties had been finally halted and reversed. The severe industrial depression of the 1930's, which was one of the prime factors driving people away from South Wales, took longer to 'work itself out' in Wales than in most parts of England and though the war led to the establishment of many new factories and to a revival in the coal and steel industries, economic opportunities in Wales were still much more restricted than they were in England. Under the Distribution of Industry Act, 1945,[1] South Wales, Monmouthshire and Wrexham were scheduled as Development areas in which it was intended to promote the growth of new and the expansion of existing industries, and if the aims of this Act are fulfilled, then there will be more varied economic opportunities than there were in the past which will help at least to retain, even if they do not attract, population. It is as yet too early to judge whether the improvement in economic conditions arising out of the war and continuing in the post-war years is likely to be maintained, or whether the Distribution of Industry Act will in the long run provide the variety of economic activity which industrialized Wales lacked in the past, but at least the outward flow of population has diminished considerably. It is, however, unlikely that Wales will see again the pattern of rapid population growth such as it had at the turn of the century.

One result of these variations in growth of county populations in England and Wales was that some counties had a much smaller proportion of native-born (i.e. born within the county) persons at each Census than others. The Census authorities

[1] The Distribution of Industry Act, 1945, gives the Board of Trade authority to build factories for letting to suitable industries, the Treasury may assist firms financially and so on, but the Government cannot direct a firm to go to any particular area. In England development areas have been established in parts of Northumberland, Durham, Cumberland and Lancashire. These are areas in which there is likely to be a danger of unemployment and which therefore may be scheduled by the Board of Trade as development areas. They are essentially the depressed areas of the 1930's.

have, since 1841, included in the Census a question on birth-place and therefore it is possible from successive censuses to make an estimate of migration between counties by comparing the proportion of native-born enumerated persons with those born outside the county of enumeration. All the counties of England and Wales, from 1841–1951 returned at least 90 per cent (and in most cases nearer 95 per cent) of their enumerated populations as having been born in England or Wales, but within each county there was a marked variation in the propor-tion of its total population resident within the county of birth at successive censuses (see Tables 28 and 29).

In the first half of the twentieth century only two counties in England, Middlesex and Surrey, have consistently been pre-dominantly composed of persons born outside the county. In both cases at each Census less than 40 per cent of the persons enumerated were born within the county, whereas in all other English counties at least 40 per cent (and in most cases over 50 per cent) of the population were 'county born'. On the other hand, not many counties could claim that the vast majority of their population was 'county born' and in England only Cumberland, Durham, Lancashire, Lincolnshire, Staffordshire and Yorkshire were able, at the Censuses of 1901, 1931 and 1951, to show that three-quarters (or slightly more) of their enumerated populations were born within the county. The trend generally has been towards a smaller proportion of 'county born' population at each Census and even Durham, Lancashire and Staffordshire (the only counties which moved up a group in Table 28) had a smaller percentage of 'county born' population in 1951 than in 1931.

The pattern in Wales was less varied – no county had an abnormally low percentage of persons born within the county and the trend towards a smaller proportion of 'county born' was not as complete as it was in England. Whereas in every English county the proportion of 'county born' was smaller in 1951 than in 1931 in Wales, two counties (Glamorganshire and Monmouthshire) had a greater proportion of 'county born' in 1951 than in 1931 (though the increase was insufficient to affect the grouping in Table 28) while the remaining counties followed the downward trend. The probable reason for the two excep-tions in Wales was that many of those who left Glamorganshire

TABLE 28

*Percentage of enumerated persons born within the county of
enumeration at the Censuses of 1901, 1931 and 1951*

Per cent		1901	1931	1951
30 and under 60		Essex; Mddx; Surrey.	⟵ do. ⟶	do.
	E.	⋯⋯⋯⋯⋯⋯	Berks; Bucks; Dorset; Hants; Herts; Kent; Oxon; Rutland; Sussex.	Beds; Berks; Bucks; Cambs; Dorset; Hants; Herefords;Herts;Hunts; Kent; Oxon; Rutland; Somerset;Sussex;Worcs; Westmorland; Wilts;
	W.			Brecon; Flint; Merion; Radnor.
60 and under 70		Cheshire. ⋯⋯⋯⋯⋯⋯	⟵ do. ⟶	do. ⋯⋯⋯⋯⋯⋯
	E.	Berks; Bucks; Hants; Here-fords; Herts; Hunts; Kent; London; Rut-land; Sussex; Worcs.	Beds; Cambs; Herefords; Hunts; Notts; Somerset; Worcs; Westmorland; Wilts;	Cornwall; Devon; Glos; London; Northants; Salop; Suffolk; Warwicks.
	W.	Brecon; Flint; Glam; Mon; Radnor.	Brecon; Denbigh; Flint; Merion; Radnor.	Anglesey; Caernarvon; Cardigan; Denbigh.
70 and under 80		Derbys; Leics. ⋯⋯⋯⋯⋯⋯	⟵ do. ⟶	do. ⋯⋯⋯⋯⋯⋯
	E.	Beds; Cambs; Devon; Dorset; Durham; Glos; Lancs; North-ants; Northumb; Notts; Oxon; Salop; Somer-set; Staffs; Suffolk; Warwicks; Westmorland; Wilts.	Cornwall; Devon; Glos; Lincs; London; North-ants; Northumb; Salop; Suffolk; Warwicks.	Cumberland; Lincs; Norfolk; Northumb; Notts; Yorks.
	W.	Caernarvon; Denbigh; Merioneth.	Caernarvon; Cardigan; Car-marthen; Glam-organ; Mon-mouth; Mont-gomery; Pembrokes.	Carmarthen; Glam-organ; Monmouth; Montgomery; Pembrokes.

Per cent		1901	1931	1951
80 and under 85	E.	Cornwall; Cumberland; Lincs; Norfolk; Yorks.	Cumberland; Durham; Lancs; Norfolk; Staffs; Yorks.	Durham; Lancs; Staffs.
	W.	Anglesey; Cardigan; Carmarthen; Montgomery; Pembrokes.	Anglesey.	
Lowest Highest	E.	Middlesex (35) Cornwall (87)	Middlesex (36) Durham (84)	Middlesex (34) Durham (83)
Lowest Highest	W.	Brecon (63) Anglesey (83)	Flint (62) Anglesey (80)	Flint (54) Glamorgan (78)

and Monmouthshire during the depression years had by 1951 returned to take up employment again in their 'home county'.

The decreasing proportion of 'county born' population was indicative primarily of an increase in internal migration within and between England and Wales which resulted in some interesting changes in the 'birthplace composition' of county populations. Between 1931 and 1951 the proportion of persons in England and Wales as a whole born outside the United Kingdom, Islands of the British seas and the Irish Republic increased by over 60 per cent and accounted, in 1951, for just over 2 per cent of the total population, so that in addition to the effects of internal migration all county populations in 1951 had a higher proportion of foreign-born persons than they had in 1931, but the 'foreign-born' were in all cases a very small proportion of total population.[1] In England the population of every county was made up predominantly of persons born in the county or elsewhere in England, but migration from Wales to England reduced the proportion of 'English-born' between 1931 and 1951. In 1931 only Herefordshire had less than 90 per cent of its population born in England, but by 1951 seven other counties

[1] For example the one county with the largest proportion of 'foreign-born' persons in 1931 and 1951 was London with 2·9 per cent and 4·4 per cent respectively, of its total population recorded as born in foreign countries. Even in 1951 only London (4·4 per cent), Cambridgeshire (3·1 per cent) and Oxfordshire (3·3 per cent) returned more than 3 per cent of their population as 'foreign-born'. In Wales no county had more than 0·6 per cent in 1931 and 1·7 per cent in 1951 of 'foreign-born' persons.

Variations in the Composition of the Population

(Buckinghamshire, Hertfordshire, London, Middlesex, Oxford-shire, Salop and Surrey) had joined Herefordshire and recorded more than 10 per cent of their population as having been born outside England. The unique position of Herefordshire in 1931 was in part due to the fact that just over 10 per cent of its population was born in Wales and it retained its place as the English county with the highest proportion of 'Welsh-born' persons in 1951. Every county in England in 1931 had its share of persons born in Wales, ranging from Durham with 0·3 per cent to Herefordshire with 10·6 per cent, but it was essentially the counties nearest to Wales – Cheshire, Gloucestershire, Herefordshire, Shropshire, and Somerset which had the greater share. By 1951 all the counties, except Durham and Lancashire, had increased the proportion of Welsh-born persons in their populations as compared with 1931, but the Welsh were not the only migrants to England; the Scots, the Irish, and others born in Commonwealth or foreign countries were also contributing to the inward migration with the result that in 1951 persons born in England and Wales formed a smaller proportion of every English county population than they did in 1931. (See Table 29.)

Even in Wales persons born in Wales and England constituted a smaller proportion of the population of each county in 1951 than they did in 1931, but the proportion of persons born out-side England or Wales was smaller in all Welsh counties than it was in nearly all English counties. For example, in most of the counties of England in 1951 between 91 and 95 per cent of their population had been born in England or Wales, on the other hand in only one Welsh county – Flint – had less than 96 per cent of the population been born in Wales or England. Welsh counties, obviously, had little to offer intending immi-grants between the First and Second World Wars, but at the 1951 Census the proportion of persons born in England had increased in every Welsh county except Glamorganshire and Monmouthshire, so that whilst every county in England had a greater proportion of Welsh-born so, too, did most Welsh counties have a greater proportion of English-born in 1951 than they had in 1931. Some typical examples of the changes in the proportion of the enumerated population born in the county, in England or in Wales are given in Table 29 in order to show

Variations in the Composition of the Population

more clearly the varied pattern of composition of county populations.[1]

The proportion of persons born outside England and Wales was higher in all counties at the Census of 1951 than it was in 1931, and, in most counties of those 'born elsewhere' just over half were from Scotland, Northern Ireland and the Irish Republic, and just under half were from Commonwealth and foreign countries. The increase in the number of immigrants

TABLE 29

Selected counties – distribution of population according to county and county of birth 1931 and 1951

ENGLAND

County		Year	Per cent born in:				
			The County	Rest of England	Wales	E. & W.	*Else-where
Bedfords	..	1931	64·1	32·3	0·7	97·1	2·9
		1951	52·3	37·8	2·1	92·2	7·8
Bucks	..	1931	52·1	42·8	1·7	96·6	3·4
	..	1951	42·7	45·8	3·3	91·8	8·2
Durham	..	1931	83·5	13·7	0·3	97·5	2·5
		1951	83·2	13·5	0·3	97·0	3·0
Herefords	..	1931	62·8	24·4	10·6	97·8	2·2
		1951	56·4	27·9	11·2	95·5	4·5
Herts	..	1931	47·5	46·7	1·3	95·5	4·5
	..	1951	40·0	49·7	2·0	91·7	8·3
Lancs	..	1931	82·7	12·2	1·2	96·1	3·9
	..	1951	81·9	11·6	1·1	94·6	5·4
Middlesex	..	1931	36·2	56·4	2·0	94·6	5·4
	..	1951	34·1	55·1	2·4	91·6	8·4
Norfolk	..	1931	81·2	17·2	0·3	98·7	1·3
	..	1951	72·9	21·8	0·7	94·4	5·6
Notts	..	1931	68·9	28·7	0·5	98·1	1·9
	..	1951	67·5	27·5	0·8	95·8	4·2
Warwicks	..	1931	70·5	25·8	1·3	97·6	2·4
	..	1951	66·7	23·7	2·5	92·9	7·1

[1] Any reader interested in a particular county should see the *Census 1951 – County Reports, England and Wales*, H.M.S.O.

93

Variations in the Composition of the Population

WALES

County	Year	The County	Rest of Wales	England	W. & E.	*Else-where
Brecon	1931	61·9	25·6	10·3	97·8	2·2
	1951	55·3	29·6	12·0	96·9	3·1
Denbigh ..	1931	66·8	12·3	18·8	97·9	2·1
	1951	63·4	11·6	21·3	96·3	3·7
Glamorgan ..	1931	74·9	9·8	12·7	97·4	2·6
	1951	78·2	7·3	11·2	96·7	3·3
Montgomery ..	1931	77·0	9·6	12·5	99·1	0·9
	1951	71·6	10·2	16·0	97·8	2·2

* 'Elsewhere' includes in all cases a small percentage of 'birthplace not stated'.

to this country in the war and post-war years obviously resulted in a more varied pattern of composition of county populations compared with the past, though it was no new experience for the population of England and Wales to receive settlers from 'over the border' and abroad. Counties have for centuries been affected by the ebb and flow of population, receiving new citizens from neighbouring counties and further afield and sending their own citizens elsewhere. There was in the 1940's a more rapid flow inward and outward of population than there was at the beginning of the twentieth century and there was certainly a definite trend towards a smaller proportion of persons being enumerated in their county of birth at each Census. Much of this movement was localized within relatively small areas, for example, of the 27·5 per cent of the population of Nottinghamshire in 1951 born in England outside the county over half were born in the neighbouring counties of Derbyshire, Leicestershire, Lincolnshire, Yorkshire, Staffordshire, Warwickshire and Northamptonshire, and most counties gained and of course lost population from and to their neighbours.[1] There seems to have been no clear pattern of movement, but it may be assumed that internal migration was due primarily to changes in economic conditions, except perhaps in the case of women, who tended to move from their county of birth to a greater extent than men, in part because if they married a man from another county

[1] See the *Census 1951 County Reports*, section on 'Birthplace and Nationality' for full details of individual counties.

94

they would generally reside in the husband's county. The period 1931–51 was undoubtedly one of fairly rapid movement of population from one county area to another but to what extent was this process maintained in the next decade?

THE COUNTIES – CHANGING PATTERN OF GROWTH
1951–61

Unfortunately the Census of 1961 did not include a question designed to show the proportion of the enumerated population born within the county and therefore comparisons with the past cannot be made. However, questions were asked about 'Nationality' and 'Country of Birth' so that some comparisons can be made and of course the pattern of over-all growth can be seen.

There were no significant changes in the acreage of counties in the decade so that the pattern shown in Table 26 was maintained in 1961, and in terms of population, although most counties continued to grow there were no dramatic changes in relative population groups (see Table 30 and for the previous fifty years Table 25). The only significant changes in England were that seven counties moved up into the next higher population group and in some cases recorded substantial increases, for example, Hertfordshire increased its population from just over 600,000 in 1951 to over 800,000 in 1961, and Warwickshire from just over 1,860,000 in 1951 to over 2,023,000 in 1961. Only four counties in England (Cornwall, Westmorland, London and Middlesex) suffered a decrease of population, whereas in Wales six counties (Breconshire, Caernarvonshire, Carmarthenshire, Merionethshire, Montgomeryshire and Radnorshire) had smaller populations in 1961 than in 1951. The seven Welsh counties in which population increased nevertheless experienced an annual rate of growth smaller than that of most of the English counties, for example, three quarters of the counties of England increased their populations by half per cent or more per annum, whereas in Wales the fastest growing county, Monmouthshire, had an annual rate of less than half per cent per annum.

If the periods 1901–31 and 1931–61 are compared, as in Table 31 (and for the intervening years see Table 27) then the

95

overall patterns of change are clearly discernible. In England counties like Berkshire, Bedfordshire, Buckinghamshire, Essex, Hampshire, Hertfordshire, Middlesex, Kent, Sussex, Surrey and Warwickshire have experienced sixty years of continuous and in some cases rapid growth, other counties such as Derbyshire, Nottinghamshire, and Lancashire, have continued to grow but less rapidly in the past thirty years, and counties which

TABLE 30

The size of county populations in England and Wales at the Census of 1951 and 1961

N.B. Counties above the dotted line have remained in the same population group at each census.

ENGLAND

Population	1951	1961
Under 200,000	Hereford; Hunts; Rutland; Westmorland.	do. ....
200,000 and less than 400,000	Beds; Bucks; Cambs; Cornwall; Cumberland; Dorset; Oxon; Salop. .... Wilts.	do. ....
400,000 and less than 600,000.	Berks; Norfolk; Northants; Somerset; Suffolk; Worcs.	do. .... Wilts.
600,000 and less than 800,000.	Leics; Lincs. .... Devon; Herts; Northumberland.	do. ....
800,000 and less than 1,000,000.	Derbys; Notts. .... Glos; Sussex.	do. .... Devon; Herts; Northumberland.
1,000,000 and less than 2,000,000.	Cheshire; Durham; Hants; Kent; Staffs; Surrey. .... Warwicks.	do. .... Glos; Sussex.
2,000,000 and less than 4,000,000.	Essex; London; Mddx.	do. .... Warwicks.
4,000,000 and less than 6,000,000.	Lancs; Yorks.	do. ....

Variations in the Composition of the Population

Population	1951	1961
Under 50,000.	Merionethshire; Montgomeryshire; Radnorshire.	do.
50,000 and less than 100,000.	Anglesey; Breconshire; Cardigan; Pembrokeshire.	do.
100,000 and less than 150,000.	Caernarvonshire; Flintshire.	do.
150,000 and less than 250,000.	Carmarthenshire; Denbighshire.	do.
250,000 and less than 750,000.	Monmouthshire.	do.
750,000 and less than 1 million.		
1 million and less than 1,500,000.	Glamorganshire.	do.

experienced a decrease in population in the first thirty years of this century have, with the exception of London, shown signs of a revival of growth rates in recent years. In Wales the pattern of change is quite different only three counties, Monmouthshire, Flintshire and Denbighshire, experienced continuous growth for sixty years, whilst three (Breconshire, Carmarthenshire and Glamorganshire) having grown quite substantially between 1901 and 1931 suffered a decrease in population in the next thirty years.

The extent to which these changing patterns of growth have been accompanied by changes in the proportions of the population born within and outside the county in the decade 1951–61 cannot be determined because the Census of 1961 asked for 'Country of birth' and not, as in previous censuses, for 'county and town or parish of birth'. It is not possible therefore to complete Table 29 so as to show the composition of county populations in 1961. However, for 1961 we can find out the numbers of persons enumerated in each county who were born outside the British Isles and of course for England and Wales as a whole.

Variations in the Composition of the Population

Thus of the 46,104,548 persons enumerated in England and Wales in 1961 the following were the broad divisions of where they were born (or birthplace not stated):

In the British Isles (including the Irish Republic and the Channel Islands)	44,446,642
Outside the British Isles but resident in England and Wales	1,419,526
Visitors	82,588
Birthplace not stated	
Resident in England and Wales	153,821
Visitors	1,971
	46,104,548

TABLE 31

Percentage increase and decrease of population in the counties of England and Wales in the intercensal periods 1901–31 and 1931–61

N.B. Counties above the dotted line have remained in the same group.

ENGLAND

Percentage	1901–31	1931–61
Increase	Westmorland.	do.
Under 10 per cent	Hunts; Norfolk; Northants; Salop; Somerset; Suffolk.	Cornwall; Durham; Lancs; Northumberland; Yorks.
10 and under 20 per cent	Devon.	do.
	Cambs; Dorset; Glos; Lancs; Oxon; Wilts; Worcs.	Cumberland; Derbys; Herefords; Lincs; Norfolk.
20 and under 30 per cent	Ches; Leics; Staffs.	do.
	Berks; Beds; Derbys; Durham; Lincs; Northumberland; Kent; Sussex; Yorks.	Dorset; Glos; Leics; Northants; Notts; Salop; Somerset.
30 per cent and over	Bucks; Essex; Hants; Herts; Mddx; Surrey; Warwicks.	do.
	Notts.	Berks; Beds; Cambs; Hunts; Kent; Oxon; Rutland; Sussex; Wilts; Worcs.
Decrease	London.	do.
1–40 per cent.	Cornwall; Cumberland; Herefords; Rutland.	

98

Variations in the Composition of the Population

Percentage	1901–31	1931–61
Increase		
Under 10 per cent	Brecon.	Anglesey; Caernarvon; Monmouth; Pembrokes.
10 and under 20 per cent	Denbighshire.	do.
20 and under 30 per cent		
30 per cent and over	Flintshire.	do.
	Carmarthen; Glam; Monmouth.	
Decrease 1–10 per cent	Cardigan; Montgomery; Merioneth; Radnor.	do.
	Anglesey; Caernarvon; Pembroke.	Brecon; Carmarthen; Glam.

The countries of birth of the 1,419,526 persons born outside the British Isles were broadly as follows:

Numbers in 000's

Commonwealth Countries
  (e.g. Ghana, Nigeria, Union of South Africa, India, Pakistan, Australia, Canada, New Zealand)   419
Colonies and Protectorates
  (e.g. Malta, Kenya, Jamaica, Trinidad, Hong Kong)   241
Foreign Countries and at sea
  (e.g. Austria, Denmark, Germany, France, Italy, Poland, Hungary, Sweden, Sudan, United States)   760

                                                                                                1,420

Of those born in Commonwealth Countries the largest single groups were from India (just over 157,000), Canada (just over 49,000), Cyprus (nearly 42,000), South Africa (Union of) (just over 37,000), Australia (nearly 37,000) and Pakistan (nearly 31,000), which between them accounted for approximately 84 per cent of the whole group. Of the persons born in the Colonies and Protectorates the largest single groups were from Jamaica (just over 100,000), other territories in the Caribbean (just over 52,000) and Malta and Gozo (nearly 25,000) which between them accounted for about 72 per cent of the whole group. Persons born in foreign countries and at sea are representative of most European, Asian, American and African countries with the largest single groups having been born in Germany (nearly 121,000); Poland (nearly 120,000); the U.S.A. (just over 94,000); Italy (just over 81,000); the U.S.S.R. (just over 53,000) and Austria and France (with about 30,000 each), so that these countries account for about 66 per cent of the foreign-born.

The 1961 Census Report (*Census 1961 – Birthplace and Nationality Tables*, published by H.M.S.O. in 1964) shows the distribution of county populations as 'proportions per 10,000 of the population of each sex by place of birth', and it will be found that the trend towards an increasing proportion of Commonwealth and foreign-born persons has been accentuated in some English counties. In England and Wales as a whole just over 3 per cent of the population was recorded in 1961 as having been born outside the British Isles, if therefore we examine the counties in which well over 3 per cent of the enumerated population was born in Commonwealth and foreign countries we find that in England fifteen counties (Bedfordshire; Berkshire; Buckinghamshire; Cambridgeshire; Hertfordshire; Huntingdonshire; London; Middlesex; Oxfordshire; Rutland; Suffolk; Surrey; Sussex; Warwickshire and Wiltshire) came into this category. In Wales, however, every county recorded a 'Foreign- and Commonwealth-born' population of well under 3 per cent so that clearly it is in the fifteen English counties that the heaviest concentrations are to be found.

In some of these counties, notably London, there are quite high proportions of foreign- and Commonwealth-born in particular areas. Thus in the Metropolitan Boroughs of Hampstead, Kensington and Paddington between a fifth and a quarter of their populations in 1961 were born abroad. However, for most of the fifteen counties persons born abroad accounted for about 5 per cent of the total population. There are of course some counties which though they have a low proportion of foreign- and commonwealth-born in the county as a whole nevertheless have higher proportions within some towns, for example, Yorkshire had less than 3 per cent in the county as a whole but in the Boroughs of Bradford, Huddersfield and Leeds about 6 per cent, 5 per cent and just over 3 per cent respectively of the males were born abroad.

Inward migration to England in the decade 1951–61 has obviously altered the nationality distribution of some of the counties but in view of the proposals which began to be made in the late 1950's for a reorganization of local government areas the county may be less important in future than it has been in the past. Under the Local Government Act, 1958, the Local Government Commission for England (and one for Wales) was established to examine the adequacy and effectiveness of existing local government areas and though no drastic changes had occurred by 1961 nevertheless there may yet be radical revisions. In the early 1960's some counties (notably Middlesex, Hertford- shire, Kent and Essex) were affected by the re-organization of local government in Greater London and as from 1965 London as an administrative county disappears and the pattern of county boundaries in this area will be very different from that of the past.

In future years 'the county' may well lose much of its signi- ficance and be replaced by 'the region' especially if the tendency continues for concentrating population in a relatively few large cities or 'urban agglomerations'.

THE CONURBATIONS

The rapid massing of populations in a few giant urban centres was (apart of course from the unique case of London) a nineteenth-century development associated with the spread of industrialization, but it was in the twentieth century that the six main living and working areas, with heavy concentrations of population, centred on London, Birmingham, Liverpool, Leeds–Bradford, Manchester and Newcastle-on-Tyne, began to extend their limits far beyond the administrative boundaries of the cities which formed their core by the building of outer suburbs which linked up neighbouring towns. The importance of this outward growth was recognized early in the century when the term 'conurbation' was applied to these areas of population which even by 1921 housed more than one-third of the population of England. 'Conurbation' has been defined in a variety of ways, but it is now generally understood to mean a group of neighbouring towns which have grown by peripheral development into a single continuous built-up area with common industrial or commercial and social interests, and in the 1951 and 1961 Census this term was applied to Greater London, South-east Lancashire, the West Midlands, West Yorkshire, Merseyside and Tyneside.[1]

The conurbation has to a considerable extent submerged the county or counties of which it forms a part, for example, the West Midlands conurbation centred on Birmingham straddles parts of three counties, Warwickshire, Worcestershire and Staffordshire, and in this century has accounted for over half of their combined populations, while the County Borough of Birmingham alone, in 1951 and 1961 accounted for over one quarter of the total population of these three counties. There is in fact only one conurbation – West Yorkshire centred on Leeds and Bradford – which is wholly contained within one county so that in the main 'the conurbation' has to a considerable extent obliterated the boundaries between the fourteen counties[2] which now have the doubtful privilege of being a part of the six conurbations at present identified in England.

There are wide differences in the sex, age and marital distributions of those living in these conurbations and there are a variety of other distinctive economic and social features, but they have in common the fact that they all contain very large numbers of people in relatively small areas of land. (See Table 32). By 1951, for example, 41·1 per cent of the population of England lived in the six conurbations although their combined areas of land and inland water represented only 4·1 per cent

[1] See *Census 1951 – Report on Greater London and Five Other Conurbations*, H.M.S.O., for a disussion of the history of the term, the principles of definition and the division, and characteristics of the present English conurbations.

[2] Viz, the whole or parts of Cheshire, Durham, Essex, Hertfordshire, Kent, Lancashire, London, Middlesex, Northumberland, Staffordshire, Surrey, Warwickshire, Worcestershire, Yorkshire.

of the total acreage of England.[1] The result was that the density of population in the conurbations was very high, in 1951 whilst the density in England as a whole was approximately 1·2 persons per acre it was 18·1 in Greater London, 10·0 in South-East Lancashire, 13 in the West Midlands, 5·5 in West Yorkshire, 14·5 in Merseyside and 14·5 in Tyneside. The relatively low density in West Yorkshire was due primarily to the hilly nature of much of the area which resulted in continuous urban development being confined to the valleys, but even within this conurbation there were extremely high densities of population particularly in Leeds and Halifax. A very heavy concentration of population in a relatively small area of land is not, however, a twentieth-century phenomenon. The most important of the older industrial towns and commercial centres of England nearly all of which are in one or other of the conurbations, have for the past 100 years suffered from the effects of continuously growing populations with relatively little increase in the land area available to meet their housing and other needs, and in one sense the conurbation by linking up towns through continuous urban development has probably reduced the density of population which might otherwise have resulted had each town remained completely independent of the others. Yet the fact remains that just over four-tenths of the population of England was crowded into about one twenty-fifth of the available land.

The proportion of the English population living in these areas which are now identified as conurbations changed only slightly between 1871 and 1951. In 1871, for example, approximately 39 per cent of the population of England (compared with approximately 41 per cent in 1951) were living in these conurbations though of course the aggregate population in 1871 amounted to about half the number in 1951. During the nineteenth century the conurbation populations grew rapidly, for example, from 1871–91 while the population of England and Wales increased by 14·4 per cent the conurbations increased by between 17·1 and 23·1 per cent, and in the last three decades

[1] In the 1951 Census Report on the conurbations their population and acreage is shown as a percentage of that for England and Wales, viz. 38·7 per cent of the population and 3·6 per cent of the acreage. Wales, however, has no part of its land or its population in any of the conurbations, therefore it is appropriate to ingore the Welsh portion of the population and acreage of England and Wales.

of the nineteenth century the populations of most of the conurbations increased at a rate greater than that of the total population of England and Wales. After 1911, however, most of the conurbations recorded rates of increase lower than that for England and Wales and in the period 1931–51 whilst the percentage increase of population in England and Wales was 9·5 per cent, five of the conurbations increased by less than 3 per cent and only one – the West Midlands – had a percentage increase (15·7 per cent) greater than that for England and Wales as a whole.[1] It is clear, therefore, that the populations of the conurbations expanded much more rapidly in the nineteenth century though the fact that the absolute size of the population in 1951 was nearly twice that of 1871 means, if we accept the same acreage, that their density of population was higher in the twentieth century than it was in the nineteenth century.

In the decade 1951–61 the limits appear to have been reached for further growth of population in the conurbations. Whereas the population of England increased by about 5½ per cent the conurbations decreased by about 0·1 per cent, but the overall decrease was accounted for entirely by a reduction of nearly 2 per cent in the Greater London Conurbation (see Table 32). Only the West Midlands where the population grew by nearly 5 per cent kept pace with the national rate of growth, and the percentage pattern of change was as follows:

Conurbation	Population increase or decrease per cent 1951–61
Greater London	− 1·98
S.E. Lancashire	+ 0·21
West Midlands	+ 4·89
West Yorkshire	+ 0·65
Merseyside	+ 0·13
Tyneside	+ 2·37
Total	− 0·11

One result of these variations in patterns of growth was to alter slightly the density of population, thus the persons resident per acre in Greater London fell from 18·1 in 1951 to 17·7 in 1961 whereas in the West Midlands the density increased from 13·0 in 1951 to 13·6 in 1961, South-East Lancashire (10·0),

[1] *Report on Greater London and Five other Conurbations* (1951).

Merseyside (14·4) and West Yorkshire (5·5) had virtually the same density in 1961 as in 1951, and Tyneside increased slightly from 14·5 to 14·8. However, it is very unlikely that the inhabitants of these areas noticed much difference in the amounts of 'elbow room' available to them in 1951 as compared with 1961.[1]

The absolute growth of population in the conurbations since 1871 is shown in Table 32, and though there has been some variation in rate of growth and in the size of populations it is obvious that continued expansion has, in most cases, led to considerable problems of providing housing and other amenities for the inhabitants. Already Greater London and the West Midland conurbations have experienced the greatest difficulties in ensuring adequate housing and other essential facilities for their residents, and with the resurgence of interest in Town and Country Planning which is concerned in part with improving living areas and preventing the obvious defects which arise out of the haphazard growth of communities, it is to be hoped that conurbations will not be allowed to develop again as they did in the latter part of the nineteenth century. Having been allowed to grow so fast in the past it is, of course, difficult now to restrict their growth. They have become firmly established living and working areas which not only retain but attract population from other parts of the country. Their future expansion or contraction will depend therefore on the extent to which economic opportunities and desirable living conditions are developed elsewhere through, for example, the Distribution of Industry Act, the rigorous operation of Town and County Planning legislation, and perhaps of re-distribution of population in Regions.

URBAN AND RURAL POPULATION

The conurbation is essentially a method of dividing the country into divisions which are convenient for statistical, administrative and other purposes. It may well be that in the course of time they will have acquired characteristics which will give them a character and purpose which the counties achieved in the past, but any method of dividing the country into divisions or regions is open to innumerable objections on statistical,

---

[1] For fuller details of the variations in the age, sex and marital condition of the populations in the conurbations see *Census 1961 – Age, Marital Condition and General Tables*, H.M.S.O., 1964.

Variations in the Composition of the Population

TABLE 32

Population growth in the conurbations of England, 1871–1961

Conurbation	Population in 000's					Acreage (1961)
	1871	1901	1931	1951	1961	
Greater London ..	3,889·5	6,586·3	8,215·7	8,348·0	8,182·5	461,885
S.E. Lancashire ..	1,385·9	2,116·8	2,426·9	2,422·7	2,427·9	242,921
West Midlands ..	968·9	1,482·8	1,933·0	2,237·1	2,346·6	172,007
West Yorkshire ..	1,064·3	1,523·8	1,655·4	1,692·7	1,703·7	310,105
Merseyside	690·2	1,030·2	1,346·7	1,382·4	1,384·2	96,025
Tyneside	346·1	677·9	827·1	835·5	855·3	57,712
Total	8,344·9	13,417·8	16,404·8	16,918·4	16,900·2	1,340,655
England	21,299·0	30,516·0	37,358·0	41,159·0	43,461·0	32,212,353

geographic and utilitarian grounds, and that which attempts to divide the population into those who live in rural and those who reside in urban areas is perhaps the subject of more objections than any other. Yet for the past 160 years it has been customary to analyse the population into rural and urban with a view particularly to tracing the movement of population from the country to the towns and to examine the variations between the structure of urban and rural populations.

The definition of rural population is by now extremely difficult because the expansion of town areas and the merging of what were formerly rustic parishes with the outer suburbs of large towns has to a considerable extent removed the characteristic distinctions between 'town' and 'country'.[1]

In the middle of the twentieth century it is by no means unusual to find, for example, farms in the middle of large housing estates belonging to a great town, nor indeed is it unusual to find villages, which in the past would have been isolated, independent and completely rural, acting as dormitory suburbs for

[1] There is a tendency among sociologists even now to look upon rural populations as being synonymous with populations engaged almost wholly in farming. It would certainly be unwise to regard the rural population of England and Wales as essentially a farming population. Many rural districts nowadays are industrialized and the majority of the population of some of our rural villages are employed in manufacturing establishments rather than on the land. For a recent study of the measurement of rural population see John Saville: *Rural Depopulation in England and Wales, 1851–1951* (Routledge, 1957). See, too, *Census 1961 – Preliminary Report, England and Wales*, H.M.S.O., a comment in the Introduction (page 8) on the problems involved in distinguishing urban and rural areas.

urban populations. The official, that is to say, the Census method of distinguishing between those who live in urban and rural areas is to accept the local government boundaries as the lines of demarcation, hence rural dwellers are those who live in areas which are under the control of rural district councils.

The constitution, powers and areas of urban and rural district councils were firmly established by the Local Government Act, 1894, and even though the more important services of local government have since come under the control of county or county borough councils the urban and rural district councils still have a wide range of functions and responsibilities within their areas. At the Census of 1901 which was of course the first to be taken after the drastic reorganization of local government in the 1890's, there were in existence 664 rural district councils and 1,094 urban authorities (i.e. county and municipal boroughs and urban district councils). During the twentieth century there were further changes in local government boundaries particularly after the Local Government Act of 1929 which brought about a reduction in the number of local authorities so that by the Census of 1951 there were 965 urban areas and 477 rural areas, by 1961 there were 993 urban and 474 rural areas. These modifications of local government boundaries have obviously affected the numbers and proportion of the population deemed to be rural or urban at different times, for example, it has been estimated that as a result of the operation of the 1929 Act something like a million people were on balance transferred from the rural to the urban category. It is, therefore, extremely difficult to measure with any degree of accuracy the changes in the number and proportion of urban and rural populations in modern times and at best it is possible only to show the broad trend of movement from rural to urban areas.

In the nineteenth century the labour demands of newly developing industries attracted population to the towns and from 1851 the urban industrialized population continuously outgrew the rural element. The drift from the country to the town was rapid and continuous and by the end of the century about three-quarters of the population of England and Wales was living in urban areas. The respective numbers and proportions deemed to be living in rural and urban areas of England and Wales since 1901 are shown in Table 33.

Variations in the Composition of the Population

TABLE 33

Urban and rural populations of England and Wales

(Population in 000's)

	1901		1931		1939		1951		1961	
	Pop.	%	Pop.	%	Pop.	%	Pop.	%	Pop.	%
Urban	25,058	77·0	31,952	80·0	34,183	82·4	35,322	80·7	36,872	80·0
Rural	7,469	23·0	8,000	20·0	7,277	17·6	8,423	19·3	9,233	20·0

The 1939 figures are based on estimates but they are included because the reorganizations brought about by the Local Government Act, 1929, were by then complete and they are particularly important because they reveal a reversal of the trend, which had existed for a hundred years, for the proportion of the population living in rural areas to decline. Whether the change since 1939 indicates a definite movement of population from town to country is difficult to determine, it may well be that it reflects little more than the fact that the more generous scale of housing now demanded by the population has stimulated development outside the congested town areas and that a large part of the additional rural population is essentially a 'town employed' population which resides in a rural area. However, the fact remains, that if we accept the conventional division between urban and rural that in recent years the decline in the proportion of the population living in rural areas has been halted.

The proportion of the population of Wales living in rural areas is, of course, greater than that of England; for example, in the twentieth century roughly one-third of the Welsh compared with about one-fifth of the English population resides in rural areas. There are, too, differences within counties ranging from those which have predominantly urban populations, notably Essex, London, Middlesex, Lancashire, Surrey, Warwickshire and Monmouthshire (with about 10 per cent or less of their populations classed as rural in 1961), to those which are mainly rural such as Huntingdonshire, Norfolk, Rutland, Anglesey, Breconshire, Cardiganshire, Montgomeryshire and Radnorshire which in 1961 had 55 per cent or more of their population living in rural areas. The populations of Berkshire,

Buckinghamshire, Cambridgeshire, Herefordshire, Norfolk, Shropshire, Westmorland, Flintshire and Pembrokeshire in 1961 were almost equally divided between urban and rural districts while the remaining counties were essentially urban.

Since 1931 there have been slight changes in the ratio of urban to rural population and from 1931–51 only three counties in England (London and Middlesex which had no rural population at either Census and Cornwall with 45·7 per cent rural population) failed to register any change in the proportion of urban and rural residents, while twenty-five counties recorded a slight increase and twelve a decrease in their rural element. In Wales on the other hand nine counties had a slightly smaller and four a slightly larger percentage of rural population in 1951 than they had in 1931. The changes in this period were, however, by no means dramatic; for example, the county which changed most was Huntingdonshire, whose rural population increased from 53·4 per cent in 1931 to 61·6 per cent of the total population in 1951. Between 1951 and 1961 further minor changes occurred, for example, the rate of growth of rural population was greater than that of the urban population in eleven English counties viz. Bedfordshire, Berkshire, Buckinghamshire, Derbyshire, Durham, Hertfordshire, Kent, Lancashire, Leicestershire, Nottinghamshire, and Surrey, whereas in Wales in all the counties except Monmouthshire the rate of decrease of rural population was greater than the rate of decrease of urban population. (See *Census 1961 – Age, Marital Condition and General Tables*). However, none of these changes were sufficient to affect dramatically the ratio of urban to rural populations. The era of rapid movement from rural to urban living undoubtedly reached its peak in the nineteenth century, for example, the rural population of England and Wales expressed as a percentage of total population fell from 49·8 per cent in 1851 to 28·0 per cent in 1891. In the twentieth century the balance of urban and rural has remained relatively stable and unless there are drastic changes in local government boundaries, it is unlikely that we shall see again any violent fluctuations in the distribution of urban and rural populations.

The tendency in modern times is clearly to reduce the differences between urban and rural life. The development of rapid means of communication, the gradual extension to rural areas of what were formerly town amenities such as piped water supplies, electricity and gas for domestic purposes, and the establishment of national services of one kind and another, have all tended to break down the distinctions between town and country. There are, of course, still some deficiencies in the physical amenities of some rural areas, and there may be some value in showing that, for example, rural populations differ from urban in their rates of birth, marriages and deaths, but the gap between urban and rural peoples is now in most respects so much less wide than it was in the past that it is probable that in one respect only is there a very big difference between them and that is in their density of population.

In 1951 the rural districts of England and Wales occupied about 32 million acres of land and housed about $8\frac{1}{2}$ million people, whereas the urban areas had about $5\frac{1}{3}$ million acres and a population of $35\frac{1}{4}$ million, by 1961 with roughly the same acreages the urban population had grown to 36·9 million and the rural to 9·2 million. So that in urban areas there were in 1951 approximately seven persons per acre compared with 0·26 persons per acre in rural areas and in 1961 just over 7 and about 0·3 persons per acre respectively in urban and rural areas. Such a difference in the density of population is a revealing commentary on the degree of urbanizations of the population of England and Wales where, in broad terms, the 80 per cent of the population which is urban is squeezed into about 15 per cent of the land area, while the 20 per cent which is rural spreads over about 85 per cent of the land area.

It is, perhaps, this vast difference in the density of urban and rural population which epitomizes the degree of variation in the distribution of the peoples of England and Wales. Although we are by now predominantly a nation of town dwellers there is still a great deal of variation in the pattern of growth within towns, conurbations, counties and urban and rural areas and it is this variety which contributes to the complexity of our social structure. We have in the 1960's a population which is larger and in many respects quite different in its composition from that which we had in the 1870's, but one of the most remarkable features of the change which has taken place in those years is the varied pattern of growth and distribution within such a relatively small area of land.

CHAPTER V

THE INDUSTRIAL
AND OCCUPATIONAL DISTRIBUTION
OF THE POPULATION

THE variations in the distribution of the population over the towns, districts and regions of England and Wales are due, in part at least, to inequalities in the distribution of industrial facilities. People settle where there are opportunities for earning a living, and where new opportunities are created in an area (as they have been in modern times) there will be changes in the geographical distribution of population.[1] There can be no doubt that in the past 160 years internal migration within England and Wales has been intimately connected with changes in opportunities for employment. Until the middle of the eighteenth century we were predominantly an agriculturally employed population, and as the facilities for agriculture were more or less evenly spread over the whole country there was no necessity for very uneven concentrations of population. The development of industries which had of necessity to be localized in certain areas (e.g. coal mining), and of those which either by accident or design became localized in a particular area (e.g. the cotton industry) led to concentrations of population in relatively small portions of the available land area, and hence to the unequal distribution of population.

We cannot be concerned in this book with the reasons for the establishment of specified industries and industrial populations in particular areas,[2] but we must examine the industrial and

[1] See, for example, J. M. Mogey's: *Neighbourhood and Family* (Oxford University Press, 1956) for a brief account of the effect on the City of Oxford of the growth of the motor-car industry.

[2] See the *Report of the Royal Commission on the Distribution of the Industrial Population* (the Barlow Report), Cmd. 6153, H.M.S.O., 1940, for an analysis of the changes in the distribution of the industrial population in modern times.

occupational distribution over time because the changes which have occurred have a direct bearing on the development of the social structure. By the middle of the nineteenth century the variety of industrial establishments and the range of opportunities for employment were greater than ever, but the rate of technical progress was to be considerably accelerated in the next 100 years and though the rate of population growth slackened, the variety of industries and the range of occupations expanded continuously. We have only to look around our homes to be aware of numerous products, useful and otherwise, now in daily use (and often accepted as necessities) which are the result of technical processes developed in the twentieth century,[1] and there are equally many occupations and professions which are twentieth-century creations. To be aware of such developments does not mean that it is possible to measure accurately the changes which have occurred in the industrial and occupational distribution of the population. There are still innumerable difficulties involved in classifying satisfactorily industries and occupations, but we can nevertheless obtain data sufficiently useful to show the broad patterns of change.

Attempts were made to record the occupations of the people in the first Census, but it was not until 1851 that a scientific system of classification was introduced. Throughout the nineteenth century the Census authorities concentrated on improving the information concerning occupational distribution, but it was not until 1921 that a separate industrial classification was made.[2] To some extent the occupations of the people bear a relationship to their industrial distribution, but there may well be substantial differences between the numbers employed in separate industries and the numbers in distinct occupations. For example, carpenters are employed in a variety of industries, but occupationally the thousands of carpenters in this country at any one time form one occupational group. The basis of the industrial classification, therefore, was that 'the industry in

---

[1] It must not be assumed that a twentieth-century product in common use is necessarily a twentieth-century invention; for example, the first 'plastic' (Parkesine) was produced in 1865. It is the large-scale production of products of this kind which has been the main feature of this century.

[2] An attempt was made in 1911 to classify industries, but it was not considered a success.

which any individual is engaged is determined (whatever his occupation) by reference to the business or economic activity in, or for the purposes of which, his occupation is followed' (Introduction to the *Census 1951 – Classification of Industries*). In effect gainfully employed persons were grouped together according to the nature of the employers' business, and the term 'industry' was used in the widest possible sense to denote any form of activity in which people are gainfully employed.

The industries of this country could have been classified in many different ways, but in 1948 a standard industrial classification was approved by the principal Government Departments concerned with the collection of industrial statistics and this (with only slight modifications) was used at the Census of 1951. The Standard Industrial Classification divided the whole field of economic activity into twenty-four orders or major industrial groups as follows: (1) Agriculture, forestry and fishing; (2) Mining and quarrying; (3) Treatment of non-metalliferous mining products other than coal (e.g. glass, china, earthenware, cement); (4) Chemicals and allied trades; (5) Metal manufacture (e.g. blast furnaces, iron and steel tubes, tinplate); (6) Engineering, shipbuilding and electrical goods; (7) Vehicles; (8) Metal goods not specified elsewhere (e.g. tools and implements, cutlery, needles, pins and fishhooks); (9) Precision instruments, jewellery, etc.; (10) Textiles; (11) Leather, leather goods and fur; (12) Manufacture of clothing; (13) Manufacture of food, drink and tobacco; (14) Manufactures of wood and cork; (15) Paper and printing; (16) Other manufacturing industries (e.g. tyres and tubes, other rubber goods, toys, pens and pencils); (17) Building and contracting; (18) Gas, electricity and water; (19) Transport and communications; (20) Distributive trades (e.g. coal merchants, builders' merchants, wholesale and retail distribution of grocery, meat, fish, vegetables, boots and shoes, clothing, confectionery and tobacco; (21) Insurance, banking and finance; (22) Public administration and defence, i.e. national and local government service, including police and fire services, and the armed forces; (23) Professional services (e.g. accountancy, education, law, medicine and religion); (24) Miscellaneous services (e.g. cinemas, theatres, horse and dog racing, restaurants, hairdressing, funeral direction, welfare and charitable services).

Each of these major groups was divided into principal sub-divisions, for example, Order 1, agriculture, forestry and fishing has major sub-divisions of farming (not fruit) and stock-rearing; agricultural contracting; market gardening, fruit, flower and seed growing; forestry; fishing (at sea); fishing (in inland water); and each of the constituent elements of these sub-divisions are recorded in a classified list. The classified list contained nearly 9,000 separate designations of in effect identifiable industries, and, for example, under farming (not fruit) and stock-rearing there were fifty-three distinct items ranging alphabetically from Angora rabbit breeding and bee-keeping to withy growing and yeoman, whilst the sub-group welfare and charitable services (of Order 24) had forty-nine items ranging from almshouses to youth centre.[1]

This method of classifying industries treats the Y.W.C.A. and a zoo in the same way as coal-mining or the making of motor-cars, and provides in effect a picture of all identifiable avenues of gainful employment, and between 1931 and 1951 there were obviously many significant changes in the opportunities for employment in a growing number of varied industries.[2] Thus the numbers of people employed in chemicals and allied trades expanded rapidly, so did they in industries concerned with metal manufacture, engineering, electrical goods and vehicles, whereas the numbers engaged in agriculture and coal mining, for example, tended to contract. It seems doubtful whether the measurement of the industrial distribution really tells us much more than we can find from the changes in the distribution of occupations and therefore the detailed analysis of the industrial distribution has been omitted from this edition.

THE OCCUPATIONAL DISTRIBUTION OF THE POPULATION

The industries in which people are employed are perhaps of greater importance to the nation than the occupation of each employed person, but to the individual the occupation which

[1] See *Census 1951 – Classification of Industries*, for the full list and method of classification.

[2] See the previous edition of this book (*The Changing Social Structure of England and Wales, 1871–1951*) for the changing pattern.

he or she follows is probably as (if not more) important than the industry in which he or she is engaged. There are, of course, some occupations which can be followed only in specified industries but many may be followed in any one of a variety of different industries, and it is in part because of this that there are differences between the industrial and occupational distribution of the population. If every single occupation could be followed only in a particular industry then the industrial and occupational distribution would be identical, but there is in fact no industry in England and Wales which is limited to any one occupation.

It would seem a relatively simple matter to classify the population on the basis of the occupations of its members. Each one of us presumably knows our own occupation, even if we may have doubts as to who are our employers.[1] But one occupation is often known by different names in different parts of the country and in different industries, or it may be a localized occupation with a distinctive local name, or a generic term may be used for what are in fact many separate occupations and, of course, over time an occupation may well acquire a new title and many new occupations may come into being. Differences and difficulties of these kinds aggravate the problems of classification and the task of the Census authorities is made even more difficult by the failure of individuals to describe accurately on a Census form what they believe their occupation to be. For example, there are people who when confronted by an official document give themselves what they deem to be higher social status by describing themselves as being in an occupation very different from that which in fact they follow. In short the measurement of occupations is not as easy as it seems at first sight to be, but we can nevertheless get from the censuses a reasonable picture of what most of us say we have done, and are doing, for a living.

Questions relating to occupations have been asked at every Census in England and Wales, but because of classification and other changes it is still not possible to compare accurately the occupational distribution of the population in the nineteenth

---

[1] Strange as it may appear, an investigation in 1955 into the problems of human relations in a nationalized industry revealed that some employees did not know who their employers were.

and twentieth centuries. In 1851 a genuine attempt was made to classify scientifically occupations and for the Census of 1851 a classified list was compiled for the use of the Census clerks.[1] The total number of separate occupations identified was by modern standards relatively small, for example, about 7,000 in 1851. In subsequent years there were continual modifications and almost complete revision, by 1881 about 12,000 different occupations were listed which in part reflected greater precision in Census-taking and in part recognized the emergence of new branches of industry. By 1901 the list had grown to about 15,000 designations, and though this showed a commendable effort of improvement in classification it also made comparison from one Census to another extremely difficult. In 1911 not only were greater varieties of occupations recorded but the 'punched card' system of processing Census data was introduced, which increased greatly the scope of analysis and reduced the risk of human errors. Henceforth greater precision and detail was possible and it is therefore advisable to examine the occupational distribution in three stages, covering the periods 1881–1901, 1931–51, and 1951–61.

1881–1901 The Census classification of occupations in the latter part of the nineteenth century was, in the main, based on 23 major groups of occupations as follows: (1) Occupations concerned with General or local government of the country (including Civil Servants and the police); (2) Defence services, i.e. the Army and Navy; (3) Professional occupations and their subordinate services, i.e. those connected with the Church, the law, medicine, teaching, literature, the arts, engineering and surveying; (4) Domestic offices or services, including private service, residential clubs and hospitals, and gamekeepers; (5) Commercial occupations, including merchants, bankers and shopkeepers; (6) Conveyance of men, goods and messages, including railways, coaches and cabs, tramways, the Merchant Marine and telegraph services; (7) Agricultural occupations, i.e. on farms, woods and gardens; (8) Fishing; (9) In and about and dealing in the products of mines and quarries, including coal,

---

[1] See *Census Reports of Great Britain, 1801–1931*, Guides to Official Sources, No. 2, for a good account of the earliest attempts to classify occupations, and the report of *The Census of Great Britain, 1851, Population Tables, Vol. I – Ages, Civil conditions, Occupations and Birthplace of the People.*

iron, tin, and lead mines, coal and coke merchants, etc.; (10) Metals, machines, implements and conveyances, including iron and steel manufacture, engineering and machine making, ship and vehicle building; (11) Precious metals, jewels, watches and instruments, including goldsmiths, silversmiths, jewellers, musical instrument and toy makers and dealers; (12) Building and works of construction, including house, canal, railway and road building; (13) Wood, furniture, fittings and decorations, i.e. makers of; (14) Brick, cement, pottery and glass, i.e. makers of; (15) Chemicals, oils, grease, soap, resin, etc.; (16) Skins, leather, hair and feathers, including furriers, tanners, saddlers and dealers in skins, etc.; (17) Paper, prints, books and stationery; (18) Textile fabrics, i.e. cotton, wool, silk, hemp and twine manufacturers and dealers in, e.g. drapers; (19) Dress, i.e. manufacture of straw and felt hats, milliners, dressmakers, boot and shoe makers, etc.; (20) Food, tobacco, drink and lodging; (21) Gas, water, and electricity supply and sanitary services; (22) Other general[1] and undefined makers and dealers; (23) Without specified occupations or unoccupied, including retired from business, pensioners and persons living on own means.

The order in which these groups of occupations were placed may or may not have had any particular significance but to the twentieth-century reader they would doubtless suggest a certain degree of class consciousness on the part of those responsible for the classification, and throughout the reports and tables of the nineteenth century censuses one can detect that certain groups of occupations are considered to be of higher social standing than others.[2] The main defect of this type of division, however, is that the distinction between an occupation and the industry in which it is followed is not made sufficiently clear, but in the General Report of the 1901 Census an attempt was made to compare the occupational distribution of the population in 1881, 1891 and 1901, and Table 34 summarizes the data for 1881 and 1901 in order to show broadly the numbers engaged in different occupations in England and Wales in the latter part of the nineteenth century.

[1] Includes, for example, cattle dealers, chimney sweepers, rag gatherers, pawn-brokers, general shopkeepers, costermongers and general labourers.

[2] Compare the twentieth-century classification (later in this chapter) in which there is no suggestion of ranking of occupations.

In Table 34 the whole of the population aged 10 years and over is included, but a large proportion of the females was in fact without specified occupation or unoccupied and these women were, of course, in the main married without gainful occupations, for example, in 1901 of the 9,018,000 unoccupied women just over 6 million were married. The proportion of the population under 10 years of age in gainful occupations was, according to the Census reports, exceedingly small, so that the distribution of the population of all ages in England and Wales in 1881 and 1901 was as follows:

TABLE 34

Occupations of males and females aged 10 years and over in England and Wales at the Census of 1881 and 1901

Occupations	Numbers in 000's			
	Males		Females	
	1881	1901	1881	1901
1. General and local government ..	97	172	7	26
2. Defence	107	168	—	—
3. Professional	231	312	188	295
4. Domestic, etc.	88	141	1,519	1,691
5. Commercial	308	531	8	60
6. Conveyance of men, goods, etc. ..	782	1,248	11	19
7. Agriculture	1,288	1,159	64	58
8. Fishing	29	24	(0·294)	(0·166)
9. In mines, etc.	521	800	8	5
10. Metals, machines, etc.	775	1,167	38	61
11. Precious metals, jewels, etc. ..	68	134	10	19
12. Building, etc.	763	1,126	2	2
13. Wood, etc.	162	233	18	25
14. Brick, etc.	104	142	24	33
15. Chemicals, etc.	62	102	8	27
16. Skins, etc.	66	80	15	25
17. Paper, etc.	116	188	42	91
18. Textiles	482	492	613	663
19. Dress	346	415	606	712
20. Food, etc.	550	774	161	299
21. Gas, water, etc.	25	68	(0·182)	(0·114)
22. Other, etc.	788	681	60	61
23. Without, etc.	1,555	1,977	6,590	9,018
Total	9,313	12,134	9,992	13,190

N.B. The occupational groups are as shown in the text above.

Industrial and Occupational Distribution of the Population

	Numbers in 000's			
	1881		1901	
	M.	F.	M.	F.
Under 10 years of age:				
Unoccupied	3,327	3,343	3,595	3,609
10 years of age and over:				
With specified occupations ..	7,758	3,402	10,157	4,172
Without specified occupations				
or unoccupied*	1,555	6,590	1,977	9,018
Total population	12,640	13,335	15,729	16,799

* Those without specified occupations or unoccupied were classified in 1901 (but, unfortunately, no similar information is available for 1881) as follows:

	000's	
	M.	F.
Retired from business (but not Army, Navy, Church or		
Medicine)	262	82
Pensioners	26	1
Living on own means	93	362
Others aged 10 years and over including students ..	1,596	8,573

The proportion of the population with specified occupations was slightly larger in 1901 than in 1881 and the increase of 28 per cent in the 'occupied' population was greater than the increase in the total population of England and Wales, which amounted to 25 per cent. It must not, however, be assumed that all persons shown at the Census as having an occupation were in fact employed, because it was (and is) the practice of the Census authorities to classify individuals according to their stated occupation irrespective of whether they are employed or not at the time of the Census.[1] If, therefore, true returns were made and recording was accurate then the occupied population had grown substantially in this period of twenty years, but what were the main changes in the types of occupations?

Accurate analysis of the changes in the types of occupations and the numbers engaged in them is not possible, but if we accept that the degree of comparability between the groups as

[1] Henceforth the term 'occupied' is used to denote persons claiming a specified occupation even though they may be unemployed at the date of the Census.

shown in Table 34 is reasonable, then we can at least obtain an idea of emerging trends in occupational distribution at the turn of the century. The largest group of male occupations were those concerned with manufacturing (i.e. Groups 10, 11, 13, 14, 15, 16, 17, 18, 19 and 20), which in 1881 accounted for about 35 per cent of all occupied males and in 1901 for about 36 per cent. Unfortunately the Census authorities did not differentiate between dealers and makers so that the numbers engaged in manufacture are overstated by the inclusion of, for example, dealers in metals, machines, skins and leathers, timber merchants, chemists, drapers and booksellers. It would seem that about 363,000 of the 2,731,000 shown under the manufacturing groups in 1881 and about 538,000 out of the 3,727,000 in 1901 were dealers and sellers rather than makers, but nevertheless about one-third of all the occupied males in both years were engaged in some form of manufacturing.

The major increases in manufacturing occupations over the period were in those connected with the manufacture of iron and steel, vehicles (particularly cycles and motor-vehicles), electrical apparatus and chemicals – an indication of the trend towards an even more rapid growth in the twentieth century of occupations in the newer manufacturing industries. On the other hand, one of the main late eighteenth and early nineteenth century manufacturing industries – textile fabrics – showed relatively little increase in the number of persons who claimed to have occupations connected with it, again an indication of the changes in industrial and occupational distribution to come in the twentieth century.

Whilst occupations connected with manufacturing were increasing steadily the others concerned with making things, viz. the building of houses and other works of construction were also expanding. There may well have been serious errors of classification in the 1881 data on the numbers occupied in these occupations (i.e. those in Group 12) especially in those returned as builders' labourers, but there was clearly a real increase in the number of carpenters and joiners (from 235,000 in 1881 to 271,000 in 1901), bricklayers and bricklayers' labourers (from 125,000 in 1881 to 213,000 in 1901), plumbers (from 37,000 in 1881 to 65,000 in 1901), and painters, decorators and glaziers (from 100,000 in 1881 to 160,000 in 1901). Occupations connected with the building trades were obviously attracting large numbers of males and the results were to be seen in, for example, the fact that between 1891 and 1901 the number of inhabited, uninhabited, and houses in course of erection increased by 15·5 per cent in this decade.

Male occupations connected with central and local government also attracted greater numbers in this period, for example, officers, clerks and messengers employed by the central Government more than doubled from about 46,000 in 1881 to about 100,000 in 1901. In the second half of the nineteenth century there were radical changes in the methods of appointment and conditions of service of Civil Servants following the Northcote–Trevelyan report of 1855, and towards the end of the century the functions of government were being enlarged. Part of this expansion in the numbers of Government servants was accounted for by a substantial increase in the numbers employed by the Post Office, but Government service as a whole was obviously demanding greater numbers of employees than ever before. Local government also underwent far-reaching reforms in this period which in part accounts for the increase in the numbers of municipal, parish and other local or county officers, from about 51,000 in 1881 to 72,000 in 1901. In addition the strength of the Police Force (shown separately under Local Govermnent in the Census reports) increased from about 32,000 in 1881 to 45,000 in 1901, which improved the ratio of policemen per head of population to 'one policeman to every 724 of the population in 1901, as against one to every 799 of the population in 1881' (the General Report of the 1901 Census).

The armed forces in 1901 were considerably larger than they had been at earlier censuses and this expansion was due primarily to the South African War. The impact of this war on the services may be gauged from the fact that the United Kingdom Army at home and abroad numbered 441,935, and the Royal Navy 90,559 in 1901, an increase of 98·3 per cent in the size of the Army and 70·9 per cent in the Navy between 1891 and 1901. There were, of course, no women in the armed forces of those days, and by the standards of the First and Second World Wars this was a relatively small military force.

'Professional occupations and their subordinate services' covers not only those occupations requiring some form of training, such as that necessary even then for clergymen, lawyers, doctors, teachers, engineers and surveyors, but others such as church, chapel and cemetery officers, law clerks, shorthand writers and showmen whom (according to the Registrar-General's report for 1901) 'it would be absurd to class as professional persons according to the ordinary acceptation of that term.'[1] Other occupations which would certainly now be classed as professional, such as those of qualified accountants and pharmacists, were excluded though they were shown separately under Commercial and Chemical occupations respectively in 1901. However, the most interesting feature of the changes in the numbers claiming professional status between 1881 and 1901 are the relatively modest rates of increase in clergymen (for example, clergymen of the Established Church numbered 22,000 in 1881 and 25,000 in 1901), barristers and solicitors (from 17,000 in 1881 to 21,000 in 1901), civil and mining engineers (from 9,000 in 1881 to 11,000 in 1901) and teachers (from 46,000 in 1881 to 59,000 in 1901), all of whom expanded at a rate less than that for occupied males as a whole who increased at an average rate of 1·5 per cent per annum. On the other hand, male physicians, surgeons and general medical practitioners increased from 15,000 to 22,000 and architects from 7,000 to 11,000 between 1881 and 1901, a percentage increase of 46 per cent and 59 per cent respectively, compared with the 30 per cent increase in occupied males as a whole. One of the few professional occupations which decreased in this period was that of veterinary surgeon, whose numbers dropped from 7,000 in 1881 to 3,000 in 1901, which was probably due in part to the decline in the importance of agriculture.

The gradual decrease in the numbers employed in agriculture was noted (in Table 34) and confirms the downward trend. In the General Report of the Census, 1901, the Registrar-General discusses in some detail the decline in agricultural occupations and shows that it had been in operation at least since 1851.[2]

---

[1] The Registrar-General avoided the problem of defining a professional occupation, a difficult task at any time. See page 137 for a further discussion of this problem in modern times.

[2] See the *Census 1901 – General Report and Appendices*. It is interesting to find that in discussing the decrease in the numbers engaged in agriculture the comment is made that the decrease had been to some extent offset by an increase in the use of agricultural machinery, a trend which was to be strongly followed in later years.

Industrial and Occupational Distribution of the Population

On the other hand, the extractive industry of coal-mining was developing rapidly and the number of persons returned specifically as coal-miners increased substantially in this period, for example, of the 800,000 males shown as working in or about mines and quarries in 1901 (in Table 34) about 650,000 were coal-miners as compared with 514,000 in 1891 and 379,000 in 1881. The increase in the number of coal-miners was particularly marked in the Counties of Nottinghamshire, Monmouthshire, and Glamorganshire, where the numbers rose by more than 100 per cent between 1881 and 1901.[1] Tin, lead, and copper-miners, however, declined appreciably in the latter half of the nineteenth century, but the decrease in these forms of mining was more than offset by the growth of coal-mining, so that the occupation of mining in general increased substantially.

Occupations concerned with the conveyance of men, goods and messages grew appreciably in the nineteenth century, and in particular the results of the 'railway mania' of the 1840's and 1850's were to be seen in the great increase in the number of railway workers in succeeding years, for example, railway officials or clerks, engine-drivers and stokers, guards, signalmen, pointsmen, level-crossing men and porters numbered 25,000 in 1851, 139,000 in 1881 and 277,000 in 1901.[2] Road transport occupations, too, grew rapidly and there was a spectacular increase in the numbers employed in the tramway services from 2,600 in 1881 to 18,000 in 1901. The motor-car, however, was still a novelty and even in 1901 there were apparently only 623 males whose occupation was that of motor-car driver, on the other hand there were 12,000 livery-stable keepers, coach and cab proprietors, and 113,000 coachmen, grooms (not domestic) and cabmen.[3] The numbers engaged in transport occupations on the seas, rivers and canals remained relatively stable, but the telegraph and telephone service was

[1] A comment in the 1901 report on output of coal in relation to the number of miners may well have been prophetic – the number of miners between 1891 and 1901 increased by 24·7 per cent but the output of coal increased by 16·4 per cent.

[2] Changes in classification make it difficult to compare all types of railway occupations – see the *Census 1901 – General Report.*

[3] The number of domestic coachmen and grooms in 1901 was 75,000, which gives some indication of the extent to which the upper and middle classes retained the hall-mark of their status – the coach.

growing rapidly, and by 1901 about 14,000 men were occupied in it as compared with 7,000 in 1881.[1]

Occupations concerned with the provision of gas, water and electricity and the maintenance of sanitary services were already beginning to expand by the turn of the century. It is not possible to distinguish in 1881 the occupations concerned with the supply of electricity because makers and sellers of electrical apparatus were classified in the same group; in any case the electrical industry was still in its infancy and the bulk distribution of electricity for power and lighting did not become widespread until the twentieth century. Even in 1901 the Census records that there were only 2,888 males whose occupations were concerned with the supply of electricity and another 47,000 were electrical apparatus makers. The gas industry, however, was firmly established with about 18,000 men in 1881 and 47,000 in 1901, stating that they were occupied in 'gas works service'. The waterworks service provided occupations for relatively few men, about 2,500 in 1881 and 5,700 in 1901, but the numbers occupied in drainage and sanitary services increased markedly from 1,300 in 1881 to 7,200 in 1901, and there were in addition 2,700 (in 1881) and 8,500 (in 1901) scavengers and crossing-sweepers.

Occupations which are assumed to 'oil the wheels' of industry by facilitating the exchange of goods and services between producers and consumers, for example, those connected with banking, finance and insurance, grew rapidly in the period 1881 to 1901. The number of commercial or business clerks rose from 175,000 to 308,000, bank officials and clerks from 16,000 to 30,000, and insurance officials, clerks and agents from 15,000 to 55,000. Their rate of increase was much greater than that of occupied males as a whole and was due probably to the expansion of trade and the predominant position of the City of London as an international financial centre.

The other group of commercial occupations separately identified in the censuses was that of accountants, merchants and agents, but most of the latter were essentially dealers and sellers

[1] Yet the first telephone capable of reproducing speech had been exhibited only in 1876. The numbers shown as employed in this service may be inaccurate because there were problems involved in distinguishing them from other occupations connected with the Postal service.

not assigned to any operation or commodity classified in specific groups, and had there been a more systematic classification of wholesale dealers and merchants, retail shopkeepers and dealers they would have been included in these categories. Despite requests from the Board of Trade the Census authorities considered that it was impracticable to identify traders of this kind, therefore it is not possible to show clearly occupations concerned primarily with selling things. We saw earlier that dealers were included among some of the manufacturing occupations and there were, too, a large number of shopkeepers, pawnbrokers and the like included in Group 22; the only guide we have to the number of dealers rather than makers is that in 1901 about 988,000 men were in occupations which dealt in food, drink, tobacco, textile fabrics and dress, metals, wood, furniture, chemicals and general shopkeeping. Similar information is not available for 1881, but it would appear that in 1901 about one out of every ten occupied males was in an occupation which could be described as dealer, shopkeeper or shop assistant.

As an indication of some of the social customs of the late nineteenth century the increase in the number of male pawnbrokers from 8,000 in 1881 to 11,000 in 1901 is significant. There is some doubt about the accuracy of these figures, but pawnbroking was obviously on the increase at the turn of the century, whereas fifty years later it had practically disappeared as an occupation and presumably as a means of regular financial support for many citizens.[1]

Male occupations which could be classed as 'domestic service' would appear (from Table 34) to have increased substantially between 1881 and 1901, but considerable changes in classification were made in 1901 which reduce the degree of comparability with earlier years. In the *General Report of the Census of 1901*, however, an attempt was made to measure the changes in some branches of domestic service and it would appear that male domestic servants (indoor) in hotels, lodging and eating-houses, and private homes had increased relatively little from 56,000 in 1881 to 64,000 in 1901. Indeed from 1851 to 1901 there had probably been a decrease because in 1851 (when domestic indoor servants were first recorded separately) there

[1] See pages 142–3 for a discussion of the decline of pawnbroking in the twentieth century.

were 74,000, but some doubt is cast on this figure because it probably included 'retired' domestic servants. Nevertheless it would seem that the occupation of indoor domestic servant for males was on the decline by the turn of the century. The other occupations included in 'domestic offices' (Group 4) were college and club servants, hospital and institution servants, cooks (not domestic), others and outdoor domestics, viz. gamekeepers, and these increased from 31,000 in 1881 to 77,000 in 1901.[1] It is, therefore, the indoor domestic servants and the 'others' who are shown in Table 34 and if we wish to isolate the male domestic staff in private homes then we can do so only for 1901, when they amounted to 47,000.

Other occupations which could well be classified as domestic service were, for example, domestic coachmen and grooms, but in 1881 they were shown under Group 6 and though they were separately identified in 1901 they have been included in Group 6 in Table 34. If they were added to the domestic service group then the total of males in occupations of this kind in 1901 would have been well over 200,000, but domestic service was (and is) a predominantly female occupation and, despite the relatively large number of males engaged in it in 1901, they were still only a small proportion of the total occupied males.

The number of women with specified occupations increased by 22 per cent between 1881 and 1901, but this was less than the increase (of approximately 32 per cent) in the total female population aged 10 years and over. The result, of course, was that of all women aged 10 years and over a slightly smaller proportion (about 32 per cent) was occupied in 1901 than in 1881 (about 34 per cent), but the difference may well have been due to changes in classification, particularly of domestic servants.[2]

Unlike the males, who were well spread out over nearly all occupational groups, the females tended to be concentrated into a few groups with a very marked predominance of one occupation, viz. domestic service, which in 1881 absorbed 44 per cent and in 1901 about 40 per cent of all the occupied women. Of

---

[1] In earlier censuses domestic gardeners were included under outdoor domestic service, but in 1901 (and in Table 34) they were included in Group 7, Agriculture.

[2] See comments on the changes in the classification of domestic servants in the *Census 1901 – General Report*, pages 76 and 77.

the women in domestic service the majority were engaged in indoor service, and of the remainder the two largest sub-groups were charwomen and laundresses and washing-women. The other major occupational group for women was the manufacture and sales of textile fabrics, dress, and food, drink and tobacco (Groups 18, 19 and 20 in Table 34), and these accounted for a further 40 per cent in 1881 and 1901 of all occupied women. In 1881, therefore, 84 per cent of all occupied women were concentrated into these four groups of occupations, but by 1901 the proportion had dropped to 80 per cent, which was an indication of the trend towards the spreading out of women over a greater variety of occupations in the twentieth century.

The occupations in which the number of females expanded most in this period were Commercial (Group 5), especially those of commercial or business clerks in which the number of women increased from 6,000 in 1881 to 56,000 in 1901;[1] Central and local government service in which women numbered 4,000 in Central and 3,000 in local government in 1881 and about 16,000 and 10,000 respectively in 1901;[2] and the manufacture of chemicals (Group 15). The percentage increases in these occupations of about 650 per cent in Commerce, 270 per cent in government and 240 per cent in chemicals between 1881 and 1901 were spectacular, and there were also major increases in paper, printing, books and stationery (Group 17) of 117 per cent, and precious metals and jewellery (Group 11) of 90 per cent. Women were obviously beginning to spread out into commerce and manufacturing, but more significantly they were infiltrating into what had previously been male preserves, for example, transport and communications (Group 6) where their numbers increased by about 70 per cent over the two decades. This increase was due primarily to the expansion of the telephone and telegraph service, in which the number of women rose from 2,000 in 1881 to 9,000 in 1901. It is, however, in the professional groups that the evidence of the emancipation of the female is most clearly to be seen, where the number of women increased by 57 per cent between 1881 and 1901.

The professional occupations in which women were to be

---

[1] In this period office machinery, especially the typewriter, was becoming more common and women typists were replacing the male clerk.

[2] There were no women police in 1881 or 1901.

found in much greater numbers in 1901 than in 1881 were nursing and subordinate medical services (68,000 in 1901 and 38,000 in 1881) and teaching (172,000 in 1901 and 123,000 in 1881). These were predominantly female occupations in both years, which expanded because of the growth of public health services and the extension of educational facilities following the passing of the Education Act, 1870.[1] Even though it was these predominantly female occupations which so enlarged the numbers of professional women there were definite signs of breaches in hitherto male professional strongholds; for example, in 1881 there were only 25 female physicians, surgeons and general practitioners (compared with 15,000 men), whereas in 1901 there were 212 (compared with 22,000 men); in 1881 there were only 100 female (compared with 25,000) law clerks, but in 1901 there were 367 (as compared with 34,000 males); and in 1901 there were 6 women architects (out of nearly 11,000 males and females), whereas there were none in 1881, but there were as yet no women barristers or solicitors or civil engineers as there are today.[2]

Of the occupied women the proportion who were married cannot easily be determined from the nineteenth-century censuses. The Registrar-General suggested (in the 1901 General Report) that the proportion of occupied married women was smaller in 1901 than in 1881. At the Census of 1901, of the 4,172,000 women recorded as having a specified occupation, 918,000 were married or widowed, so that 22 per cent of all occupied women were married or widowed. Of all married and widowed women in England and Wales, however, only 13 per cent had a specified occupation and the occupations which had the greatest number (but not necessarily proportion) of married or widowed women were domestic services, textile fabrics,

---

[1] The Registrar-General commented on the expansion of the education services in his report of the 1901 census and showed that in 1871 there was one teacher for every 67 persons aged 3 to 20 years in England and Wales, whereas in 1881 there was one teacher for every 58 and in 1901 one for every 50 persons. Equally the proportion of persons who could not sign the marriage register other than by mark fell from 194 to 25 per 1,000 males and 268 to 29 per 1,000 females between 1871 and 1901 'coincidentally with the great increase in the number of teachers' (*Census 1901 – General Report*).

[2] For some interesting comments on the status of women in the professions at the end of the nineteenth century see the biography of Florence Nightingale by Cecil Woodham-Smith. (*Florence Nightingale, 1820–1910*, Penguin Books, 1955).

dress, food, drink and tobacco, and lodging-house keeping, whilst those with the greatest proportion were agriculture,[1] dealing in coke and coal, and food, drink, tobacco and lodging in which 40 per cent or more of the occupied women were married or widowed. In all other occupations the proportion of occupied women who were married or widowed varied from 10 to 25 per cent, with the notable exception of the few women engaged in building and works of construction (excluding gas-fitting makers and lock and key makers) who, for some obscure reason, were nearly all married or widowed.

It is perhaps surprising to find that the proportion of occupied women who were married or widowed was (in 1901) relatively low in domestic service (19 per cent), and textiles (21 per cent), but the over-all figures were affected by marked variations, even within areas providing roughly similar occupational possibilities; for example, in the County Borough of Blackburn 76 per cent of all the unmarried women aged 10 years and over, and 38 per cent of the married and widowed had specified occupations, but in Bolton 72 per cent of the unmarried and only 15 per cent of the married and widowed women were occupied. The variations throughout England and Wales were very marked,[2] but what does seem clear is that the trend towards a large proportion of married women having a specified occupation had not been firmly established at the turn of the century.

The pattern of occupational distribution (despite the imperfections of classification) in England and Wales in the last two decades of the nineteenth century was probably as follows:

Out of every 100 males and females with specified occupations about 12 in 1881 and 9 in 1901 were engaged in agriculture or fishing; about 5 in 1881 and 6 in 1901 were in mining or quarrying; about 36 in 1881 and 1901 were concerned with making things in factories, workshops, or on building sites; about 7 in 1881 and 9 in 1901 conveyed persons, goods or messages or provided gas, water and sanitary services; about 6 in 1881 and

---

[1] Agricultural occupations present difficult problems of classification in that it is not easy to determine whether the wife of a farmer should be classified as having a separate occupation.

[2] See *Census 1901 – General Report*, Table 31, for details by areas and age-groups of the proportions of occupied married and widowed women.

8 in 1901 were engaged in selling things or in banking or insurance; about 14 in 1881 and 13 in 1901 gave personal service as domestic and other servants; about 4 in 1881 and 1901 gave professional services; about 2 in 1881 and 3 in 1901 were in occupations connected with Government or defence; about 6 in 1881 and 7 in 1901 were either making or selling food, drink and tobacco, or providing lodging; about 8 in 1881 and 5 in 1901 were general dealers, labourers or in undefined occupations.

1931–51. The kinds of occupation and the numbers engaged in them were to change appreciably in the twentieth century and so too did the method of classification for Census purposes. In 1921 a new classification covering about 30,000 separate occupations was adopted and the principles upon which it was based were retained for the Censuses of 1931 and 1951. The main principle of the new method was that of classifying an occupation almost entirely upon the nature of the work performed and considerations of an industrial nature were left to the newly introduced industrial classification. After the Census of 1931 the problems of occupational classification were again reconsidered, and for the Census of 1951 a new classification ol occupations was adopted which whilst retaining the essentiaf principles of 1921 modified some of the detailed allocations of particular occupations, and therefore created some difficulties of comparison but not sufficient to affect the broad picture of occupational distribution in 1931 and 1951.

The 1951 classification of occupations consisted of twenty-seven Orders of groups of occupations having at least one common characteristic and 'the basic factor of all groups is the kind of work done and the nature of the operation performed'.[1] A twenty-eighth Order contains the retired or not gainfully occupied, but it is the twenty-seven Orders and their sub-orders which show the occupational distribution of the population. The twenty-seven Orders with some indication of their sub-orders are as follows: Order I – Fishermen; Order II – Agricultural, horticultural and forestry occupations, 3 sub-orders covering agricultural and horticultural occupations, occupations ancillary to Agriculture, e.g. land agents and foresters and

[1] *Census 1951 – Classification of Occupations* published by the General Register Office.

woodmen; Order III – Mining and Quarrying occupations, 2 sub-orders covering coal mines and other mines, quarries, oil wells, etc.; Order IV – Workers in the treatment of non-metalliferous mining products other than coal, 3 sub-orders covering makers of bricks, tiles, pottery, glass and other products; Order V – Coal-gas and coke makers and workers in chemical and allied trades, 2 sub-orders; Order VI – Workers in metal manufacture, engineering and allied trades, 18 sub-orders including foundry workers, coppersmiths, shipwrights, metal machinists, plumbers, vehicle makers, electrical apparatus makers, etc.; Order VII – Textile workers, 7 sub-orders, including spinners, doublers, winders, weavers, bleachers, dyers; Order VIII – Tanners, etc., leather-goods makers, fur dressers, 3 sub-orders, including fell-mongers, leather tanners and boot and shoe makers; Order IX – Makers of textile goods and articles of dress (not boots and shoes), 4 sub-orders, including garment workers, hat and cap makers, upholsterers, coach trimmers and mattress makers; Order X – Makers of foods, drink and tobacco, 4 sub-orders; Order XI – Workers in wood, cane and cork; Order XII – Makers of and workers in paper and paper-board, bookbinders and printers, 3 sub-orders; Order XIII – Makers of products not elsewhere specified, 4 sub-orders, including workers in rubber, plastics and makers of musical instruments; Order XIV – Workers in building and contracting; Order XV – Painters and decorators; Order XVI – Administrators, directors, managers (not elsewhere specified); Order XVII – Persons employed in transport and communications, 5 sub-orders, including railway, road, water and air transport workers, and workers in communications; Order XVIII – Commercial, finance and insurance occupations (excluding clerical staff), 2 sub-orders; Order XIX – Professional and technical occupations (excluding clerical staff); Order XX – Persons employed in defence services, 2 sub-orders covering armed and civilian services; Order XXI – Persons professionally engaged in entertainment and sport; Order XXII – Persons engaged in personal service (including institutions, clubs, hotels, etc.); Order XXIII – Clerks, typists, etc; Order XXIV – Warehousemen, storekeepers, packers, bottlers; Order XXV – Stationary engine-drivers, crane-drivers, tractor-drivers, etc. stokers, etc.; Order XXVI – Workers in unskilled occupations (not elsewhere specified); Order XXVII – Other and undefined workers, 2 sub-orders covering workers in the distribution of gas and electricity and others.

Each of these orders and sub-orders contains, in most cases, large numbers of separate occupations amounting in all to over 40,000,[1] and some of them have strange and fascinating names; for example, in Order III – Mining and quarrying, Sub-order 1, coal-mining, there are over 1,000 separate occupations, including that of dragger-down, hitcher-up, lasher-on, turner-out, gal driver, back stripper, bottom cutter, joy loader, pom-pom man, pin boy and pit-brow girl; Order VI – Workers in metal manufacture, engineering and allied trades has in its sub-orders over 4,500 separate occupations, including that of bogeyman, dogger-on, pin knocker-out, putter-in, runner-through, jumper-over, plier minder, pump doctor, facer (hand), second bender (clog irons) and sickle tedder; Order XIV – Workers in building and contracting – has over 600 occupations, including over 40 different kinds of bricklayers ranging alphabetically from boiler fixer to tuck pointer, and about 100 different types of masons and stone-cutters; Order XIX – Professional and technical has over 1,300 separate occupations, including about 70 kinds of trained nurses and midwives, over 60 types of civil, structural and municipal engineers and 50 varieties of electrical engineers; but it is in Order XVII – Transport and communications – that we find some of the most picturesque occupational titles, especially in Sub-order 3, water transport workers where among the 500-odd listed occupations there is that of supercargo, ingeniero, carpintero, cassab, contramaestro, cubierta, timonel, bandady and topas. Many of these distinctive terms are probably 'job names' rather than titles of quite separate occupations, but they help to make the new classification more detailed and precise than anything previously published and, of course, they indicate the range and variety of occupations which may be followed.

The full report on the occupations followed by occupied persons in England and Wales at the Census of 1951 was published at the end of 1956 and it is from this and the Occupation Tables of the 1931 Census that we can gauge the changes which took place in the occupational distribution of the population

---

[1] As compared with about 35,000 separate occupations identified in 1931.

in those years.[1] Despite the fact that some modifications were made in the allocation of certain occupations in 1951 and that, therefore, absolute comparability between the two Censuses is not possible, the major changes are discernible. The number of persons with specified occupations (though not necessarily in employment at the date of the Census) was greater in 1951 than in 1931, but the rate of increase of males in occupations was less than the rate of increase of males aged 15 and over in the population as a whole, as shown below:

	Numbers in 000's			
England and Wales	Males		Females	
	1931	1951	1931	1951
Total population	19,133	21,016	20,819	22,742
Population aged 15 years and over	14,325	16,067	16,108	17,999
'Occupied' population aged 15 and over	13,085[1]	14,064	5,484[1]	6,272
Percentage increase 1931–51: in the population aged 15 and over	12%		12%	
in the total occupied population aged 15 and over ..	7%		14%	

[1] The school-leaving age was 14 in 1931 and the population aged 14 and over 'occupied' was as shown in Table 35, page 135.

The substantially smaller percentage increase in 'occupied' males as compared with all males aged 15 and over is a reflection of the changing age structure of the population and of the spread of retirement schemes for the working man. The marked difference in the ratio of 'occupied' to total males in 1951 as compared with 1931 is, therefore, accounted for in Order XXVIII – Retired or not gainfully occupied – as shown below:

The pattern of retirement from gainful employment obviously changed substantially, in 1931 only 5 per cent of all males aged 14 and over had retired, whereas in 1951 about 8 per cent of males aged 15 and over had retired, and between 1931 and 1951 the number of retired males increased by 70 per cent. Females on the other hand constitute only a small

[1] Preliminary results were published in the *One Per Cent Sample Tables* in 1952, but the final results show the full picture.

	Numbers in ooo's			
Order XXVIII	Males		Females	
	1931	1951	1931	1951
Retired or not gainfully occupied (age 14 and over in 1931 and 15 and over in 1951): Students	278	280	248	234
Retired from previous gainful occupation	803	1,365	172	277
No gainful occupation stated ..	292	335	10,382	11,210
Persons occupied outside U.K.	13	23	3	5
	1,386	2,003	10,805	11,726

proportion of the retired from gainful employment, but 'occupied' women increased at a rate greater than that of all women. Of all females aged 15 and over the proportion 'occupied' increased slightly from 34 per cent in 1931 to 35 per cent in 1951, but the significant feature of this modest increase is that the proportion of 'occupied' women who are married has grown rapidly.

The employment of married women was encouraged during the Second World War and it may well be that the impetus then given to their employment outside the home established a pattern which has since been maintained. Whatever the reason the fact is that of all 'occupied' females aged 14 and over in 1931 and 15 and over in 1951 the proportion married increased from 16 per cent in 1931 to nearly 40 per cent in 1951, and in terms of all married women the proportion 'occupied' increased from 13 per cent in 1931 to 23 per cent in 1951. In other words whereas in 1931 something like one out of every eight married women was 'occupied' and of the 'occupied' women about one in seven was married, by 1951 nearly one in four of all married women was occupied and of all 'occupied women' nearly one out of every two was married. This radical change is in part a reflection of the increase in the proportion of married women in the population as a whole, but there is clearly a greater tendency for married women to continue in gainful employment outside the home. Many of them are employed part-time[1] and

[1] Part-time employment for the purposes of the 1951 Census was defined as paid employment or work for less than 30 hours a week.

in 1951 of the 'occupied' married women about one-quarter were part-timers; unfortunately there is no comparable data for 1931.

The occupations followed by men and women in England and Wales in 1931 (aged 14 and over) and 1951 (aged 15 and over) at the time of the Census are summarized in Table 35 and it is apparent that even in this short period there were significant changes. The most marked expansion in the occupations followed by males was in those concerned with manufacturing (Orders IV, V, VI, X, XII and XIII, but not VII, VIII, IX and XI); defence (Order XX); building and contracting, and painting and decorating (Orders XIV and XV); professional and technical services (Order XIX); administrators, etc. (Order XVI); clerks and typists (Order XXIII); warehousemen, etc., and stationary-engine drivers, etc. (Orders XXIV and XXV). Within these groups there were significant variations which require individual (though brief) examination.

TABLE 35

The Occupations of Males and Females aged 14 and over at the Census of 1931 and aged 15 and over in 1951 – England and Wales

Occupations	Numbers in 000's			
	Males		Females	
	1931	1951	1931	1951
Order				
1. Fishermen	27	15	(less than 100)	(less than 50)
2. Agricultural	1,117	961	56	97
3. Mining and quarrying:				
(i) In coal mines ..	888	549	2	1
(ii) Other	72	41	—	—
4. Workers in ceramics, glass, cement, etc.	77	81	44	46
5. Coal, gas and coke-makers and workers in chemical and allied trades ..	47	93	4	11
6. Workers in metal manufacture, engineering, etc. ..	1,557	2,260	142	198
7. Textile workers	298	198	582	359
8. Tanners, etc., leather goods makers, fur dressers ..	167	117	63	65
9. Makers of textile goods and articles of dress (not boots and shoes)	151	124	506	437

Occupations	Numbers in 000's			
	Males		Females	
	1931	1951	1931	1951
Order				
10. Makers of food, drink, tobacco	136	149	56	84
11. Workers in wood, cane and cork	442	433	7	13
12. Makers of and workers in paper, paperboard, bookbinders, printers..	159	162	93	81
13. Makers of other products, e.g. rubber, plastics	58	85	32	41
14. Workers in building and contracting	646	840	(less than 500)	1
15. Painters and decorators ..	242	299	13	10
16. Administrators, directors, managers	355	406	27	46
17. Transport and communications	1,566	1,404	69	130
18. Commerce, finance and insurance ..	1,469	1,228	605	758
19. Professional and technical	404	714	394	523
20. Defence services – armed and civilian	282	685	(less than 500)	20
21. Entertainment and sport ..	91	82	22	22
22. Personal service	472	466	1,934	1,464
23. Clerks and typists ..	711	862	571	1,271
24. Warehousemen, storekeepers, packers ..	245	348	147	181
25. Stationary-engine drivers, stokers, crane drivers, etc.	162	226	(less than 500)	2
26. Unskilled ..	1,292	1,119	198	379
27. Other and undefined	114	117	36	32
Totals	13,247	14,064	5,606	6,272

Note – Strict comparison between some of the orders is not possible and particularly for the females in 1931 the constituent items shown are less than the total.

Among the manufacturing occupations those concerned with engineering and metal manufacture, especially those connected with machine-shops and electrical work increased appreciably. They are indicative of the advance of the 'machine age' just as the expansion of the number of workers in the chemical trades and in the manufacture of rubber and plastics signifies the growth of large-scale production of the 'newer' products of the twentieth century. The number of males engaged in manufacturing occupations increased by about 24 per cent over the period which is much greater than the increase in 'occupied' males as a whole, and if the number of males in occupations connected with some of the older industries, for example, textiles and leather (Orders VII and VIII) had not decreased, the proportion of all males following manufacturing occupations would have increased even more significantly. On balance manufacturing occupations (Orders IV to XIII inclusive) accounted for about 26 per cent of all male occupations in 1951 as compared with 23 per cent in 1931.

The increase in the number of men engaged in the armed forces and the civilian defence services is accounted for by the expansion of the Army from about 102,000 in 1931 to 241,000 in 1951, and the Air Force from 22,000 in 1931 to 198,000 in 1951 stationed at home. In the civilian defence services the Police Force increased slightly, but the great expansion was in the Fire Service where the number of officers and firemen rose from 6,000 in 1931 to 25,000 in 1951. The war and the succeeding 'cold war' were responsible for the growth of these services which were larger than they had ever been before in peace-time.

Building and contracting occupations have been expanding continuously for the past eighty years and they probably reflect the changing standards of living of an economically developed community. The demand for buildings of all kinds has been continuously growing, but whether the increase of 30 per cent in twenty years in these occupations has been accompanied by a comparable increase in output is open to question. Some of the processes in building operations are still carried out by hand and the substitution of human labour by machines has probably not proceeded as rapidly in these kinds of occupations as in many others. There is, however, an indication that in the building trade the trend is away from the craftsman who built in stone to the builder who is primarily concerned with laying bricks; for example, for every one stonemason there were in 1921 about two, in 1931 about three and in 1951 about seven bricklayers, which may indicate the decline of the craftsman or a radical change in building methods or perhaps both.[1]

---

[1] The actual numbers were (000's):

	1921	1931	1951
Males returned as bricklayers ..	87	118	142
,, ,, ,, stonemasons..	36	38	21

The growth of the numbers engaged in professional and technical occupations (Order XIX) by about 76 per cent symbolizes the increasing specialization required in this technological age and the more widespread demand for professional status. It is by no means easy to define satisfactorily 'professional' and it would certainly be difficult to obtain universal agreement on which occupations should be classed as professions, but if we accept the Census method of classification which is based in the main on the possession of technical qualifications then it is apparent that the over-all increase obscures the quite marked variations within the professional group.[1]

Professional occupations concerned with religion have, on the whole declined; for example, the number of Anglican clergy fell from 22,000 in 1921 to 20,000 in 1931 and to 17,000 in 1951, but Roman Catholic priests and monks increased from about 3,000 in 1921 to 4,000 in 1931 and to 6,000 in 1951, whilst ministers of other religious bodies decreased slightly from just over 10,000 in 1921 to just below that number in 1951. Lawyers increased slightly, the number of judges, stipendiary magistrates and barristers rose from 2,966 in 1931 to 3,084 in 1951 and solicitors from 15,777 in 1931 to 19,689 in 1951. The third of the ancient professions, medicine, showed a substantial increase in most branches; for example, the number of registered medical practitioners and radiologists grew from about 26,000 in 1931 to 36,000 in 1951, and (male) trained, assistant and student nurses numbered 25,527 in 1951 as compared with 15,173 in 1931, but dental practitioners decreased from 11,092 in 1931 to 10,697 in 1951. Male teachers (other than teachers of music) also increased from about 79,000 in 1931 to 119,000 in 1951, which was not unexpected in view of the expansion in education services following the Education Act, 1944.

It is, however, in the newer professions connected with science and technology that the most significant increases occurred; for example, civil and structural engineers numbered about 22,000 in 1931 and 54,000 in 1951; mechanical, electrical and chemical engineers rose from 11,000 in 1931 to 50,000 in 1951;

---

[1] See Carr-Saunders and A. P. Wilson: *The Professions* (Clarendon Press, 1933); and Roy Lewis and Angus Maude: *Professional People* (Phoenix House, 1952); and *The English Middle Classes* (Phoenix House, 1949) for a discussion of the problems of definition and classification.

and scientists including chemists (not pharmaceutical), metallurgists, physicists, mathematicians and economists numbered 88,000 in 1951 compared with about 25,000 in 1931.[1] This broad group of 'scientists' contains a large number (about 47,000 in 1951) of laboratory assistants and technicians so that the real increase in highly qualified scientific manpower is not as substantial as would appear.[2] In any case the demand for scientists and technologists in the middle of the twentieth century is, apparently, far greater than the supply and a variety of measures designed to increase rapidly the supply of scientific manpower in the national interest have been adopted.[3]

The growth of most of the scientific and technical professions is in part a response to and of course responsible for the so-called atomic revolution which has been gathering momentum in recent years with the application of atomic energy for warlike and more recently for peaceful purposes,[4] but some professions have grown not because of scientific advances but as a result of radical changes in social policy. Two professional groups whose expansion has been due primarily to a widening of the functions of Government and the development of the so-called 'Welfare State' are those of Civil Servants and social workers. The number of Civil Service administrative and executive officers (male) increased from 19,000 in 1931 to 59,000 in 1951 and local authority officers from about 15,000 to 26,000, and though the Census classification shows them as being in Order XVI (Administrators, directors, etc.) they could with justification claim that theirs is a professional occupation. This rapid expansion in the number of higher Civil Servants can perhaps be justified, but some critics would question the necessity for the degree of increase and might suggest that part of it at least was due essentially to the operation of 'Parkinson's Law'.

[1] Physicists were first classified separately in 1931, but economists were identified separately in 1921, which indicates to some extent the rapid advance of physics in recent years.

[2] Of the scientists in 1951 approximately 20,000 were chemists (not pharmaceutical), 4,000 were metallurgists, 1,000 were biological scientists, 2,500 were physicists and 2,600 were mathematicians and economists.

[3] See, for example, *Britain: An Official Handbook*, H.M.S.O. 1955, section on 'The Promotion of the Sciences', Chapter XII, for a good account of the proposals made and methods suggested to increase scientific manpower.

[4] The opening of Calder Hall power station in 1956 established the development of nuclear energy as a source of power.

Industrial and Occupational Distribution of the Population

This law was first propounded in *The Economist* of 19th November, 1955, in a light-hearted article which nevertheless may have more substance in it than at first glance appears. Very briefly (but see the full article) it is suggested that 'the number of officials and the quantity of work to be done are not related to each other at all. The rise in the total of those employed is governed by Parkinson's Law, and would be much the same whether the volume of work were to increase, diminish or even disappear,' and this it is claimed operates especially in Central Government Departments. The substantial increase in the number of higher Civil Servants during a short span of twenty years does at least create a suspicion even in the minds of unbiased observers that Parkinson's Law was in operation to some extent.

Whether social welfare work is a professional occupation could be a subject of considerable argument but the Census authorities do classify social workers in the professional group. In 1931 there were nearly 4,000 male social workers and in 1951 just over 9,000, a remarkable increase particularly in view of the fact that in the nineteenth century and even in the 1930's social work was a predominantly female occupation. Those who bemoan the rise of the 'Welfare State' would doubtless regard the exceptional increase in the number of social workers as an indication of the growth of parasitic occupations having little or no direct contribution to make to the material wealth of the community, but less biased observers could contend that such an increase is symbolic of the awakening of the social conscience to the needs of individuals who require personal help and guidance in order to surmount the difficulties involved in living in an increasingly complex society. Whatever may be one's views on the usefulness or otherwise of any particular occupation it seems that the demand for social workers has increased and is unlikely to diminish in the near future.[1]

Other professional occupations which increased between 1931 and 1951 were those of qualified accountants (from about

---

[1] On the demand for and supply of social workers see the *Report on the Employment and Training of Social Workers* by Eileen Younghusband and published by the Carnegie United Kingdom Trust in 1947, and a second report by the same author, *Social Work in Britain* in 1951; and the *Report of the Ministry of Health Working Party on the Proper Field of Work and the Recruitment and Training of Social Workers at all Levels in the Local Authority Health and Welfare Services*, 1959.

27,000 to 32,000); officials of political, industrial and trade associations (from about 4,000 to 7,000) ; and other professional and technical occupations, e.g. business efficiency consultants, dietitians, labour managers, methods engineers, numismatists, personnel managers, and time study engineers, from 6,000 to 17,000. The trend clearly was for professional occupations to grow and with increasing specialization and the prestige and status attached to membership of a professional body there appears to be no end to the range and variety of occupations which are likely to lay claim to the term professional. It may well be that one of the distinctive features of change in occupational distribution in the twentieth century is the apparently never-ending birth of professions.

There is, in most cases, justification for the expansion of many of the professions and certainly national policy is now directed towards enlarging still further the numbers of persons with technical qualifications particularly in the applied sciences, but it is difficult to see why the number of male clerks and typists should have increased by about 20 per cent.[1] Many of them are employed in Government service and in local government departments whose functions have widened so much that an increase in the clerical labour force was inevitable, but this growth may again signify a partial operation at least of Parkinson's law.

Male occupations which declined follow to a considerable extent the pattern of the industries which have contracted in modern times, for example, occupations connected with fishing and mining decreased by about 40 per cent between 1931 and 1951, and those connected with agriculture, transport and communications, commerce and finance, entertainment and sport, and personal service decreased by between 2–16 per cent. The fall in the number of transport workers is the result primarily of a reduction in occupations concerned with horse-drawn vehicles (from about 129,000 drivers of horse-drawn vehicles in 1931 to 13,000 in 1951) and water transport workers (notably merchant seamen and dock labourers). On the other hand air transport workers increased in number substantially, though it is difficult to measure precisely the degree of change because in

[1] Even more difficult to see why female clerks and typists should have increased to the extent they have, see page 147.

1931 they were a relatively insignificant proportion of the transport group.[1] The decrease in most of the commercial, financial and insurance occupations is attributable mainly to smaller numbers of brokers, agents and factors, commercial travellers and canvassers, owners of retail greengrocery, meat, fish, and confectionery shops, newspaper sellers, costermongers and other hawkers. Many small retail shopkeepers suffered from the depression of the 1930's and from the effects of war-time controls on consumer goods, and since the war they have had to meet increasing competition from chain stores, multiple stores and co-operative societies,[2] but other occupations connected with finance and insurance (except stockbroking, money-lending and pawnbroking) increased their numbers from 125,000 in 1931 to 130,000 in 1951.

The steady rise in financial (mainly banking) and insurance occupations bears little relation to the great increase in the use of banking facilities and the demand for insurance cover of all kinds, for example, in England and Wales for the year 1931 about £37 million was cleared through the Banker's Clearing Houses, in 1946 the amount was £70 million and by 1951 just over £111 million; the premium income of life assurance companies established in the United Kingdom rose from £91 million in 1938 to £156 million in 1948 and to £213 million in 1951, and premium income for motor-vehicle insurance business rose from £37 million in 1938 to £70 million in 1948 and to £119 million in 1951. During these years the value of money fell appreciably, but it is probable that the growth in the volume of business was an indication of the spreading of banking and insurance facilities among a larger proportion of the population.

These relatively modest changes in most of the occupations concerned with commerce and finance conceal a significant change in one kind of financial transaction which reflects improvements in the standard of living, viz. the decline of pawnbroking. At the turn of the century there were about 11,000 men and 2,000 women occupied as pawnbrokers, and even in 1931 there were 3,613 men and 708 women returned as 'money-

[1] The only really comparable air transport occupation figures available for 1931 and 1951 are for air crew who in 1931 numbered 457 and 2,477 in 1951.

[2] For details of retail trade establishments see *The Census of Distribution and Other Services, 1950*, the reports published in 1953 and 1954.

lenders and pawnbrokers', but by 1951 there were only 1,252 men and 255 women. The pawnshop is, presumably, now less in demand than it was, for example, in 1899 when, according to Seebohm Rowntree in his *Poverty : a Study of Town Life,* 'the pawnshop often plays a most important part in the lives of . . . those who live in the slums, where the stream of people coming to the pawnshop on a Monday morning is a characteristic sight'. The custom of pawning clothes on a Monday morning and redeeming them on the week-end is not quite extinct, but the services provided in a Welfare State have undoubtedly reduced the need for regular recourse to the pawnbroker.

The numbers engaged in entertainment and professional sport have never accounted for more than a small proportion of all occupied males and the decrease from 1931–51 in Order XXI is accounted for almost entirely by the fall in the number of professional musicians from 19,612 to 11,036. On the other hand, males engaged in personal service have always formed a fairly large occupational group and the reduction in their number cannot be accounted for by the decline of any one occupation. Between 1931 and 1951 there were decreases in gamekeepers and game-watchers (from about 11,000 to 4,000); in publicans and innkeepers (from about 69,000 to 62,000); in barmen and waiters (from about 52,000 to 34,000); in barbers and hairdressers (from about 49,000 to 38,000); in chimney sweeps (from about 6,000 to 4,000); in domestic in-door servants (including chefs, kitchen-hands, servants in institutions, clubs and private homes) from about 80,000 to 66,000; and in others in personal service, e.g. beach, cloakroom and cinema attendants, and private detectives (from about 37,000 to 32,000). The personal service occupations which increased were those of managers and proprietors of restaurants (from about 26,000 to 40,000); hospital and ward orderlies and attendants (from 26,000 to 40,000);[1] caretakers and office keepers (from about 32,000 to 42,000); office cleaners (from about 5,000 to 13,000); and laundry workers, dry-cleaners and carpet cleaners (from about 15,000 to 21,000). The pattern of male personal service occupations is obviously changing and the tendency is for personal service to be identified less with

[1] The precise figures for hospital and ward orderlies and attendants were 26,374 and 39,754, and for managers and proprietors of restaurants 26,052 and 39,846.

residential service than it was in the past, and for it to continue to be a predominantly female occupation.

The occupational distribution of women changed appreciably between 1931 and 1951, and the outstanding features of change were the increase in nearly every occupation of the number of women occupied, and the elimination of the concentration of women into relatively few occupations. In manufacturing occupations (Orders IV to XIII) as a whole the number of women decreased by about 13 per cent due primarily to a substantial decline in the number of women in textile occupations. It was, however, only in Orders VII and IX that the number of women fell and there were substantial increases in, for example, occupations concerned with metal manufacture and engineering (Order VI) which increased by 40 per cent, and makers of food, drink and tobacco (Order X) where the numbers increased by 50 per cent. As a result of the over-all decrease the proportion of all occupied women engaged in manufacturing occupations was lower in 1951 (about 21 per cent of all women) than in 1931, when about 27 per cent of all women had manufacturing occupations. The over-all reduction may of course indicate a much higher degree of mechanization in 1951 and possibly is a reflection of the increasing opportunities for the employment of women in other than manual jobs within manufacturing establishments.

Women engaged in mining occupations (above ground only) were fewer in 1951, but in agricultural occupations the number of women increased by about 70 per cent between 1931 and 1951. The greater part of this increase is to be found in market-gardening occupations, but it would seem that the efforts made during the Second World War to attract women on to the land (e.g. through the Women's Land Army) achieved some success and that women continued to be attracted by agricultural occupations after the war. Equally the predominantly male building and contracting occupations attracted more women and in 1951 there were 153 female bricklayers, 72 bricklayers' labourers and 8 plasterers, whereas there were none in 1931, and even the 30 female masons and stone-cutters recorded in 1931 had increased to 77 in 1951. Unlike the position at the turn of the century when nearly all the women in building and contracting were married or widowed, nearly half the female builders and contractors in 1931 and 1951 were single.

The increase in the number of women engaged in the defence services indicates a radical change in attitudes towards the employment of women. In 1931 there were no women in the armed forces, but in 1951 there were nearly 17,000 stationed at home, and the extent to which the Women's Forces have become an integral part of our military system may be gauged from the fact that when (during the war of 1939–46) they were first enrolled in the Army they were looked upon as an auxiliary force (the Auxiliary Territorial Service), whereas by 1951 they had become the Women's Royal Army Corps.[1] Women police, too, increased their numbers appreciably from 231 all ranks in 1931 to 1,784 in 1951. In entertainment and sport, however, the over-all numbers remained relatively stable, decreases in the number of actresses, entertainers and musicians were offset by increases in occupations connected with cinemas, on the production side of theatres, and especially in women book-makers, whose number increased from 422 in 1931 to 1,853 in 1951.

The greater part of the increase of nearly 90 per cent in women following occupations in transport and communications is to be found in railway transport workers, where, for example, women railway porters increased from 170 in 1931 to 2,369 in 1951, and above all in the postal and telephone services, in which the number of postwomen and post office sorters rose from 1,512 in 1931 to 5,990 in 1951, and telephone operators numbered 63,155 in 1951 compared with 27,606 in 1931. The growing popularity of the telephone as a means of communication is presumably responsible for this increase in telephone operators; in 1931 there were just under 2 million telephones in the United Kingdom, in 1951 there were nearly 5 million and the number of local and trunk calls rose from about 1,371,000,000 in the year 1931 to about 3,326,000,000 for the year 1951.

The rapid rate of increase of women in the Post Office services was by no means exceptional. The entry of women into other branches of the Civil Service proceeded even more rapidly though the absolute numbers were smaller, for example, in 1931 there were 1,245 female administrative and executive officers, whereas in 1955 there were 14,103 in England and

[1] The Navy and the Air Force, of course, had their W.R.N.S. and W.R.A.F.

Wales. The majority were executive or higher clerical officers, but by the 1950's even the highest posts were within the reach of women, and in 1954 the first woman permanent secretary was appointed.[1]

Women increased their representation in commercial and financial occupations during this period, and not only as shop assistants in retail trade. There were more women owners of wholesale and retail businesses in 1951 than in 1931, more company directors; bankers; stockbrokers and jobbers (17 in 1951 and 8 in 1931);[2] but, like the men, so too were there fewer newspaper sellers,[3] costermongers and pawnbrokers in 1951 than in 1931.

The number of women in professional and technical occupations increased by about 35 per cent and the greater part of this increase was attributable to a rise in the number of nurses of all kinds (from about 138,000 to 210,000), registered medical practitioners and radiologists (from 2,810 to 6,649), industrial designers and draughtsmen[4] (from 5,030 to 13,811), chemists (not pharmaceutical) and metallurgists (from 568 to 1,710), and social workers (from 3,439 to 10,170). In 1951 there were, too, greater numbers of female mechanical, electrical, chemical and gas engineers (310 in 1951 and 22 in 1931); architects and town-planners (658 in 1951 and 107 in 1931); and judges, stipendiary magistrates, barristers and solicitors (677 in 1951 and 195 in 1931); but the predominantly female occupation of teaching (not music) increased its numbers only slightly from 181,806 in 1931 to 182,409 in 1951, whilst women teachers of music fell from 17,754 to 8,807. Despite these increases the ratio of women to men in professional and technical occupations was lower in 1951 than in 1931, and it would seem that if the output of technologists is to be greatly increased in the future, then more women will need to be trained.

---

[1] Dame Evelyn Sharp was appointed the permanent secretary to the Ministry of Housing and Local Government.

[2] Stockbroking and jobbing was still, however, a male stronghold, and even in 1956 a woman was refused membership of the all-male Birmingham Stock Exchange.

[3] On the other hand it would seem that the newspaper delivery girl was rapidly replacing the newspaper boy in the 1950's, but this matter of common observation would not be recorded in the Census since the main occupation of these youngsters would be that of student.

[4] Should the female be a draughtswoman?

The largest single group of occupations followed by women in 1951 was, as it has been for at least the past eighty years, personal service, but within Order XXII there were significant changes between 1931 and 1951. The most striking change was the decrease in the number of indoor domestic servants (in hotels, institutions and private homes) from about 1,333,000 to 724,000. Most other female personal service occupations increased, especially those of proprietors and managers of restaurants (from about 20,000 to 43,000); waitresses (from 71,000 to 81,000); hairdressers and manicurists (from 34,000 to 49,000); and office cleaners and charwomen (from 140,000 to 215,000). Many of them were employed part-time and in 1951 of the 744,000 women returned as part-timers some 314,800 were in Order XXII, of whom 234,000 were married. It may well be that these kinds of occupation will have to rely even more in the future on the part-timer, and this would seem to apply particularly to domestic service, where the trend away from this kind of job had by 1951 been firmly established.

Whereas in the past, and even as late as 1931, personal service occupations stood out as by far the largest single Order for women, by 1951 it was being closely challenged by Order XXIII – clerks and typists. The increase of 122 per cent in the number of female clerks and typists in England and Wales between 1931 and 1951 is astounding and no simple explanation for this mammoth growth can be offered. Presumably a not inconsiderable proportion of the new army of clerks was to be found in the service of Central and local government, in which case 'Parkinson's Law' might provide a partial explanation, and there has been since the war an enormous extension of statutory controls which rely on 'forms' of one kind or another for their implementation. 'Forms and form-filling' require clerks, indeed they might be said to generate clerks, so perhaps the explanation for the increase is after all very simple, but it is still difficult to believe that this country required for its economic development one out of every five of its occupied women or one out of every ten occupied persons to be a clerk or typist, which was in fact the position in 1951.

The changing pattern of occupational distribution in England and Wales between 1931 and 1951 may be summarized broadly as follows:

Industrial and Occupational Distribution of the Population

Out of every 100 males and females with specified occupations:

approximately 6 in 1931 and 5 in 1951 had occupations connected with agriculture or fishing;

approximately 5 in 1931 and 3 in 1951 were mining or quarrying;

approximately 29 in 1931 and 30 in 1951 were making things in factories, workshops or on building sites;

approximately 9 in 1931 and 8 in 1951 were in transport and communications;

approximately 11 in 1931 and 10 in 1951 were selling things or in banking and insurance;

approximately 13 in 1931 and 10 in 1951 were providing personal services or in entertainment or sport;

approximately 4 in 1931 and 6 in 1951 provided professional or technical services;

approximately 1 in 1931 and 4 in 1951 were in the armed or civilian defence forces or in the police force;

approximately 2 in 1931 and 2 in 1951 were administrators in central or local government, or managers or directors of businesses;

approximately 7 in 1931 and 10 in 1951 were clerks or typists;

approximately 3 in 1931 and 3 in 1951 were stationary-engine drivers, crane drivers, warehouse-keepers or bottlers;

approximately 9 in 1931 and 8 in 1951 were unskilled or in ill-defined occupations.

The main conclusions to be drawn about the changing pattern of occupational distribution between 1881 and 1951[1] are that the proportion of the occupied population engaged in agricultural, fishing, mining, quarrying, and personal service occupations declined; the proportion engaged in manufacturing, building, transport and communications remained relatively stable; that there was an appreciable increase in the proportion concerned with administration, defence, commerce and finance, and a slight increase in professional and technical

---

[1] If the list on pages 129–30 for 1881 and 1901 is compared with that for 1931 and 1951 above due regard must be paid to the changes in methods of classification, the variations in the accuracy of the returns and of the recording and analysis of the results. Absolute comparisons certainly cannot be made.

occupations; that the occupied population (despite the raising of the school-leaving age and more general retirement schemes) grew at a rate greater than that of the total population; that the ratio of occupied males to occupied females remained relatively stable; and that a much greater proportion of occupied women were married and women were to be found in a greater variety of occupations than in the past.

Accompanying the variations in the numbers following the different occupations there were significant changes in the age structure of the occupied population and in the industrial status of occupied persons. The age structure of the occupied population was affected by the changes in age balance of the population as a whole and by the raising of the minimum age of entry into employment and the introduction of retirement schemes, the result was that the age distribution of occupied persons in 1951 was quite different from that in 1901, as shown in Table 36.

TABLE 36

Distribution of occupied persons by age-groups in England and Wales at the Censuses of 1901, 1931 and 1951

Age-group	Per cent					
	Males			Females		
	1901	1931	1951	1901	1931	1951
Under 25 years ..	32	25	18	53	46	33
25 and under 35 ..	24	22	22	20	22	19
35 ,, ,, 45 ..	19	19	23	11	13	20
45 ,, ,, 55 ..	13	17	20	8	10	17
55 ,, ,, 65 ..	8	12	13	5	6	9
65 and over	4	5	4	3	3	2
All ages	100	100	100	100	100	100

N.B. – The occupied population in Table 36 refers to persons occupied aged 10 and over in 1901, 14 and over in 1931, and 15 and over in 1951.

The trend towards a smaller proportion of young and a larger proportion of middle-aged occupied persons has been firmly established in the twentieth century, and this was to be expected in view of the changes in the age distribution of the population as a whole and in social policy. The most marked movement in balance of age-groups was in the female occupied population where in 1901 the majority were in the young groups, whereas by 1951 the proportion aged 35 and over was nearly as large as that under 35, and this no doubt was due to the increase in the numbers of occupied married women.

The movement towards a greater proportion of middle-aged persons was common to all occupational groups, but there were substantial changes in the proportion of elderly (i.e. aged 55 years and over) persons in the various occupational groups, as shown in Table 37.

TABLE 37

Occupational groups in which 20 per cent or more of the occupied persons were aged 55 years and over at the Censuses of 1901, 1931 and 1951.

ENGLAND AND WALES

Males

	1901	1931	1951
	Per Cent	Per Cent	Per Cent
Agricultural	22	25	22
Personal service	—	21	25
Makers of textile goods and articles of dress	—	23	22
Building and contracting	—	21	—
Professional	—	21	—
Painting and decorating	—	20	—
Textile workers	—	—	20
Leather workers and fur dressers	—	—	25
Administrators, directors and managers ..	—	—	22
Commerce and finance	—	—	20
Warehousemen, storekeepers, etc.	—	—	23
Unskilled	—	—	22

Females

Agricultural	20	26	—
Personal service	—	—	21

In 1901 there was no occupational group, other than agricultural, in which 20 per cent or more of its occupied persons were aged 55 years or more, and only two male groups ('professional occupations and their subordinate services' and 'domestic offices and services') in which just over 10 per cent of their occupied persons were elderly. By 1931 five other groups had joined 'agriculture' among the males, but even so the occupied population was predominantly in the younger age-groups. In

1951, building and contracting, professional, and painting and decorating had reduced their proportions of elderly to 18, 14 and 17 per cent respectively, but six other groups had not joined the ranks of the 'elderly male occupational groups'. Among the women, however, agriculture had lost its unique position by 1951 and was replaced by personal service in which elderly persons were to be found mainly as charwomen and indoor domestic servants. The trend towards a larger proportion of middle-aged persons had been firmly established, and, even though retirement schemes were more widespread than in the past, there was a modest increase in the number of males (from 215,000 in 1921 to 238,000 in 1951) aged 70 and over still engaged in an occupation. This increase was not evenly spread over the occupations in which 70-year-old and over males were engaged, for example, in 1921, 1931 and 1951 the number of men aged 70 and over in agricultural occupations fell from 50,745 to 49,152 to 39,792; textile workers from 4,608 to 4,391 to 3,251; makers of textile goods and articles of dress from 9,059 to 8,320 to 3,981; whilst in building and contracting they varied from 12,368 to 13,296 to 11,960; in commerce and finance they increased from 23,992 to 30,981 to 36,242; and in professional occupations they increased (due mainly to relatively large numbers of older clergymen, lawyers and doctors) from 8,420 to 11,381 to 13,058. The proportion of over 70-year-olds was smaller in 1951 than in 1921 and if the system of compulsory retirement continues it will continue to fall.

The industrial status, that is the division of occupied persons into employers, employees and workers on own account, appears to have changed comparatively little in recent years, but exact measurement is difficult because the Census authorities have revised their methods of classification from time to time. In the nineteenth century an attempt was made to distinguish the employers from the employed and in 1891 an additional division was made of persons working on own account, but the results were considered to be 'excessively untrustworthy'[1] and as the majority of occupied persons were in any case employees it will be sufficient for our purpose to look at the change in industrial status since the First World War.

For the Census of 1921 occupied persons were classified into

[1] See the comments in the *Census 1901 – General Report*.

employers, employees and workers on own account, and presumably (though it is by no means certain) persons out-of-work were included; in 1931, on the other hand, the terms managerial and operative were used for employers and employees and the out-of-work (all classes) were specifically identified, but in 1951 yet another distinction was drawn between employers and managers, and operatives were sub-divided in order that apprentices and articled clerks, part-time workers, and unpaid assistants could be identified. The reason for reintroducing the separate categories of employer and manager was to enable the National Insurance class of self-employed persons to be identified in the Census results.[1] The effect, however, is that for the three censuses only workers on own account (and the retired) are strictly comparable, but in Table 38 the available data (apart from the retired) is summarized to show broadly the changes in the industrial status of the occupied population.

Ordinary observation would lead us to believe that most of us were, and are, employees, but Table 38 reveals two significant trends, viz. the decrease between 1921 and 1951 in the proportion of the occupied population who were employers and in women working on own account. One of the reasons for the reduction in employers is that some occupations are now followed in nationalized industries, for example, in mining and quarrying there were 1,181 male employers in 1921 whereas there were only 22 in 1951. The growth of the limited liability company since the middle of the nineteenth century, and the incursion of central and local government authorities into trading activities of many kinds has obviously reduced the number of employers and in 1951 it was only in agriculture, building and contracting, professional occupations, commerce and finance, and personal service that male employers constituted a not inconsiderable proportion of all occupied males. In 1921 they were in addition more commonly found in manufacturing especially in metal manufacture and the manufacture of textile goods and articles of dress, but the limited company had by 1951 replaced them in these fields.

---

[1] The number of self-employed persons in the U.K. in respect of whom contributions were payable under the National Insurance Acts during the year 1951 were males (in 000's) 1,300 and females 160; see the *Annual Report of the Ministry of Pensions and National Insurance*.

TABLE 38

Industrial status of the occupied population of England and Wales at the Censuses of 1921, 1931 and 1951

Status	Numbers in 000's and status group per cent					
	Males					
	1921		1931		1951	
	No.	%	No.	%	No.	%
Employers ..	563	5	—	—	376	3
Managers.. ..	—	—	922	8	625	5
Operatives ..	10,800	89	9,806	85	11,940	86
On own account ..	749	6	835	7	842	6
Total.. ..	12,112	100	11,563	100	13,783	100
	Females					
Employers ..	74	1	—	—	52	0·8
Managers	—	—	138	2	135	2·2
Operatives ..	4,665	92	4,664	91	5,739	93
On own account ..	327	7	321	7	231	4
Total.. ..	5,066	100	5,123	100	6,157	100
Out of work – all classes	M.	F.	M.	F.	M.	F.
	—	—	1,684	483	281	115

Workers on own account have steadfastly maintained their place in the economic system despite the advance of mass production and the limited company; in 1951 they were most commonly to be found (as they were in 1921) in agriculture, boot and shoe making and repairing, the manufacture of textile goods and articles of dress, printing, building and contracting, painting and decorating, road and water transport, retail trade, personal service (particularly in restaurants and public houses, as window cleaners and hairdressers), professional occupations, and to a lesser extent in some branches of manufacturing. Even in coal-mining there were, in 1951, thirty-eight men working on own account as hewers and getters of coal, presumably with the consent of the National Coal Board, so that despite the public corporation and the impersonal limited company the worker on own account still survived and showed no tendency to give in to the giants of economic progress.

Industrial and Occupational Distribution of the Population

1951–61. For the Census of 1961 the Classification of Occupations, and indeed of industries, were revised yet again. (See the *Standard Industrial Classification,* H.M.S.O. 1958 and *Classification of Occupations 1960,* H.M.S.O.). As a result of these revisions the 1961 Census reports will show the economically active or former active population by occupation, industry, employment status and economic position. Occupation is defined as the kind of work a person 'performs due regard being paid to the conditions under which it is performed; and this alone determines the particular group in an occupation classification to which a person is assigned'. Twenty seven orders and unit groups are classified as follows: 1. Farmers, foresters and fishermen; 2. Miners and quarrymen; 3. Gas, coke and chemical makers; 4. Glass and ceramics makers; 5. Furnace, forge, foundry, rolling-mill workers; 6. Electrical and electronic workers; 7. Engineering and allied trades workers N.E.C.; 8. Woodworkers; 9. Leather workers; 10. Textile workers; 11. Clothing workers; 12. Food, drink and tobacco workers; 13. Paper and printing workers; 14. Makers of other products; 15. Construction workers; 16. Painters and decorators; 17. Drivers of stationary engines, cranes, etc.; 18. Labourers N.E.C.; 19. Transport and communications workers; 20. Warehousemen, storekeepers, packers, bottlers; 21. Clerical workers; 22. Sales workers; 23. Service, sport and recreation workers; 24. Administrators and managers; 25. Professional, technical workers, artists; 26. Armed forces (British and Foreign); 27. Inadequately described occupations.

These groups differ in many respects from those identified in 1951,[1] and there are fewer (about 30,000 compared with 40,000 in 1951) separately identified occupations. Furthermore for the 1961 Census questions about occupation were asked of only 10 per cent of the population, so that problems arise in making strict comparisons with the past.

The male population aged 15 and over in England and Wales increased by just under 6 per cent in the decade 1951–61, and the female population by just under 4 per cent, but the 'occupied' population (classified as 'economically active' in the 1961 Census) showed an increase of just over 4 per cent for males and just over 12 per cent for females. Very broadly (and bearing

[1] Compare the 1951 groups on p. 130 above.

in mind the fact that the 1961 data was obtained from a 10 per cent sample and therefore the absolute figures may be liable to slight errors) the pattern of change was as follows:

England and Wales	Numbers in 000's					
	Males			Females		
	1951	1961	Inc. % 1951–61	1951	1961	Inc. % 1951–61
Total population aged 15 years and over ..	16,067	16,992	6	17,999	18,706	4
'Occupied' (economically active) population aged 15 years and over	14,064	14,244	4	6,272	7,045	12

The relatively low rate of increase in the population aged 15 and over is a reflection of the low birth-rates of earlier years, and the decline in the rate of increase of occupied males is due in part to a considerable increase in the numbers of students in educational establishments from about 280,000 in 1951 to about 488,000 in 1961, and the retired from about 1,365,000 in 1951 to about 1,646,000 in 1961. On the other hand the occupied females increased at a rate much greater than that of females aged 15 and over which was to be expected in view of the trend established in the war and immediate post-war years for married women to remain in or take up again gainful employment.

The extent to which married women are now engaged in gainful employment may be gauged from the fact that of all women 'economically active' in 1961 nearly 52 per cent were married compared with nearly 40 per cent in 1951, and of all married women in 1961 about 30 per cent were 'economically active' compared with about 23 per cent in 1951. In other words nearly 1 in 3 in 1961 (compared with nearly 1 in 4 in 1951) of all married women were gainfully occupied and of all 'occupied women' more than 1 in 2 in 1961 were married compared with less than 1 in 2 in 1951. Some of course are employed part-time, for less than 30 hours per week, and in 1961 nearly 40 per cent of all married women 'occupied' were part-timers compared with about 25 per cent in 1951.

The exact changes in the occupations followed by males and

females in 1961 as compared with 1951 (or earlier) cannot easily be measured because of changes in classification and grouping, but the broad pattern of occupational distribution in 1961 was as shown in Table 39.

TABLE 39

The Occupations of males and females aged 15 and over in England and Wales, at the Census of 1961.

Occupations	Numbers in 000's	
	Males	Females
1. Farmers, foresters, fishermen	754	78
2. Miners and quarrymen	458	(Less than 400)
3. Gas, coke and chemical makers	118	13
4. Glass and Ceramics makers	66	36
5. Furnace, forge, foundry, rolling-mill workers ..	205	10
6. Electrical and electronic workers	433	55
7. Engineering and allied trades workers	2,157	253
8. Woodworkers	393	11
9. Leather workers	87	63
10. Textile workers	147	252
11. Clothing workers	86	361
12. Food, drink and tobacco workers	253	88
13. Paper and printing workers	203	100
14. Makers of other products	174	118
15. Construction workers	514	(500)
16. Painters and decorators	294	12
17. Drivers of stationary engines, cranes, etc. ..	280	3
18. Labourers	1,100	92
19. Transport and communications workers ..	1,236	131
20. Warehousemen, storekeepers, packers, bottlers	478	275
21. Clerical workers	1,045	1,796
22. Sales workers	1,165	898
23. Service, sport and recreation workers	740	1,513
24. Administrators and managers	563	39
25. Professional, technical workers, artists	1,173	707
26. Armed forces (British and Foreign)	296	12
27. Inadequately described occupations	231	129
Total	14,649	7,045

If broad comparisons are made with the occupational distribution in 1931–51 (Table 35 *ante*, p. 135) then it would seem that the male groups which maintained the trend towards expansion established in that period were Orders 3, 4, 5, 6, 7, 12, 13, 14, 17, 21, 24, and 25 of the 1960 Classification. Orders 3 to 7 and 12 to 14 are of course those concerned with manufacturing and in view of the emphasis placed on manufacturing goods especially for export in recent years it is understandable that they should continue to expand. Some of the most substantial increases are to be found in the newer occupations concerned with electronics and male electrical and electronic workers increased from about 312,000 in 1951 to about 433,000 in 1961, in the same way there were substantial increases in the occupations connected with the 'new' materials, for example, 'workers in plastics' increased from about 12,000 in 1951 to about 26,000 in 1961. As in the past manufacturing occupations constitute a significant proportion of the occupied population but whereas in 1951 of all occupied males 26 per cent were following these kinds of occupations in 1961 the proportion was about 25 per cent. In part this relative proportional decrease was due to a decline in some of the older manufacturing occupations such as textile workers who fell from about 197,000 in 1951 to 145,000 in 1961, and of course to the seemingly ever-increasing demands from other occupations. As the total male labour force increased only slightly then clearly if some occupational groups expanded rapidly then others must remain stable or contract.

Two groups of male occupations expanded substantially in the decade and they were professional and technical occupations and clerical workers. Again we would expect professional occupations to expand as they did for males from about 714,000 in 1951 to about 1,173,000 in 1961. Some of the older professions such as those of clergy, ministers and members of religious orders which experienced a relative decline in earlier years appear to have regained some of the lost ground in that they seem to have increased from about 35,000 in 1951 to about 41,000 in 1961, and lawyers whose rate of increase from 1931 to 1951 was relatively small have increased quite substantially from about 23,000 in 1951 to about 28,000 in 1961. It is, however, the newer professions which have increased most, thus the number of mechanical engineers rose from about 25,000 in 1951 to about 46,000 in 1961, electrical engineers from about 20,000 to about 40,000; chemists, physical and biological scientists from about 29,000 to about 45,000 and social welfare and related workers from about 9,000 to about 20,000. Yet there appears still to be serious shortages in these professions in the

1960's and grave concern has been expressed about the supposed 'brain drain' of scientists to other countries, the serious shortage of social workers and the like.

The growth in the numbers of male clerical workers maintains the trend firmly established in earlier years and the number recorded in 1961 about 1,045,00 is considerably larger than that of 1951 where there were about 862,000. However, there were some changes in classification, for example, Civil Service executive officers and some local authority officers were recorded under clerical workers in 1961 whereas in 1951 they were allocated to the administrators, directors and managers group. Nevertheless even if they were excluded from the 1961 totals it would still be true that about 1,000,000 males were clerical workers.

There is obviously a tendency for 'white collar' workers to increase at a rate faster than that of the male occupied population as a whole and it is therefore not surprising to find that some of the long-standing 'manual worker' occupations continue to show a decline. Thus the numbers of fishermen fell slightly from about 15,000 in 1951 to about 14,000 in 1961; agricultural workers from about 411,000 to about 300,000; and coalminers and quarrymen from about 590,000 to about 458,000.

Other male occupational groups have remained relatively stable in the years 1951 to 1961, for example, transport and communications workers, though there are some variations within the group such as decreases in the numbers of railway guards and an increase in postmen and mail sorters; and sales workers (as they were classified in 1961 whereas they were shown under commercial occupations in 1951) where the group as a whole numbered between 1,100,000 and 1,200,000 in both years.

The changes in the patterns of male occupational groups reflect the changes which have occurred in economic and social conditions in recent times. The move away from the economically depressed conditions of the 1930's through the disturbed years of war and then to the supposedly affluent society of the 1950's with the technological revolution gathering momentum was bound to result in, and in part be caused by, variations in occupational patterns. But the extent to which particular occupations attract or fail to attract new recruits depend on a whole complex of factors and overall there is a limit imposed on the rate and extent of change by the growth of total population. The supply of male workers of different kinds is limited and it would seem that by the 1960's the demands for all kinds of labour exceed the supply and this is perhaps in part why there have been such radical changes in the varieties of occupations followed by women.

The trend established between 1931 and 1951 of women spreading into a greater variety of occupations than in the past was firmly maintained in the decade 1951–61. A glance through the occupational tables in 1961 shows that in every group there were considerable numbers of women and in some groups they clearly represented a more than reasonable proportion of the whole occupational group. In manufacturing occupations especially in engineering they showed marked increases over 1951 especially as workers in rubber and plastics, but as in 1951 there was a decrease of textile workers, and whereas women increased in number in agricultural occupations between 1931 and 1951 they showed a decrease between 1951 and 1961. As 'clothing workers', workers in 'food, drink and tobacco', and paper and printing workers they recorded increases between 1951 and 1961, but as 'construction workers' they fell substantially. Thus there were far fewer women bricklayers and stone masons in 1961 than in 1951, on the other hand women painters and decorators increased slightly in number.

In transport and communications occupations where the number of women increased substantially between 1931 and 1951 there was very little change in the next ten years. They declined as railway workers, for example, there were apparently no female railway guards in 1961 as compared with 86 in 1951 and there were only just over 1,700 railway porters and ticket collectors in 1961 as compared with over 2,500 in 1951, but the number of telephone operators increased from about 63,000 in 1951 to about 84,000 in 1961.

Where women increased substantially in numbers was as warehousemen, storekeepers and packers, clerical workers, sales workers and in professional and technical occupations. In 1951 there were about 1,270,000 female clerks and typists and in 1961 about 1,780,000 (if we exclude the executive grade

Civil Servants and local authority minor officials). Unlike 1951, however, when about 28 per cent were married by 1961 nearly 43 per cent were married women. If we take male and female clerks together then as in 1951 they comprised more than 10 per cent of the total working population, and by 1961 clerical workers were the largest group of all women workers.

The number of women in professional and technical occupations increased from about 523,000 in 1951 to about 707,000 in 1961 a rate of increase of about 35 per cent as it was between 1931 and 1951. As in the earlier years there was an increase in the number of nurses (from about 210,000 in 1951 to about 263,000 in 1961); medical practitioners (from about 6,400 to about 8,300); and lawyers (from about 677 to 1,030). The number of women engineers of all kinds, however, appears not to have increased, but chemists, physical and biological scientists have increased from about 2,400 to about 3,300. Women teachers who increased only slightly in numbers from 1931 to 1951 have, however, grown substantially from about 182,000 in 1951 to about 262,000 in 1961 and social welfare and related workers from about 10,000 to about 18,000. However, the ratio of women to men scientists has again fallen in this decade as it did in the previous twenty years.

Personal service occupations were, until 1951, the biggest single group of occupations followed by women, but by 1961 they had lost their pride of place to clerical occupations. However, there were still over 1,500,000 women who were 'service, sport and recreation workers' in 1961 and there were substantial increases in, for example, the numbers of barmaids (from about 29,000 in 1951 to about 39,000 in 1961), in waitresses and others engaged in serving food and drink, and of course in hairdressers, manicurists and beauticians from about 47,000 to about 99,000.

All occupations concerned with maintaining the supply of goods and services to the community have clearly maintained the trends established in the post-war years, but those which are concerned with defence have equally shown a tendency to decline, despite the 'cold war', in recent years. Thus the number of women in the armed forces has fallen from about 16,000 in 1951 to about 11,000 in 1961 and men from about 527,000 to about 268,000.

Industrial and Occupational Distribution of the Population

The broad patterns of change between 1951 and 1961 were that proportionally occupations related directly to agriculture, fishing, mining, transport and communications and the armed forces declined; occupations related to the making of things in factories, workshops or on building sites, selling things or in banking and insurance, and providing personal or clerical services tended to remain stable; and that occupations concerned with administration, management and professional and technical services tended to increase.

Just as there were significant variations in the age structure of the occupied population in 1951 as compared with earlier years (see Table 36, p. 149 *ante*) so, too, were there differences between 1961 and 1951 as shown in Table 40.

TABLE 40

Distribution of Occupied persons by age-groups in England and Wales, 1951 and 1961.

Age-group	Per cent			
	Males		Females	
	1951	1961	1951	1961
Under 25 years	18	17	33	29
25 and under 35	22	20	19	16
35 ,, ,, 45	23	21	20	19
45 ,, ,, 55	20	22	17	21
55 ,, ,, 65	13	17	9	12
65 and over	4	3	2	3
All ages over 15	100	100	100	100

The trend established in the years 1931–51 for the occupied population to be predominantly middle-aged was firmly maintained between 1951 and 1961, but the occupations in which 20 per cent or more of the persons following them were 55 years of age or over tended to change only slightly. Thus of the male occupational groups shown in Table 37 *ante*, p. 150 for 1951 all except administrators, directors and managers still had 20 per cent or more of their workers aged 55 years or over in 1961 and the only additional occupational groups to enter the list for the first time in 1961, were 'miners and quarrymen', and 'drivers of stationary engines, etc.'. However, the number of males aged

161

70 years and over shown as 'economically active' in 1961 was very much smaller than in 1951, they decreased from about 238,000 to about 188,000.

As in 1951 the 70-year-olds and over were to be found in relatively few occupational groups and the main group in 1961 and in 1951 was that concerned with agricultural occupations. There were slightly more professional and technical workers in the older age-groups in 1961 (about 15,000 compared with about 13,000 in 1951) and in the main they were still to be found among clergymen, lawyers and doctors. But the spread of retirement pension schemes is undoubtedly tending to reduce the numbers of elderly persons in occupations.

The classification of occupied persons by industrial status in previous censuses (see p. 151 *ante*) was replaced in 1961 by a system of classification by employment status (see *Classification of Occupations*, 1960). The economically active in 1961 were therefore classified as follows:

	Numbers in 000's	
	M.	F.
Self-employed without employees	722	213
„ „ with „ (large establishments)	4	(0·3)
„ „ „ „ (small establishments)	523	93
Managers (large establishments)	517	76
„ (small establishments)	495	120
Foremen and supervisors (manual)	489	43
„ „ „ (non-manual)	170	92
Apprentices, articled clerks, etc.	623	130
Professional employees	377	51
Other employees	10,324	6,060
Out of employment – sick	188	72
„ „ „ other	217	95
Totals	14,649	7,045

This more detailed classification is clearly much more valuable than those used in previous censuses, but to show the broad pattern of change between 1951 and 1961 Table 41 has been constructed by merging all the different self-employed groups in 1961 into 'workers on own account', all foremen and employees into 'operatives' and making the assumption that managers include employers. For comparison with earlier censuses see Table 38 (*ante* p. 153).

TABLE 41

Employment status of the economically active population of England and Wales at the Censuses of 1951 and 1961.

Status	Numbers in oo's and status group per cent.			
	Males			
	1951		1961	
	No.	%	No.	%
Employers ..	376	3	} 1,012	7
Managers.. ..	625	5		
Operatives ..	11,940	86	11,983	84
On own account..	842	6	1,249	9
Total	13,783	100	14,244	100
Out of work ..	281		405	
	Females			
Employers ..	52	0·8	} 196	3
Managers.. ..	135	2·2		
Operatives ..	5,739	93	6,376	93
On own account..	231	4	306	4
Total	6,157	100	6,878	100
Out of work ..	115		167	

The employment status of females has not changed at all in the decade but among males there is the significant change in the increased numbers and proportions of self-employed persons. The occupations in which they are to be found were broadly similar in 1961 to those of 1951 (see p. 153 *ante*).

The changing pattern of occupational distribution is obviously related to the changes in industrial distribution, but there were modifications yet again in the industrial classification for 1961 (see *Standard Industrial Classification*, H.M.S.O., 1958) which make exact comparisons with the past rather difficult. However, the full reports of the Censuses of 1951 and 1961 on Occupations and Industries provide a wealth of detail.[1] Additionally a great

[1] The Census reports are of course not infallible and must be used judiciously. For example it is most unlikely that in 1951 there were 2 clergymen (Church of England), 4 solicitors, 4 registered medical practitioners, 1 dentist, 10 opticians, 23 chiropodists and 34 accountants (all males) under the age of 16 as recorded in the Occupational Tables, 1951. And that in 1961 of the males who were at the time of

deal of information can be gained from the annual reports of the Ministry of Labour and National Service and especially from the monthly *Ministry of Labour Gazette* which provides a moving picture over time. It may well be, too, that as from 1964 with the establishment of a Ministry of Economic Affairs and Regional Economic Development Councils that henceforth even more elaborate data on industrial and occupational distribution will be made available.[1]

[1] In 1964 the first in a series of Manpower studies made by the Ministry of Labour's Manpower Research Unit was published. See *Manpower: Studies No. 1. The Pattern of the Future*, H.M.S.O. 1964.

---

the Census '15 last birthday' there were about 10 'deck, engineering officers and pilots, ships'; about 270 commercial travellers and manufacturers' agents; about 10 pharmacists and dispensers (presumably qualified); about 30 mechanical engineers (qualified); about 30 'accountants, professional', company secretaries and registrars; and about 30 surveyors and architects (presumably qualified). Even more unlikely are the numbers of girls 'age 15 last birthday' at the Census of 1961 who claimed to be (or were wrongly recorded and analysed as) 'proprietors and managers, food sales' about 50 of them; about 10 girls shown as 'managers in mining and production, not elsewhere classified'; about 70 who claimed to be 'pharmacists and dispensers' (presumably qualified); about 10 'surveyors and architects' (presumably qualified); and about 10 who were shown as 'social welfare and related workers'.

It is most unlikely, too, that of the boys and girls at the Census of 1961 whose ages were shown as '16–17' last birthday about 240 boys and about 50 girls were in fact 'judges, barristers, advocates and solicitors'.

CHAPTER VI

OCCUPATIONAL
AND OTHER ASSOCIATIONS

FOR many centuries past the people of England and Wales have formed themselves into associations to pursue some common interest whether it be in religion, the advancement of knowledge, the furtherance of trade or industry or for almost any purpose or cause, and in the nineteenth century the urge to band themselves into industrial, occupational, political and 'social' associations became particularly strong among all sections of society. It is, perhaps, the fact that so many came into being among the 'lower orders' which distinguishes associations in the nineteenth from those of earlier centuries, and having once established themselves (in some cases against the law) their range and variety was to become even greater in the twentieth century.

The measurement of the types and sizes of associations in our society is by no means easy. We cannot, unfortunately, call to our aid the Census because on no occasion have householders been asked to state the associations to which they belong or even the kinds of association of which they are nominal members.[1] But there are other sources which give at least an indication of the kinds, and with less precision the size, by membership of associations in this country, and it is on these that we have to rely if we wish to make an assessment of the significance of occupational and other associations in the social structure.

Occupational associations in the form of guilds (or gilds) of merchants or craftsmen had been a common feature of the

[1] An attempt was made in the Census of 1851 to determine the religious affiliations of the population but objections were raised to compulsory questions and so it became a voluntary inquiry. Refusals were, however, relatively few and in 1853 a separate report on *Religious Worship: England and Wales* was published. The experiment has never been repeated.

social structure of medieval England, but by the eighteenth century they had lost most of their power and influence, and apart from the continuance (even in the twentieth century) of the Livery Companies in the City of London (with very different functions from those they originally possessed) the ancient gilds had ceased to be of importance in the economic and social system. In the nineteenth century, however, new kinds of occupational associations emerged designed to cater on the one hand for the common interests of employees, and on the other for the mutual interest of employers, and these were of course Trade Unions and Associations of Employers.

The twentieth-century system of Trade Union organization is a product of the mid-nineteenth century and the Trade Union Act, 1871, is still 'the principal Act on which the present-day status of Trade Unions is based',[1] so that it is essentially in the period with which we are concerned that Trade Unionism as it exists at present has grown up. The objects of a Trade Union are, primarily, to protect, maintain and improve the status of its members and to safeguard their conditions of employment, and the need for protection of employed persons became especially great with the spread of industrialization in the nineteenth century. But that does not mean that Trade Unions were (or are) limited to members in industrial establishments (in the narrow sense), it is simply that Trade Unionism was born out of the first industrial revolution, and that in the twentieth century it is to be found in a variety of industries and among nearly all kinds of occupations. It is, however, difficult

---

[1] *Industrial Relations Handbook* of the Ministry of Labour and National Service, first issued for general publication in 1944 by H.M.S.O., should be consulted for a brief account of the development of Trade Unions and Employers' Associations and for modern methods of Collective Bargaining and Joint Negotiations between employers and employees. See, too, the report of P.E.P. on *British Trade Unionism* published in 1948 for an interesting series of studies on trade union structure and functions in the twentieth century. The standard history of Trade Unionism up to 1920 is of course S. and B. Webb: *History of Trade Unionism* (Longmans, 1920); see also, G.D.H. Cole and Raymond Postgate: *The Common People* (Methuen, 1946) for a good account of Trade Unionism in its social setting. In recent years a number of new studies on Trade Unionism have been published see e.g. B. C. Roberts: *Trade Unions in a Free Society* (Institute of Economic Affairs, 1959); A. Flanders and H. A. Clegg: *The System of Industrial Relations in Great Britain* (Blackwell, 1954); H. A. Turner: *Trade Union Growth, Structure and Policy* (Allen & Unwin, 1962); and H. A. Clegg, A. Fox and A. F. Thompson: *A History of British Trade Unions since 1889, Vol. I, 1889–1901* (Oxford University Press, 1964).

in some cases to distinguish between Trade Unions and Professional Associations whose members contend that they do not belong to a Trade Union because they are primarily concerned with safeguarding their professional interests. The only test which can be applied in cases of this kind is, does the Professional Association negotiate in the interests of its members to protect their conditions of employment? If it does then it is a Trade Union. In this sense the British Medical Association and the National Union of Teachers are Trade Unions, but there are of course Professional Associations who have no other object than that of maintaining the professional standards of their members. The distinctions between a Trade Union and a Professional Association are, in many cases, by no means clearcut and the best that can be done is to accept the definition adopted by the Ministry of Labour which classifies as Trade Unions all organisations of employees – including salaried and professional workers and manual wage earners – which include among their functions that of negotiating with employers with the object of regulating the conditions of employment of their members.[1]

The precise membership of Trade Unions in England and Wales cannot be determined. In part this is due to the fact that a Trade Union may have members in other parts of Britain, or even in other countries, and the only available figures which are assumed to be complete are for organizations of employees with headquarters in the United Kingdom, and the number of such Trade Unions and their membership is shown in Table 42. This table has been compiled from data given in the *Industrial Relations Handbook* of the Ministry of Labour and the *Annual Abstract of Statistics* and if these figures are compared with information relating to Trade Unions in recent years in, for example, *the Ministry of Labour Gazette,* or for the turn of the century the *Abstract of Labour Statistics* issued by the Board of Trade (Labour Department) or even with previous issues of the *Annual Abstract* some differences will be found. The fact is that precise and accurate data appears to be unobtainable.

[1] One cannot, unfortunately, accept the fact that all Unions registered with the Chief Registrar of Friendly Societies are Trade Unions of Employees since Associations of Employers may also be registered with him as Trade Unions in order that supervision may be exercised over their rules and funds. In any case not all Unions of employees nor all Unions of employers are registered.

Occupational and Other Associations

The numbers and membership of Trade Unions registered as such with the Chief Registrar of Friendly Societies are smaller than those shown in Table 42, for example, at the end of 1951 there were in Great Britain 413 registered Unions of Employees with a total membership of 8,286,881 and in 1961 there were 393 registered Unions with 8,545,000 members. The Chief Registrar estimated that the membership of registered Unions of Employees represented about 90 per cent of that of the whole of the Trade Union movement in Great Britain.

Despite the fact that we cannot make strict comparisons between the membership of Trade Unions given in Table 42 or by the Chief Registrar of Friendly Societies with the occupational and industrial distributions of the population of England and Wales shown in Chapter V, we can still affirm that even in 1951 and 1961 less than half the occupied population of England and Wales were members of a Trade Union. But, on the other

TABLE 42

Number of Trade Unions and membership (at the end of the year) in the United Kingdom

Year	Number of Trade Unions	Membership in 000's at end of year		
		Males	Females	Total
1896 ..	1,358	1,466	142	1,608
1906 ..	1,282	1,999	211	2,210
1920 ..	1,384	7,006	1,342	8,348
1930 ..	1,121	4,049	793	4,842
1941 ..	996	5,753	1,412	7,165
1951 ..	730	7,742	1,789	9,531
1961 ..	635	7,898	1,985	9,883

hand, it is equally clear that since the turn of the century Trade Union membership has increased appreciably and there has been a conspicuous increase in the proportion of the occupied population who are Trade Union members. In broad terms, it would seem that at the end of the nineteenth century something like 1 out of every 7 occupied males and 1 out of every 33 occupied females in England and Wales were members of a Trade Union, whereas in 1961 something like 1 out of every 2 occupied males and 1 out of every 4 occupied females were Trade Unionists.

Trade Union membership varies appreciably in different industries and occupations. There are some industries which operate a 'closed shop' which means that all persons employed in that industry have to be members of a Trade Union and equally there are some occupations which are restricted to members of a particular Union. The restriction of entry into a particular occupation is of course by no means new and some of the Craft Unions which continue this practice are merely perpetuating a custom which was certainly accepted in the Middle Ages. The 'closed shop', on the other hand, is a relatively new device which has become common in recent years and is found especially in the 'nationalized' industries and among the larger public companies. It is, perhaps, a sign of the growth in the power and influence of the Trade Union movement in the mid-twentieth century, which in part is due to the emergence of the 'big' Trade Unions.

At the beginning of the twentieth century there were a large number of Unions each with a relatively small membership, but by a gradual process of concentration and amalgamation the number of separate Unions has been reduced (as shown in Table 42) with the result that by 1951 more than half the Trade Union membership was controlled by a very few large Unions. For example, in 1951 there were 141 Trade Unions with less than 100 members each and a combined membership of about 7,000, but at the other end of the scale there were 17 Unions each with over 100,000 members and a combined membership of over 6 million or about two-thirds of the total of all Trade Union members. Between 1951 and 1961 the pattern did not change appreciably, thus the number of small Unions with less than 100 members had been reduced by 1961 to 120 with a combined membership of about 6,000, and the number of Unions with over 100,000 members was still 17 in 1961 as it was in 1951 but their combined membership had grown to just over 6½ million, and still accounted for about two-thirds of the total of all Trade Union members. In 1901, on the other hand, there was only one Union (The South Wales Miners Federation) with more than 100,000 members and the extent to which concentration and amalgamation has changed completely the pattern of Trade Unionism may be gauged from the fact that in 1961 there were two Unions – the Transport and General

Workers Union and the Amalgamated Engineering Union which each had over 1 million members, the equivalent of the total of Trade Union membership in 1901.

The trend towards concentration of membership has become particularly marked since 1945, when, for example, a number of separate Unions of miners combined to form the National Union of Mineworkers (with over 600,000 members), and this trend seems likely to continue, but that does not mean that co-operation between separate Trade Unions is of very recent origin.[1] As early as 1868 the Trade Union movement had formed a central co-ordinating body – the Trades Union Congress – whose objects were, *inter alia*, to promote the interests of its affiliated organizations, generally to improve the economic or social conditions of workers in all parts of the world and to settle disputes between its members or between its members and their employers.[2] The Congress is constituted by delegates of the affiliated Unions, and though not all Trade Unions have been (or are) affiliated to the T.U.C., its membership (i.e. the membership of the Unions affiliated to it) has grown from 118,367 in 1868 to 1,250,000 in 1900 and by 1961 it was 8,312,875. Despite the fact that only about one-quarter of the separate Unions in 1961 were members of the T.U.C., they included all but two[3] of the largest Unions, so that most Trade Unionists were in fact in its membership, and in recent years the General Council of the Trades Union Congress has been firmly accepted as the representative of the Trade Union movement as a whole in, for example, discussions with the Government in respect of national economic policy.

The formation of a central co-ordinating body was a logical step in the evolution of nineteenth-century Trade Unionism in which federations of Unions with similar interests had become common. Within most federations each Union was still respon-

[1] For recent figures of the number of Trade Unions and their size see the *Annual Abstract of Statistics*, and the *Ministry of Labour Gazette*.

[2] In 1897 the Scottish Trades Union Congress was established, whose objects are similar to those of the T.U.C. and with which it works in close co-operation.

[3] The two exceptions were the National Union of Teachers and the National Association of Local Government Officers. In 1964, however, N.A.L.G.O. formally became affiliated to the T.U.C. For up-to-date figures of membership of the Unions affiliated to the T.U.C. see the Annual Reports of the Trades Union Congress or *Whitaker's Almanack*, published annually.

sible for its own policies and decisions and the object of forming a Federation was essentially to provide strength of bargaining power. The tendency towards amalgamation has to a considerable degree reduced the need for Federations with the result that whereas in 1901 there were 109 Federations of Trade Unions, by 1961 there were only forty-three.

Trade Union organizations of various kinds have, in the past 100 years, obviously become extremely important voluntary[1] associations whose influence extends over the whole industrial, occupational and (as we shall see later) political system of this country. The 'new model' Trade Unions of the mid-nineteenth century which began in a relatively small way and among particular crafts, have by now spread into almost every occupation and all industries.[2] It is, perhaps, this extension of Trade Unionism to almost all kinds of occupations and industries which is the outstanding feature of the changing pattern of Trade Unionism in modern times. For most of the latter half of the nineteenth century it was to be found mainly in particular crafts and these Craft Unions accepted only skilled workers as members, but gradually many new Unions came into being to cater for the semi-skilled and the unskilled. These were usually either industrial Unions covering all workers in an industry or general labour Unions for workers in a variety of industries, and it is in the main these industrial and general Unions which became in later years the 'big Unions'. Trade Unionism in the nineteenth century was confined essentially to manual wage earners and it is in the twentieth century that the movement has spread to non-manual and salaried workers. In 1901, for example, the twenty-five largest Trade Unions were predominantly 'manual worker' associations, such as the Amalgamated Society of Carpenters and Joiners (with 67,000 members), the Durham Miners Association (with 82,000 members), the Amalgamated Society of Engineers (with 91,000 members), and the National Union of Gas Workers and General Labourers of Great Britain

---

[1] The voluntary element in Trade Union membership may in modern times be less strong than it was since in many industries and occupations today membership of a Trade Union is often a *sine qua non* of employment.

[2] The Amalgamated Society of Engineers (now the Amalgamated Engineering Union) is usually regarded as the outstanding example of the 'new model' Trade Unionism of the 1850's.

and Ireland (with 46,000 members),[1] but by 1961 some of the largest Unions are representative of the 'black-coated' (or 'white collar') workers, such as the National Union of Bank Employees (with 53,000 members), the Civil Service Clerical Association (with 143,000 members) and the Inland Revenue Staff Federation (with 41,000 members).

The list of Unions affiliated to the T.U.C. in the 1960's is certainly much more varied than it was at the turn of the century, and though 'manual worker' Unions are still predominant it would be quite wrong to regard Trade Unionism nowadays as being confined to manual occupations. If the marked trend towards an increasing proportion of non-manual workers' Unions being members of the T.U.C. continues then it may not be too long before it becomes a predominantly non-manual worker organization.

Occupied females were slow to recognize the advantages of combining together in their mutual interest and it was primarily after the First World War that Union membership by women became common.[2] Presumably the fact that for most women gainful occupation covered a relatively short period between childhood and marriage accounted for their apparent reluctance to join Trade Unions, and of course they were not engaged in large numbers in the occupations or industries in which Trade Unionism was first firmly established. There was, too, some opposition to female membership of male Trade Unions[3] which was only gradually broken down, but by now females have, in the main, been absorbed into hitherto predominantly male Unions and have not established 'all-female' Unions.

The spreading of Trade Unionism to nearly all kinds of occupations and grades of workers is one of the outstanding features of the changing social structure of modern England, and whilst employees have been combining to protect their common interests employers, too, have formed Associations of a

[1] See *Eleventh Abstract of Labour Statistics of the United Kingdom for 1905–06* published by the Board of Trade (Labour Department), which shows the membership, from 1896–1905, of the twenty-five largest unions.

[2] See G. D. H. Cole and Raymond Postgate: *The Common People (1746–1946)* for some interesting examples of the attempts by women in the 1890's to organize themselves into Trade Unions.

[3] ibid.

similar kind. Associations of employers vary enormously in their objects and functions. Some are concerned purely with matters of trade, joining together to determine the prices of the products or services they sell, or to restrict competition, and though such measures may, since 1948, be subject to inquiry by the Monopoly and Restrictive Practices Commission it does not follow that their effect on the public interest is necessarily any worse than that of Trade Unions of employees who restrict the supply of labour or impose restrictive conditions of employment.[1] However, it is not usual to regard Trade Associations as being comparable with Trade Unions, since the former are primarily concerned with goods and services, and it is their supply and price which forms the subject of inquiry, but Associations of Employers whose main purpose is to deal with questions of industrial relations are in essence the counterpart of Trade Unions.

Precise information on the number of Employers' Associations whose main purpose is to engage in collective bargaining with Trade Unions is not easily obtainable, but it would seem that in 1900 there were 43 Federations and National Associations of Employers and 810 Local Associations in the United Kingdom (including Ireland). They were to be found mainly in the Building Trades, the Mining Industry, Metal, Engineering and Shipbuilding Industries and the Textile and Clothing Trades.[2] In 1919 the British Employers' Confederation was established to secure the co-operation of the Employers' National Federations and in effect this is the counterpart of the Trades Union Congress.[3] It has remained as the central organization of Employers Associations, though it is believed that the number of separate National, Regional and Local Associations had grown by 1961 to about 1,800. The establishment of nationalized industries in recent years has of course modified its membership and the British Employers' Confederation now represents

---

[1] See the reports published by the Monopolies Commission from time to time of the results of inquiries made into a variety of firms or combinations of firms which have been investigated. See too the Annual Report which the Board of Trade has to publish on the working of the Monopolies and Restrictive Practices (Inquiry and Control) Act, 1948, and its amendments.

[2] See *Eleventh Abstract of Labour Statistics of the United Kingdom for 1905–06.*

[3] The British Employers' Confederation must not be confused with the Federation of British Industries (founded in 1916) which is an Association of Manufacturers for the encouragement, promotion and protection of British industries of all kinds but it does not deal with problems of labour relations.

nearly all 'private' industries, whilst the Boards of the nationalized industries negotiate independently with the Trade Unions.

In the middle of the twentieth century it is, perhaps, unrealistic to think of employers as persons, since they would in the main be limited companies or other corporate bodies and the individuals designated as employers in most Employers' Associations would be no more than paid managers or directors acting on behalf of the shareholders who, in theory at least, 'own' the company. The term 'employer' is by no means synonymous, as it probably was in the early nineteenth century, with 'owner' and the position of 'employer' in the case of nationalized industries is even more obscure, since the State owns the 'firm' and presumably it is the employing authority. In practice the members of the Board (or Commission) who are themselves paid employees of the State are the employers, but it does seem rather incongruous that, for example, the members of the National Coal Board who are themselves employees of the State should in turn be the employers of coal-miners, who, as taxpayers, presumably own the Coal Board and therefore employ its members. The individual employer is rapidly becoming a rarity and Associations of Employers are by now essentially Associations of representatives of employing authorities, which is in itself a distinguishing feature of the changing pattern of occupational and industrial Associations.

The relationship of Unions of employees to Unions of employers has undergone remarkable changes in recent years. In the past, formal negotiations between both sides were arranged on an *ad hoc* basis as and when the occasion arose, but towards the end of the nineteenth century voluntary machinery for dealing with disputes by conciliation and arbitration had been established in a few industries, particularly those in which the Craft Unions were strong. In the first two decades of the twentieth century more systematic negotiating machinery was established by legislation through, for example, Trade Boards and Whitley Councils, but it was not until 1939 that the British Employers' Confederation and the Trades Union Congress were brought together on a permanent basis for closer and more regular consultation in a National Joint Advisory Council.[1] In

---

[1] See *The Industrial Relations Handbook* for the historical development of negotiating machinery and present-day schemes.

many ways the bringing together of both sides of industry has changed their pattern of relationships and certainly it has established these 'voluntary' Associations as essential factors in economic development and the maintenance of industrial peace. The Trade Unions and Employers' Associations are by now powerful instruments of economic change and indeed of political pressure, and the fact that they have become such potent bodies in a relatively short period of time is one of the outstanding features of the changing social structure of modern England.

The growth of the Trade Union movement is usually regarded as the prime example of the rise of 'the working classes' (undefined) through mutual aid associations, but another kind of 'working class' association was also growing strongly in the nineteenth century and that was the Co-operative movement. The history of the Consumers' Co-operative movement in this country has been well documented,[1] and it remains for us to examine, briefly, its growth as an association. The idea of retail customers joining together to form an association which would purchase goods essential for daily living and would sell them to the members so that they would be able to share in the profits of combined purchasing and selling was firmly established in this country in the first half of the nineteenth century. By 1881 there were about 965 Consumers' Co-operative Societies in Great Britain registered under the Industrial and Provident Societies Acts and the Friendly Societies Acts which had given the movement a legal basis. Throughout the remainder of the nineteenth century the number of Societies and the membership continued to grow, so that by 1901 there were in Great Britain 1,455 Societies with a total membership of 1,789,358.

In the nineteenth and the early years of the twentieth century membership of a Co-operative Retail Society was probably confined to persons who would generally have been regarded as working class. Indeed the official statistics of those years relate to 'Workmen's Co-operative Societies' and there is no doubt that the aims and objects of co-operation in retail trade were essentially linked with the aspirations of the working class movement as a whole. To what extent membership of a

---

[1] See, for example, A. M. Carr-Saunders, P. Sargant Florence and R. Peers: *Consumers Co-operation in Great Britain* (Allen & Unwin, 1938).

particular Society was an indication of active participation in the attempt to attain the broad objectives of the movement is difficult to determine, because there were very few restrictions imposed on those who wished to become members, and even the minimum shareholding was not intended to restrict members but was a device for financing the Society. The entrance fee payable was often as low as 6d. or 1s., and after payment full rights of membership could usually be exercised, but the available evidence suggests that most members were interested primarily in the advantages to be derived from co-operative purchasing with 'the dividend' on purchases as the main benefit and only a small proportion were prepared even to attend occasional meetings.[1] This is, of course, by no means unusual, since in most associations the active members are invariably a small proportion of the total membership, and in recent years when most associations have grown appreciably the proportion of active members is usually small and does not necessarily increase proportionately with the growth in membership'[2]

The main feature of growth of Consumers' Co-operation since the end of the nineteenth century has been the decrease in the number of Societies, the marked expansion in the number of members and in the total sales made by Retail Co-operative Societies, as shown in Table 43.

The decrease in the number of societies is due primarily to amalgamation and absorption of small societies and the trend has been (as in the Trade Unions) towards an increase in the average size of societies and to the development of a few very large concerns so that, for example, by 1961 just over a third of the total membership was provided by the nineteen largest societies, each of which had over 100,000 members. The increase in the number of members particularly in recent years is remarkable and it would seem that nominal membership at least must now extend beyond what would usually be regarded as the

[1] See, for example, *Consumers Co-operation in Great Britain*, Chapter 16 – 'Democratic Control of Retail Societies'; and more recent studies, e.g. G. A. Bankes and G. N. Ostergard: *Co-operative Democracy* published by the Education Department, Co-operative Union Ltd. in 1955.

[2] For example, the non-attendance of Trade Unionists at meetings and the fact that the control of most Unions rests in the hands of a few active members became a subject of considerable interest in the 1950's.

TABLE 43

Co-operative Retail Societies – Great Britain

Year	Number of Societies	Number of members (000's)	Sales for year £ million
1901 ..	1,455	1,789	53
1921 ..	1,300	4,501	219
1931 ..	1,159	6,532	208
1951 ..	1,045	10,700	648
1961 ..	879	12,788	1,017

'working classes'. If we assume that most members are repre-sentatives of 'households' or 'families', then clearly the majority of families in this country are Co-operative members, but it seems probable that a not inconsiderable proportion of all members are 'occasional' purchasers only, who use 'the Co-op' for convenience, or for purchasing 'branded products', in effect at lower prices than elsewhere because of the dividend they re-ceive on purchases. The figures of total sales are, unfortunately, not necessarily an index of the purchases per member, since in any case in the past sixty years there have been marked variations in prices, and in the past twenty years the value of sales has been affected by inflationary conditions. It would be unwise to draw too many conclusions from the total sales figure in view of such changes, for example, 1921 was a year of high prices whereas 1931 was a year of low prices, but allowing for changes in the value of money it is obvious that total sales have increased appreciably. But it has been suggested that whereas in 1950 Co-operative Retail Societies accounted for 11·4 per cent of all retail trade by 1961 their share of national retail trade had fallen to 10·8 per cent. It would seem therefore that in the 1950's the continued progress of the past was not main-tained.[1]

The association of consumers in the form of Co-operative Retail Societies has undoubtedly become a feature of some significance in the social structure of modern Britain and with the extension of co-operative principles to the manufacture of goods and the establishment of wholesale societies the Co-operative movement as a whole has grown from very small

[1] Sidney Pollard: *The Co-operatives at the Crossroads*, Fabian Society Pamphlet, 1965.

beginnings in the early nineteenth century to become one of the major trading organizations in our society.[1]

The Trade Union and the Co-operative movements have a political side to their activities, but it was among Trade Unionists that political action was firstly strongly developed. During the nineteenth century the Trade Unions had increasingly tried to secure reforms in conditions of labour by Act of Parliament and they soon realized that to promote reforms they would need to have in Parliament their own representatives. For some time support was given to the Liberal Party, but in 1900 the Trade Union movement helped to form the Labour Representation Committee, which in 1906 became the Labour Party. Since then the political activities of Trade Unions have been intimately bound up with the growth and development of the present-day Labour Party.

The Co-operative movement, however, was less eager in the nineteenth century to take part in political activities despite the fact that as early as 1863 the Central Co-operative Board (later known as the Co-operative Union) had been formed in part at least to provide opportunity for the expression of political views. In 1880 the first Parliamentary Committee of the Co-operative Union was founded to watch legislation and protect Co-operative interests in Parliament, but it was not until 1920 that the Co-operative Party was established as an active political force designed to send its own representatives to Parliament. Since 1927 an alliance has existed between the Co-operative Party and the Labour Party, which has prevented Co-operative and Labour candidates standing in opposition to each other and where Co-operative candidates have been elected they are labelled Co-op and Labour. The number of Co-operative Members of Parliament has never been great and by now the Co-operative movement is assumed to be in the main a supporter of the Labour Party.[2]

[1] See *Consumers Co-operation in Great Britain*, for a good description of the manifold trading activities of the Co-operative movement as a whole.

[2] For example in 1957 there were twenty Co-operative members of Parliament among the Labour members in the House. On the 28th February 1957, however, it was reported in the *Manchester Guardian* that the Labour Party had decided to review their existing alliance with the Co-operative Party in view of the apparent discontent among Trade Union supporters of the Labour Party with the existing arrangements.

The Employers' Associations do not openly engage in political activities, but that does not mean that they are indifferent to political action or that they do not support political parties.[1] However, as there is no clear evidence of their political interests we can do no more than record the fact that unlike the Trade Union and Co-operative movement they do not avowedly support a political party.

The modern political party (or Association) is essentially a product of the nineteenth century and it came into being in part because of the expansion of the electorate after the Reform Act of 1832 and in part because of the political aspirations of the working-class movements and their demands for equal representation in the affairs of State.[2] It was after the Reform act of 1867 (which had considerably increased the electorate) that the Conservative and Liberal leaders in Parliament encouraged the creation of party organizations outside Parliament 'devoted to wooing the newly-enfranchised urban voters'[3] and for the remainder of the century Conservative and Liberal Clubs (even Conservative Working-men's Clubs) were established to foster support for the parties in the House.

The active membership of these associations was probably never very large and as far as the Clubs were concerned, there was always the danger, which was recognized by the Conservatives, for example, in 1882 'that the political aims of these institutions may in some cases come to be regarded as secondary to the social objects'.[4] However, organized political parties in the modern sense had been firmly established, but at the turn of the century a third political association was to come into being – the Labour Party.

Unlike the Conservative and Liberal Associations which had in effect been created by the Parliamentary Parties, the Labour Party in Parliament arose out of the Trade Unions and other

---

[1] Employers' Associations registered as Unions do in fact contribute to political funds, see the Annual Reports of the Chief Registrar of Friendly Societies.

[2] The best modern account of the growth of the political parties in this country is R. T. McKenzie: *British Political Parties* (Heinemann, 1955), and see too Herman Finer: *Goverments of Greater European Powers* (Methuen, 1956) section on 'the Government of Britain' which has brief accounts of the major parties as well as of the electoral and political systems.

[3] R. T. McKenzie, op. cit.; he does not, unfortunately, deal with the growth of the Liberal Party, but see Herman Finer, op. cit.

[4] ibid.

workers' associations. When the first two Labour Members were returned to Parliament in 1900 they were endorsed by the Labour Representation Committee, and it was not until 1906 that the Parliamentary Labour Party was formally constituted. We need not be concerned with the subsequent growth and development of the Labour Party[1] except to note the fact that in the twentieth century it replaced the Liberal Party and was to become along with the Conservatives one of the two major political parties.

The membership of the Labour Party is difficult to determine precisely because there are in effect two classes of members, those who belong directly to the Party and those who are members of affiliated organizations, notably the Trade Unions. Not all Trade Unions are affiliated, nor does it follow that even where a Trade Union is affiliated that all its members whole-heartedly support the Labour Party, but unless they 'contract out' of the political levy they will at least support the party financially.[2] In any case how should we measure the membership of political parties, by the number of paid-up members, or by the number of active working members, or even by the number of voters who support each party at elections? Whichever method or combination of methods is adopted it is unlikely that we should obtain a result sufficiently accurate to indicate anything more than the extent to which the parties have a 'hard core' of supporters in the population at any given time.

If paid-up membership is accepted as the most significant method of associating in a political party then in modern times the record for the number of paid-up members of the Conservative Party was reached in 1953, when total membership in

---

[1] But see R. T. McKenzie, op cit.; Herman Finer, op cit.; and Cole and Postgate, *The Common People*.

[2] The 'political levy' in Trade Unions has had a somewhat chequered career – after the 'Osborne Judgment' of 1909 it was illegal for a Trade Union to compel a member to contribute to the funds of a political party; The Trade Union Act, 1913, however, allowed Unions to impose a political levy subject to certain conditions and to the right of a member to 'contract out'; the Trade Disputes and Trade Unions Act, 1927, allowed a political levy on condition that a member 'contracted in' (i.e. specifically agreed to pay the levy); and finally The Trade Disputes and Trade Unions Act, 1946, repealed the 1927 Act and allows the political levy subject to the right to 'contract out'. The effect of all these changes has been to vary the affiliated membership of the Labour Party from time to time – see R. T. McKenzie, op. cit., page 483, and for the amounts contributed by Registered Unions see The Reports of the Chief Registrar of Friendly Societies.

England and Wales was 2,805,032 as compared, for example, with 911,600 in 1946. The Labour Party in 1953 had a total membership of 6,107,659 of whom 5,071,935 were members of affiliated Trade Unions (and constituted about two-thirds of the total membership of unions affiliated to the T.U.C.), but as R. T. McKenzie points out in his *British Political Parties,* the spectacular rise in the number of affiliated members after the passing of the Trade Disputes and Trade Unions Act, 1946, from about 2½ million in 1945 to about 4 million in 1947 is 'convincing evidence of the lack of significance attached to their Labour Party membership by a large proportion of those who are affiliated through their Trade Unions.'[1] The increase in paid-up members of the Conservative Party may equally indicate no more than the willingness on the part of a greater number of people to subscribe to party funds, and it should be noted that since 1946 both parties have launched vigorous campaigns designed to increase substantially the income required to maintain the party machines.

If party membership is not a particularly reliable guide to the strength of political associations the election results are still less satisfactory except to show the changes which have occurred in political representation in Parliament. The most striking change since the turn of the century has been the virtual elimination of the Liberal Party as a political force and changes in the allegiance of voters from time to time. It must be remembered that the electorate has undergone a number of changes even in the twentieth century and particularly since 1928, when women were given equality of the franchise, and there have been changes in electoral boundaries. The pattern of change in political representation may be gauged from Table 44.

The elections shown in Table 44 were not the only elections held in this century[2] but they were particularly significant in the history of the rise and fall of the major parties. The 1906 election brought the Liberals into power after almost twenty years of

[1] On the growth of membership and the absence of any correlation between party membership and votes cast at elections see R. T. McKenzie, op. cit.

[2] For a summary of all election results between 1922 and 1955 see Herman Finer, *Governments of Greater European Powers,* and see, too, D. E. Butler, *The Electoral System in Britain, 1918–1951* (Oxford University Press, 1953), and his regular publications on British elections. On the social fabric of British politics see G. Blondel: *Voters, Parties and Leaders* (Penguin Books, 1963).

Occupational and Other Associations

Conservative rule, the 1923 election resulted in the Labour Party (with the support of the Liberals) coming into power for the first time, and those held in 1935, 1945 and 1951 show the pendulum of power swinging between the Labour and Conservative Parties and the decline of the Liberals. From 1951 to 1964 the Conservative Party continuously remained in power and even at the election of 1964 they were only narrowly defeated by the Labour Party. In the same period there was clearly a revival of support for the Liberal Party to the extent that in 1964–5 the Liberal M.P.s held the balance of power in Parliament. But whether or not these swings of electoral opinion indicate equally violent changes in membership of political associations is doubtful. In all elections in this century between 70 and 80 per cent of the electorate have voted and since 1928, when universal franchise for adults was introduced it is the Conservative and Labour Parties which have commanded the majority of the votes, though there is not necessarily a relationship between total votes cast and seats obtained.

TABLE 44

Political Representation in the House of Commons as a result of the General Elections of 1906, 1923, 1935, 1945, 1951, 1955, 1959 and 1964.

Parties		Seats in House of Commons							
		1906*	1923	1935	1945	1951	1955	1959	1964
Conservative..	..	157	258	431	212	321	345	365	304
Labour	..	29	191	154	394	295	277	258	317
Liberal	..	401	159	21	12	6	6	6	9
Others	..	83	7	9	22	3	2	1	0

Percentage of Votes

		Conservative	Labour	Liberal	Others
1935 ..	..	53·6	37·8	6·6	2·0
1945 ..	..	39·8	47·8	9·0	3·4
1951 ..	..	48·0	48·8	2·6	0·6
1955 ..	..	49·7	46·4	2·7	1·2
1959 ..	..	49·4	43·8	5·9	0·9
1964 ..	..	43·4	44·1	11·2	1·3

* The division of the parties in 1906 was not as clear-cut as in the later years and the actual composition of the House was Conservative 132 + Liberal Unionists 25; Labour 29; Liberals 377 + 24 Liberal-Labour; Irish Nationalists 83 – a total House of 670 members including, of course, Irish members.

If voting behaviour[1] is an indication of political affiliation, then it would seem that by the middle of the twentieth century we have become a nation almost equally divided in our political allegiance, but that does not mean that minor parties have no part to play or that political associations are confined to the major parties. For example, since 1920 the Communist Party has achieved a position of some prominence and though its membership in Great Britain has probably never exceeded 60,000[2] and its representation in the House has not exceeded two Members at any one time, its influence industrially and politically may well be out of proportion to its size. Other minor parties, too, have from time to time appeared but none have, as yet, succeeded in establishing themselves sufficiently to rival the major parties in voting strength.

Industrial, occupational and political associations have become, especially in the twentieth century, powerful instruments of social control and of social action affecting not only their members but the community as a whole, and it is this fact which gives them a degree of prominence which is often out of proportion to their actual active membership. Other associations which have grown equally strongly in modern times are less prominent because their influence is limited to their members and this is particularly true of mutual aid associations, such as Friendly Societies.

The Friendly Society, that is a voluntary organization whose members contribute to a common fund from which they may receive financial assistance in time of need, has been in existence in this country since the eighteenth century, but it was in the latter part of the nineteenth century that the movement became particularly strong among the members of the wage-earning population. A great variety of Friendly Societies (whose main

[1] The study of voting behaviour and the analysis of election results is now deemed by some people to be a science with the distinctive name of psephology. See the publications of some modern psephologists, for example, D. E. Butler: *The British General Election of 1951* (Macmillan, 1952) and on succeeding elections, notably D. E. Butler and Anthony King: *The British General Election of 1964* (Macmillan, 1965).

[2] See Finer, op. cit. In 1957 at the Annual Conference of the Communist Party of Great Britain the membership was said to be 32,000, but it has been suggested in *The Times*, 17th February 1958, that membership declined after the Soviet intervention in Hungary in 1956 and that, for example, in 1958 there were only 25,000 members.

purpose was to provide financial assistance in times of sickness or old age and to meet the funeral expenses of the member) came into being and by 1901 there were 27,005 different Societies with a membership of about 5½ million.[1] The number gradually declined in the twentieth century, due in part to the introduction of the system of National Insurance, but even in 1951 there were 14,353 Societies, Orders and Branches in Britain with a membership of 6,794,000.[2] and in 1961 there were 10,467 with a membership of 6,012,000. There can be no doubt of the value of Friendly Societies to the lower income groups in the past and even now the additional benefit they provide in time of need and as a supplement to the National Insurance benefits cannot be ignored. It would seem however, that the introduction of comprehensive National Insurance in 1948 diminished the desire to band together in mutual aid associations of this kind and membership fell from 8,608,000 in 1947 to 6,535,000 in 1953 and just over 6 million in 1961. If the 'Welfare State' is maintained then presumably there is unlikely to be any revival in the Friendly Society movement in the future, and a notable feature of our past social structure may well become little more than material for the social historian.

There is undoubtedly a close relationship between the membership of Friendly Societies, Trade Unions, Co-operative Societies and the Labour Party, but it would certainly be most unwise to add together their separate membership figures in order to try and arrive at the proportion of the population who belong to associations of this kind. It would probably be safe to assume that the majority of Trade Unionists are in addition members of Friendly Societies, 'The Co-op' and the Labour Party but that the majority of 'Co-op' members do not necessarily belong to the others. The extent to which they are active members of one or more of these associations is difficult to determine, but again it would probably be fair to assume that most are no more than subscribing members whilst the few are the active policy-makers working with paid officials. And it is, perhaps, the rise to power of full-time paid officials which makes

[1] For an interesting analysis of Friendly Societies at the end of the nineteenth century see L. Chiozza Money: *Insurance versus Poverty*.

[2] See Annual Reports of Chief Registrar of Friendly Societies, and the *Annual Abstract of Statistics*.

these associations in the middle of the twentieth century so different from what they were in the past when they were more closely knit small groups of people with common aims and purposes working together in a common cause.

Yet there are still in our society associations which demand more of their members than the weekly subscription and among them are those concerned with education, religion, and the giving of service to others in the community.

Most associations in our society may be said to have to a greater or less degree an educational function, for example, the Trade Unions and the Co-operative Societies have always had an educational purpose in addition to their main objects, but some associations have been concerned purely with the provision of educational services to their members. In the early nineteenth century the majority of the population in this country had to rely almost entirely on voluntary organizations for such formal education as they received, but the provision of statutory education services as a result of a succession of Education Acts and the creation of Local Education Authorities had by the end of the century largely removed the voluntary element in the primary education field. Adult education movements, however, were soon to appear and among the first was the Workers' Education Association.

In 1903 'an Association to promote the Higher Education of Working Men' was formed whose main object was to construct a working alliance between the University Extension and Working Class movements, and out of this has grown the Workers' Educational Association of Great Britain. It began with 135 members but soon grew and at the end of ten years had over 11,000 members. Membership had doubled ten years later and it reached its peak in 1946–7, when it had 45,320 members. By 1951–2, however, membership had declined to 35,000 but there were still over 1,000 branches and student groups.[1] Since then there has been a tendency for membership to grow and in 1961–2 there were 38,508 members, a further 11,321 student members in 903 branches which provided 6,985 classes having 133,025 students. The influence of the W.E.A. on adult education in this country has undoubtedly been great and there are

[1] See *W.E.A. Retrospect, 1903–1953,* published to commemorate the Jubilee of the movement.

countless men of eminent standing in our middle-twentieth-century society who owe the education they received to the pioneers who so bravely brought the standards and value of University teaching to the 'working man'. The reasons for the relative decline in membership in recent years are complex, but the growth of compulsory education and the spread of a variety of mass media of communication, such as radio, television, films and newspapers, may well have had their effect on the earlier urge to obtain 'education' by active participation in educational associations. Furthermore it is very doubtful whether the movement now provides services purely for 'the working man', it has become much more an Association for adult education of all classes in society.

There are, of course, hundreds of other Associations whose aims are essentially 'educational', though they may bring people together for such diverse reasons as acting together in amateur theatricals or because of a desire to preserve rural scenery and to prevent disfigurement of the countryside.[1] The number of these associations has grown rapidly particularly in the twentieth century, despite the extraordinary expansion of 'statutory' facilities, and some of them have succeeded not only in attracting members in this country but have expanded well beyond Britain to become International Movements. A discussion of the range, scope and variety of voluntary associations is beyond the scope of this book, but the fact that so many new associations have come into being in modern times must be recorded because it is a distinctive feature of the changing social structure. It would be virtually impossible to measure their total membership at any one time, but it must run into millions in the middle of the twentieth century.

Religious associations have been a feature of our social life ever since we became, at least nominally, a Christian country, but in the nineteenth century in particular the variety of religious associations was considerably increased. The Anglican Church has for centuries past been the established Church in England, but the rights of religious freedom which are now possessed by every citizen are of comparatively recent origin

[1] See, for example, *Voluntary Social Services – Handbook of Information and Directory of Organisations*, published by the National Council of Social Service, and *Whitaker's Almanack*, published annually.

and it is this right which has enabled the variety of other denominations to establish their places of worship. Any attempt to measure precisely the membership (and especially the active membership) of religious associations is fraught with difficulty, but the variety of religious groups may be gauged from the number of religious buildings which are certified by the Registrar-General as meeting-places for religious worship.[1] As shown in Table 45 the number of buildings increased between 1921 and 1950 but in recent years there has been a reduction in part perhaps because of the re-development of living areas and of a decline in actual membership leading to the closing down of churches and chapels.

The 'other denominations' include, for example, Christian Scientists, Christadelphians, Baha'is, Jehovah's Witnesses, Seventh Day Adventists, Spiritualists, Elim Four Square Gospel Alliance, and the like, but as a building need not be certified unless it is also to be registered as one in which marriages may be solemnized[2] it is likely that the total of buildings used as meeting-places for religious worship is larger than that shown in Table 45.

The purpose of Table 45 is merely to give an indication of the distribution of meeting-places of worship but the number of buildings does not necessarily bear any direct relationship to the number of members of each denomination. In some countries the Census provides details of religious affiliation and though this may indicate no more than nominal membership at least it is a guide.[3] In this country the available evidence can be obtained only from the religious organizations themselves whose records may or may not be adequate and even with such information we may know no more than the number on the rolls. Attempts have been made to collect such data and even to measure the degree of Church attendance, but it cannot be

[1] It was by the Places of Religious Worship Certifying Act, 1852, that provision was made for places of religious worship of Protestants other than churches or chapels of the Established Church to be certified to the Registrar-General instead of the Diocesan authorities or local Justices of the Peace as required by earlier Acts.

[2] Buildings used by Jews and Quakers need not – since 1836 – be registered even for the solemnization of marriages. See the Registrar-General's Statistical Reviews for details of the buildings of religious denominations.

[3] See footnote page 165 above for the one attempt made by the Census in England and Wales.

TABLE 45

Buildings certified[1] to the Registrar-General as
meeting-places for religious worship in England and Wales

Denomination	Number of Buildings		
	1921	1950	1962
The Established Church in England and the Church in Wales[1]	16,156	16,827	16,810
Wesleyan Methodists	7,626 ⎱		
Primitive Methodists	4,360 ⎰	13,295*	⎱ 12,505
United Methodists	1,980		⎰
Congregationalists	3,364	3,615	3,791
Baptists	3,188	3,597	3,788
Roman Catholics	1,560	2,388	3,124
Salvation Army	1,136	1,569	1,289
Calvinistic Methodists..	1,299	1,417	1,463
Presbyterians	448	466	421
Jews	259	423	400
Society of Friends	431	422	407
Unitarians	184	193	225
New Church	55	61	†
Catholic Apostolic Church	70	53	†
Countess of Huntingdon's Connexion ..	47	43	†
Other denominations	3,335	7,513	7,304
	45,498	51,882	51,527

N.B. Nearly 1,000 buildings of Churches other than the Anglican Church were certified before 1852 and are not included above.

[1] Buildings of the Established Church or the Church in Wales do not have to be certified but they are included in Table 45 in order to give an idea of the distribution of denominational buildings.

* In 1932 these three denominations combined to become The Methodist Church.

† The Registrar-General appears to have re-classified the main groups in his Statistical-Review for 1962 and figures are not available for those marked † but presumably they are included in 'Other denominations'.

said that the available studies provides much more than a guide to the membership of the various religious associations.[1] John Highet[2] estimated that in 1950–1 membership of Christian

[1] See, for example, A. Carr-Saunders and D. C. Jones: *Survey of the Social Structure of England and Wales* for interesting comments on the problems of measurement and of Church membership in 1935 in England and Wales. For a recent intensive study on religious adherence in Scotland with occasional references to England and Wales see *The British Journal of Sociology*, Vol. IV, No. 2, June, 1953, article on 'Scottish Religious Adherence' by John Highet.

[2] loc. cit.

religious denominations in England and Wales amounted to 7,203,700 and was distributed broadly as follows:

Anglican Communion:	
Church of England	2,965,200
Church in Wales	196,389
Roman Catholic	2,034,600
Presbyterian Church of England	69,676
Presbyterian Church of Wales	159,627
Methodist and other Members of the Free Church Federal Council:	
Congregational Union	229,825
Baptist Union	313,023
Methodist Church	730,592
Union of Welsh Independents	125,336
Other Methodists and other Members of the Free Church Federal Council	45,931
Other Denominations: Salvation Army	100,000
Jehovah's Witnesses	27,000
Assemblies of God	20,000
Society of Friends	20,432
Miscellaneous	166,602

From other available evidence it would seem that Highet's figures are reliable, but it must be noted that the various denominations have different methods of compiling their membership, thus the Roman Catholics do not keep membership lists as such, but record the Catholic population (and in Highet's figures they cover the adult population only); the Church of England figures may be either those on the Electoral Roll (as shown above) or of Communicants at a specified time; and the Salvation Army has no roll of members, but merely provides 'unofficial estimates'.

In broad terms it would seem that in the 1950's the major religious associations in England and Wales were the Church of England and the Church in Wales with about 3 million members, the Roman Catholic Church with about 2 million members; the Methodist Church with about three-quarters of a million members and the Congregationalists, the Baptists and the Presbyterians with about a quarter of a million members, and that there were numerous other associations with membership varying from a few thousand to 100,000 members.[1] Some of the smaller religious groups, for example, the Quakers, are far more important than their small membership would suggest

---

[1] The number of Jews is not known; nor can an estimate be made of Non-Christian Associations, though it is thought that, for example, Muslims are widely represented in this country.

and it would certainly be unwise to judge the strength or power of any religious association by its nominal membership.

From the imperfect data available it would seem that about one-fifth of the adult population of England and Wales in the middle of the twentieth century belonged to a religious association, but whether this proportion was very different from that at the turn of the century is difficult to determine.[1] Ordinary observation would lead us to believe that the proportion of the adult population who were members of a religious association in 1951 was less than it was fifty years before and there is certainly evidence available to suggest that in general there was a marked decline in church attendance. For example, it has been shown that in York about 35 per cent of the adult population (i.e. persons of 17 years of age or over) attended church on Sundays in 1901 as compared with about 18 per cent in 1935 and about 13 per cent in 1948, and that the only denomination to show an increase in its Sunday attendance was the Roman Catholic Church.[2] York was probably not untypical of most towns in England, and even in Wales – a stronghold of Nonconformity and chapel-goers – there was an obvious decline in Sunday attendance from 1901 to 1951, though it is probable that membership in Wales had not decreased as much as it had in England.[3]

In the late 1950's there was considerable discussion and controversy about an assumed decline in religious adherence, and in 1960 the Church Assembly of the Church of England passed a resolution 'That the Central Advisory Council for the Ministry be instructed to consider in the light of changing circumstances, the system of payment and deployment of the clergy, and to

[1] As compared with about one-half of the adult population of Scotland according to Highet, op. cit.; and, according to the *Year Book of the American Churches*, just over half the population of America in 1951. Compare, too, Carr-Saunders and Caradoc Jones' estimate of one-quarter of the adult population in 1935.

[2] Rowntree and Lavers: *English Life and Leisure* (Longmans, 1951), Chapter XIII on 'Religion'.

[3] See, for example, T. Brennan, E. W. Cooney and H. Pollins: *Social Change in South-West Wales* (Watt & Co., 1954) in which the growth of Non-conformity in the area and its influence on Welsh life and thought is discussed, and the estimate is made that though there has been a decline in membership and attendance since the nineteenth century, even in 1950 at least 33 per cent of the adult (i.e. aged 15 years and over) population were members of the Church in Wales or of one of the four principal Nonconformist denominations.

make recommendations'. The task of making this fact-finding inquiry was given to Mr. Leslie Paul and in 1963 he produced his report on *Deployment and Payment of the Clergy* (published by the Church Information Office, November 1963). This was a landmark in the history of self-analysis by the Church of England and Mr. Paul provides substantial evidence to show the way in which 'in this country as a whole, though not everywhere to the same degree, the Church of England is facing a loss of membership and the attrition of its power and influence'. He was able to make use of the report of the Statistical Unit of the Central Board of Finance which in 1959 published *Facts and Figures about the Church of England* and this elaborate statistical data and his own investigations enabled Mr. Paul to give us a real picture of the structure and organization of the Church of England.

Quite clearly active membership of the Church of England has declined, for example, infant baptisms were 623 per 1,000 live births in 1885, rose to 717 in 1927 and then fell to 554 in 1960; the number of Confirmations per 1,000 of the population aged 12–20 has dropped from 34·5 in 1957 to 30·5 in 1962; and Easter Day Communicants fell from 98 per 1,000 of the population aged over 15 in 1911 to 63 per 1,000 in 1958. Indices of these kinds are to some extent counterbalanced by local surveys made in different parts of the country which indicate that religious adherence in the sense of infant baptisms, church marriages and burials is still strong. (See *The Deployment and Payment of the Clergy*, by Leslie Paul.) However the overwhelming impression is that the Church of England was confronted in recent years by a serious loss of membership.

Overall figures of membership comparable with those produced by Highet (op. cit) in 1951 are still not easily obtainable despite the extensive data now provided by the Statistical Unit (see *Facts and Figures about the Church of England*, 1959 and, presumably, subsequently).

From the larger number of sources of data now available (e.g. membership figures for the main religious bodies are now published in *Whitaker's Almanac* and see too *British Political Facts 1900–1960* by D. Butler and J. Freeman published in 1963) it would seem that over-all membership of the Church of England has declined relative to population growth from 1951 to 1961;

that the Church in Wales has not declined to the same extent;[1] that the Roman Catholic population has increased substantially; and that the numbers of Methodists, Baptists and Congregationalists has declined.[2] Other groups such as the Quakers, Jews and Salvationists have probably remained stable.

The plain truth is that we do not know precisely the extent to which membership of religious associations and attendance at places of worship has changed in the past 60 years. It may be that the decline is not nearly as great as we are often led to believe, but what would seem to be apparent is that (with the exception of the Roman Catholics) active participation in religious associations is now less strong than it was at the turn of the century. Since the 1930's a new form of participation in religious worship has been provided through the radio and some recent surveys, for example, T. Cauter and J. S. Downham, in *The Communication of Ideas,* have shown that though in Derby only 13 per cent of the adult population went to church once a week or more in 1953 about 80 per cent claimed to listen to a religious service on the radio at least occasionally, and Highet (op. cit.) has shown that in Scotland in 1953 a majority of the population claimed to listen to religious broadcasts. It may be that the radio has to a considerable extent replaced attendance at church but being a member of the radio-listening public is hardly equivalent to being a member of a religious association.[3]

However, the Churches still maintain a leading role in one of the fundamental features of social life and that is as institutions for the solemnization of marriage. For example, in 1961-2 for every 1,000 marriages registered in England and Wales, 704 were with religious ceremonies and 296 were civil marriages. Of every 1,000 marriages with religious ceremonies 673 were of the Church of England and the Church in Wales; 175 were Roman Catholic; 69 were Methodist; 26 were Congregationalist and 24 were Baptist. Yet it would seem that whilst the great majority of the population get married in a church this

[1] See *New Society*, Vol. 1, No. 21, 21 Feb. 1963, article on 'Church, Chapels and the Welsh,' by C. C. Harries.

[2] See Harries, op. cit., for the sharp decline in attendance at Nonconformist chapels in Wales.

[3] See a report of the B.B.C. Audience Research Unit, *Religious Broadcasts and the Public,* published by the B.B.C. in 1955. See, too, an article on 'Church Going in Scotland' by John Highet in *New Society*, 26th December 1963.

does not mean that most of them become active Church members after marriage.

Associations whose main purpose is to provide 'services for others' are more varied in this century, though they may have more specific aims than those of the past. To a considerable degree voluntary social service organizations in the nineteenth century were concerned with the predominant and overwhelming problem of poverty and membership of them was very largely restricted to those who were able to spend time and give money to those less fortunate than themselves. They were essentially associations of 'the haves' who from mixed motives were prepared to devote part of their activities to 'the have-nots', but with the growth of the Welfare State and with the raising of standards of living all round the need and the demand for associations of this kind has diminished, yet voluntary organizations have continued to come into being. Their aims and purposes, however, are now very different from those of the past and in the main their efforts are directed to improvement in the conditions of particular groups in the community, for example, the mentally and physically handicapped or the aged; or to social reform, for example, penal reform; or to the personal problems of individuals in a complex society, for example, marriage guidance.[1] We have become more aware of personal problems and are less beset by mass problems in the twentieth century and voluntary organizations have responded to (and of course they have made us more aware of) problems of this kind and if we were to summarize the changing pattern of voluntary social services we could do no better than to say that in the twentieth as compared with the nineteenth century we have moved away from mass problems and mass solutions to individual problems and individual solutions of social problems.

Yet the urge to form voluntary associations is no less strong now than it was in the past and, indeed, the main distinguishing feature of the pattern of change may well be that whereas in the past 'the few' formed societies for their own or the benefit of others, now the right and the inclination to join together is more widespread and not circumscribed by wealth or status.

[1] See *Voluntary Social Services – Handbook of Information and Directory of Organizations*, published by the National Council of Social Service, for excellent summaries of the purposes, aims and objects of the hundreds of organizations listed.

Occupational and Other Associations

We cannot measure accurately the extent to which there has been any significant change in the proportion of the population who combine to form associations, but it would be fair to assume that there is by now a larger proportion than there was in the past, but that it would still constitute a minority of the members of the population as a whole.[1]

It may well be that the strength and power of associations lies in their relatively small membership, and when one considers the influence of learned societies, such as the Royal Society (founded in 1660), the Royal Society of Arts (founded in 1704), the Royal Institution (founded in 1799) and the British Association for the Advancement of Science (founded in 1831), one may feel that it is not numbers but quality which counts. If therefore it is a large number of relatively small associations of good quality which makes the best contribution to the advancement of individual well-being, then it is clear that in our twentieth-century society we have a range, variety, number and type of associations which contribute to the maintenance of a healthy democracy. Once the right to combine together with one's fellows for whatever purpose or reason is removed an essential freedom is abolished and it is perhaps the fact that in the twentieth century we can, and some of us do, combine together in whatever walk of life we may be to form associations, which distinguishes the present social structure from that of the not so distant past.

[1] For example, Cauter and Downham have shown that in Derby, in 1953, 8 per cent of the adult population belonged to intellectual or cultural clubs or societies, 11 per cent were members of some political party, 13 per cent went to church every week and 3 per cent held some church office. See their *The Communication of Ideas* for details of the kinds of associations to which people belonged in Derby, their analysis of active membership and their assessment of the extent to which different people are influenced by and take part in the various associations in a modern town.

CHAPTER VII

SOCIAL CLASSES
AND EDUCATIONAL OPPORTUNITIES

THE novelists and social historians of the nineteenth century emphasized time and again the wide differences which existed between the various social classes in England[1] without attempting either to define 'social class' or to measure the numbers in each of the classes which were assumed to be in existence. In the twentieth century sociologists and social psychologists have devoted a great deal of attention to the concept of social class and its significance in society, but the fundamental problem of determining the criteria which distinguish one class from another is still unresolved, and it would be difficult to find a definition and form of measurement which would be universally acceptable.

We cannot be concerned with the numerous attempts which have been made to define social class and to analyse the criteria distinguishing one class from another, nor with the theories which have been propounded on the nature and significance of social classes in our society, but some consideration must be given to their existence and to the methods devised to measure them in modern times.

There can be little doubt that for centuries past the population of this country has been divided, or has divided itself, into groups each with their own interests and standards which marked them off from each other, and that where the members of a group had the same social status they formed a social class. But what were the criteria which determined membership, and how could the separate classes be identified? Was it wealth

---

[1] The social class structure in Wales was (and is) probably less complicated than in England, see Brennan, Cooney and Pollins op. cit., and Table 47 *post*.

and/or birthright which controlled entry into the upper class; was it lack of wealth or a lowly occupation which determined membership of the lower classes; and what about the middle class? Was there in fact a hierarchical system and were the boundaries clearly definable? It was, and is, questions of this kind which have exercised the minds of social scientists when attempting to identify social classes, but the answers to them are difficult to find.[1]

Pioneer social surveyors like Charles Booth in his *Life and Labour of the People of London* (1902), used income as a measure of economic status and indirectly as a determinant of social class, and this criterion has been used more recently in a variety of ways, but income groups are not necessarily social classes. The Census authorities on the other hand began, in 1911 to divide the population into occupational groups and these have traditionally become known as 'social classes'. Occupation may well be one of the determinants of social class and recent evidence suggests that different occupations have varying degrees of social ranking,[2] but it does not follow that persons in the same occupation comprise a unified group or class. In this country, however, most of us have to rely on income from an occupation to provide our material standard of living, and even though some occupations have a relatively high prestige and in comparison with other occupations a low rate of earning power, there is undoubtedly a connection between occupations and standards of living which may in turn influence the membership of a social class. What then are the patterns of occupational grouping?

The method adopted by the Census authorities is to group occupations into five classes, e.g. at the Census of 1951 they were as follows: Class 1 – Professional and similar occupations, e.g. Civil Service administrative officers, secretaries and registrars

---

[1] See T. H. Marshall: *Citizenship and Social Class* (Cambridge University Press, 1950); G. D. H. Cole: *Studies in Class Structure* (Routledge, 1955) for comments on the class structure in the past 100 years and on the measurement of social class in 1951; T. Cauter and J. S. Downham: *The Communication of Ideas* (published by Chatto for the Reader's Digest Association) for brief summaries of the methods employed to measure social classes in America and Britain.

[2] See J. Hall and D. Caradog Jones, 'Social Grading of Occupations' in the *British Journal of Sociology*, Vol. I, 1950, and Michael Young and Peter Willmott 'Social Grading by Manual Workers' in the same journal, Vol. III, No. 4, 1596; and D. V. Glass (ed): *Social Mobility in Britain* (Routledge, 1954)

of companies, ministers of religion, lawyers, doctors, and professional engineers; Class 2 – Intermediate occupations, e.g. farmers, retailers, local authority officers, pharmacists, teachers; Class 3 – Skilled occupations, e.g. coal-miners, most factory workers, shop assistants, most clerical workers, actors and actresses; Class 4 – Partly skilled occupations, e.g. plumbers' labourers, locomotive engine firemen, bus conductors, domestic servants, window cleaners; Class 5 – Unskilled occupations, e.g. dock labourers, costermongers and other hawkers, watchmen and most kinds of labourers.[1] This 'social class grouping provides a convenient arrangement of the unit groups of the Occupational Classification into five social classes based on general standing in the community, economic circumstances not being taken into account except so far as they are reflected in the Occupational Classifications' (*The General Register Office, Classification of Occupations*, 1950). Doubtless many of the persons in Class 3 had far bigger incomes than some in Class 1, but that makes no difference to this method of grouping, and there could be endless discussion about the class to which a particular occupation should be assigned. The main objections to this system are that it has too few classes, with the result that there is a heavy concentration in the middle grade, and it is a classification of occupational groups and not of persons.

For the Census of 1961 this division of five main classes was retained but substantial alterations were made in the allocation of occupations to each class. For example, University teachers were moved from Class 2 to Class 1, whereas Civil Service administrative and other higher officers were re-allocated to Class 2 from Class 1; actors and musicians were moved from Class 3 to Class 2, whilst postmen and telephone operators were moved from Class 3 to Class 4.[2] Strict comparison with the past cannot therefore easily be made, and furthermore questions about occupation in the 1961 Census were limited to the 10 per cent sample. However to show the broad changes over time Table 46 has been compiled but it should be noted that whilst there is a fair degree of comparability between 1931 and 1951

[1] For the details of the occupations in each class see the *Classification of Occupations*, 1950.

[2] For the changes made and the composition of each class see the *Classification of Occupations*, 1960.

(see The Occupation Tables, Census 1951, Table D), the data for 1961 has been derived from the 10 per cent sample and furthermore the percentage in each group has been calculated on the basis of the numbers of males actually stating an occupation. The total number of males included in the 10 per cent sample was just over 16,330,000 but just over 778,000 could not be classified, hence the percentage distribution in each social class is based on the total as shown in Table 46.

TABLE 46

Social class distribution of occupied and retired males in England and Wales at the Censuses of 1931, 1951, and 1961

Class	1931		1951		1961	
	No. (000's)	%	No. (000's)	%	No. (000's)	%
1	336	2	494	3	591	4
2	1,855	13	2,146	14	2,368	15
3	6,848	49	8,041	52	7,933	51
4	2,552	18	2,433	16	3,237	21
5	2,459	18	2,258	15	1,422	9
	14,050	100	15,374	100	15,551	100

The main positive trend is towards a reduction in Class 5 and an increase in Class 1 and 2 which is what could be expected from the changing pattern of occupational distribution. If there are five social classes in the population then they probably correspond to the divisions shown in Table 46, and as occupational differences play a fundamental part in a society like ours in attracting or repelling people towards or from each other it may well be that the Registrar-General's classification is as good a guide as any to our social class structure.[1]

The social class distribution of the population as a whole (as distinct from occupied males) is determined in the censuses by allocating heads of households to each of the five social classes

[1] See G. D. H. Cole: *Studies in Class Structure* for an interesting analysis of this method of classification, but note that his book was written before the final report of the Census, 1951, on Occupations was published. He had to rely on the One Per Cent Sample results and therefore his figures are slightly different from those shown in Table 46, but the differences are not sufficient to invalidate his conclusions.

and broadly the proportion in each class is similar to that shown in Table 46. The amount and variety of data in the Census reports on, for example, the age and marital status of the persons in each class and the regional variations is by now extraordinarily wide, yet the demands for even more detailed analyses have been quite strong in recent years. In an attempt to provide a more elaborate sub-division of occupational groups the Census authorities introduced at the 1951 Census the concept of socio-economic groups.

Thirteen socio-economic groups were identified as follows :

A.—Agricultural	1.	Farmers.
	2.	Agricultural workers.
B.—Non-agricultural		
(i) Non-manual	3.	Higher administrative, professional and managerial (including large employers).
	4.	Intermediate administrative, professional and managerial (including teachers and salaried staff).
	5.	Shopkeepers and other small employers.
	6.	Clerical workers.
	7.	Shop assistants.
	8.	Personal service.
(ii) Manual	9.	Foremen.
	10.	Skilled workers.
	11.	Semi-skilled workers.
	12.	Unskilled workers.
C.—Special groups not included elsewhere	13.	Armed forces (other ranks).

Objections can be raised against this method of division, but it had the merit of breaking-up the five broad classes into major sub-units, thus Social Class 1 was covered by socio-economic group 3; Social Class 2 contained socio-economic Groups 1, 4 and 5; Social Class 3 contained socio-economic groups 6, 7, 8, 9 and 10; Social Class 4 contained socio-economic groups 2 and 11; and Social Class 5 contained socio-economic groups 12 and 13. As this method was employed for the first time at the Census, 1951, comparisons with the past are not possible, but in 1951 the Social Class and socio-economic grouping of heads of households in England and Wales was as shown in Table 47.

The division into socio-economic groups is a most useful method of analysing the population in more detail, but it would seem that if occupation is used as the basis of social class, then the broad pattern emerges of a small upper and lower group with a predominant large middle group. Independent investigations made at the London School of Economics into social

TABLE 47

*Social class and socio-economic distribution of private households
in England and Wales classified according to the social class
of the head of the household at the Census of 1951*

Numbers in 000's								
Social Class				Socio-economic groups				
England		Wales		England			Wales	
No.	%	No.	%		No.	%	No.	%
I	357	3·3	17	2·7	3	357	3·3	17	2·7
2	1,928	18·4	131	21·0	1	235	2·2	41	6·6
					4	1,209	11·5	59	9·5
					5	522	5·0	33	5·3
3	5,257	50·0	278	44·6	6	555	5·3	20	3·2
					7	331	3·2	14	2·2
					8	438	4·2	18	2·9
					9	422	4·0	22	3·5
					10	3,660	34·8	209	33·5
4	1,697	16·2	112	18·0	2	434	4·1	17	2·7
					11	1,146	10·9	93	14·9
5	1,267	12·1	85	13·6	12	1,158	11·0	80	12·8
					13	39	0·4	1	0·2
	10,506	100	623	100		10,506	100	623	100

N.B. – 1,787 households in England and 127 in Wales could not be classified.

mobility confirm this broad pattern, for example, in the first
report it has been shown that if the population were divided
into seven occupational groups they would, in the 1950's, have
been distributed as follows:

% of men in Britain.

(1) Professional and higher administrative   3
(2) Managerial and executive 4½
(3) Upper inspectorial, supervisory and
    other non-manual workers   10
(4) Lower   ditto 12½
(5) Skilled manual workers and routine non-
    manual   41
(6) Semi-skilled 16½
(7) Unskilled 12½

This pattern is not so very different from that given by the Census for England and Wales. The important contribution made by this study, however, is that in the preliminary report;[1] it is suggested that in the twentieth century very little change has taken place in the class structure in the sense that the amount of social mobility from class to class has not varied greatly. It may well be, therefore, that the class structure based on occupation is not so very different now from that of the turn of the century.

For the Census of 1961 the thirteen socio-economic groups introduced in 1951 were replaced by 'sixteen somewhat differently derived socio-Economic groups based on the census recommendation of the Conference of European Statisticians sponsored jointly by the Statistical Commission and Economic Commission for Europe (General Register Office, Classification of Occupations, 1960, H.M.S.O.). The sixteen groups are as follows:

(1) Employers and Managers in central and local government, industry, commerce etc. (i.e. persons who employ or plan and supervise in non-agricultural enterprises employing twenty-five or more persons).

(2) Employers and managers in industry, commerce etc. – small establishments (i.e. less than twenty-five persons).

(3) Professional workers – self-employed.

(4) Professional workers – employees.

(5) Intermediate non-manual workers (e.g. employees, not exercising general planning or supervisory powers, engaged in non-manual occupations ancillary to the professions but not normally requiring qualifications of University degree standard).

(6) Junior non-manual workers (e.g. employees engaged in clerical, sales and non-manual communications and security occupations).

(7) Personal service workers (i.e. employees engaged in service occupations caring for food, drink, clothing and other personal needs).

(8) Foreman and supervisors – manual.

(9) Skilled manual workers.

---

[1] See the results in *Social Mobility in Britain* ed. by D. V. Glass.

(10) Semi-skilled manual workers.
(11) Unskilled manual workers.
(12) Own account workers (other than professional).
(13) Farmers – employers and managers.
(14) Farmers – own account.
(15) Agricultural workers.
(16) Members of the armed forces.

Each of these groups contain an array of persons of differing occupations and statuses and readers interested in the detailed allocations should consult the *Classification of Occupations*, 1960. The advantages of this method of grouping are that an attempt is made to relate employment status and occupation, and that it enables comparisons to be made with European countries. However, this new arrangement makes comparison with the past rather difficult and it is not always easy to allocate a particular socio-economic group to one social class. Thus, for example, persons in socio-economic groups 1 and 2 may be in Social Class 2 or 3 or 4 or 5; those in socio-economic groups 3 and 4 are, however, in Social Class 1; but those in socio-economic group 5 may be in Social Class 2 or 3. (See the *Classification of Occupations*, 1960). The broad pattern which has emerged from the 1961 Census is that of all males in England and Wales stating a present or former economic activity the percentage distribution in each socio-economic group was broadly as follows:

Socio-economic group	Percentage
1. Employers and managers, etc. large establishments ..	3·6
2. ,, ,, ,, ,, small	5·9
3. Professional workers – self employed	0·8
4. ,, ,, employees	2·8
5. Intermediate non-manual workers	3·8
6. Junior non-manual ,, ...	12·5
7. Personal service ,, ...	0·9
8. Foreman and supervisors – manual	3·3
9. Skilled manual workers	30·4
10. Semi-skilled manual workers	14·7
11. Unskilled ,, ,, ...	8·6
12. Own account workers (not professional)	3·6
13. Farmers – employers and managers	1·0
14. ,, – own account	1·0
15. Agricultural workers	2·3
16. Members armed forces	1·9
Unclassified	2·9
	100

Social Classes and Educational Opportunities

If other criteria are used as the main determinant of social class the evidence for the size and the degree of change is no more precise than that provided by the occupational method. Any attempt to measure social class by, for example, the distribution of wealth or physical standards of living present difficult problems of definition and assessment, but market research organizations have devised methods which use a combination of factors, such as manner of speech, appearance, occupation and type of house and district lived in as the determinants of social class. For example, the British Market Research Bureau produced for the Hulton Press a Readership Survey designed to give advertisers information on the extent to which newspapers and journals are read by each of the social classes. In the years 1947–55 a sample of the population of Great Britain was interviewed annually and the social class of every person interviewed was assessed by the interviewer on the basis of the appearance, manner of speech, occupation, type of house and district lived in. Five social classes were identified, viz. Class A – the well-to-do, which included doctors, chartered accountants, barristers, stockbrokers, farmers on a large scale, and administrative grade civil servants; Class B – the middle class, which included surveyors, qualified engineers, executive grade civil servants, and farmers of a medium-size farm; Class C – the lower middle class, which included bank clerks, teachers, commercial travellers, owners or managers of a small business or shop, and farmers of a small farm; Class D – the working class, a wide group, including skilled and semi-skilled manual workers, such as bricklayers, plumbers, machine operators, miners, postmen, shop assistants and waiters; and Class E – the poor, mainly unskilled manual workers, such as charwomen, labourers, snack-bar attendants and also old age pensioners, who relied almost entirely on the old age pension.[1] Broad income limits were assigned to each class, but these were not obtained from the survey, they were merely aids to an understanding of the approximate incomes likely to be earned by each group.

The distribution of the population of Britain in those years, according to these surveys, was as follows:

[1] These examples were taken from the Hulton Readership Survey for 1955; consult the annual surveys for fuller information and for changes in the composition of classes.

	Percentage of the population aged 16 and over in Class				
Year	A	B	C	D	E
1947 ..	5	10	20	55	10
1950 ..	3½	7½	17	63	9
1955 ..	4	8	17	64	7

In 1947 the broad income ranges assigned to each class were, Class A over £1,000 per annum, Class B between £650 and £1,000, Class C from £350 to £650, Class D from £225 to £350, and Class E not more than £225 per annum. By 1955 the ranges of income per annum which it was suggested might be typical of the head of the household in each class were, Class A probably more than £1,300, Class B between £800 and £1,300, Class C between £450 and £800, Class D between £250 and £450, and Class E probably less than £250. Approximate measurements of these kinds have their value not only as markers of social class but of the rate of change in incomes receivable as well. The broad pattern of social class distribution revealed by these surveys differs from that given by the Census primarily in the way in which occupations are grouped, but again we see the concentration in the middle and lower middle groups.

The Readership Survey provided information on material possessions, such as the type of house, furnishings, motor-cars, refrigerators and the like owned by the members of each class, and in some studies of social class determinants, especially in America, these are used as indices of social status. For example, in 1955 the Hulton Readership Survey showed that in the population of Great Britain 18·7 per cent of the men were car-owners and that within each class car ownership varied from 53·9 per cent in Classes A and B to 30·5 per cent in Class C and 10·2 per cent in Classes D and E. On the other hand, in 1951 the percentage of car ownership for each Class was AB 46·6, C 20·0, DE 4·4; the difference between 1951 and 1955 is some indication of the change in material standards of living in four years. The ownership of bicycles was, as we should expect, the inverse of that for cars, in 1955 men bicycle-owners were distributed as follows: Class AB, 18 per cent, Class C 27 per cent, and Classes D and E 40 per cent; women bicycle-owners were quite differently distributed, 21 per cent of Classes A and B, 16 per cent of Class C and 14 per cent of Classes D and E, so that whereas the car was the hall-mark of upper class status for men the bicycle was for women. Home ownership, too, had a definite class pattern: in 1955 nearly 60 per cent of Classes A and B owned (probably with the help of a mortgage) their houses compared with just over 40 per cent of Class C and about 17 per cent of Classes D and E.[1]

By 1961 Market Research organizations were using a radically revised system, for example, Research Services, Ltd. under its director, Dr. Mark Abrams,[2] identified six socio-economic grades and classified the heads of households into:

Grade A – upper middle class, i.e. those whose occupations were e.g. higher managerial, administrative or professional with incomes of £1,750 per annum and over.
Grade B – middle class i.e. those whose occupations were intermediate managerial, administrative or professional with incomes of £950 – £1,750 per annum.
Grade C1 – lower middle class i.e. those whose occupations were supervisory or clerical and junior managerial, administrative or professional with incomes of under £950 per annum.
Grade C2 – skilled working class i.e. skilled manual workers with incomes of £650 – £1,000 per annum.
Grade D – working class i.e. semi-skilled and unskilled workers with incomes of £350 – £625 per annum; and Grade E, i.e. those at the lowest levels of subsistence such as State pensioners or widows and casual or lowest-grade workers with incomes under £340 per annum.

Obviously the income limits used in this method of classification must be changed regularly when economic conditions result in continuous fluctuations of wages and salaries, and as a measure of the speed of change in the supposedly affluent society of

[1] See the Hulton Readership Survey for other variations in the social class habits and customs, for example, the newspapers and journals they read, the alcoholic beverages they consume, their smoking habits and their attendances at cinemas.
[2] I am indebted to Dr. Mark Abrams of Research Services, Ltd. for giving me information on the commonly accepted socio-economic grades and their determinants.

Heads of Household percentage in each Socio-Economic grade in Great Britain in 1961

Grade	Per cent
A	4
B	8
C1	20
C2	35
D	25
E	8

the late 1950's and early 1960's the ranges of income used in 1961 and 1964 are compared as follows:

Range of income p.a.

Grade	1961	1964
A	£1,750 and over	£2,000 and over
B	£950 – £1,750	£1,250 – £2,000
C1	Under £950	Under £1,250
C2	£625 – £1,000	£780 – £1,250
D	£340 – £625	£416 – £780
E	Under £340	Under £416

Home and car ownership have equally been subject to change and in 1964 the percentage in each grade owning or buying their homes and cars were as follows:

Grade	*Percentage, in Households, in Great Britain owning (or buying) houses and cars*	
	Houses per cent	*Car per cent*
A	88	89
B	80	78
C1	60	55
C2	38	42
D	24	22
E	26	3
All	43	42

The rates of change in income levels and in the ownership of material possessions has been particularly rapid since the second world war but how far they have affected the class structure is an open question.

Social Classes and Educational Opportunities

There are obviously a variety of factors which contribute to the determination of social classes in this country and with the development of systematic investigations we may be in a position in the near future to determine more accurately the nature and size of social classes in our society. It may then be possible to measure accurately and make comparisons over time, but as far as this book is concerned since we cannot make adequate comparisons with the past and as this is our main purpose we can do no more than admit the inadequacy of our knowledge on the changing social class structure of England and Wales.

EDUCATIONAL OPPORTUNITIES

There is undoubtedly a connection between the formal education one receives and the social class to which one belongs (or hopes to belong) and recent surveys have shown that a not inconsiderable proportion of the population believes that education is one of the most important criteria of social class.[1] Certain occupations demand particular kinds of education and, therefore, entrance into them is dependent (in part at least) on the opportunities for obtaining that kind of education. If occupation is a determinant of social class then clearly the distribution of educational opportunities will have a bearing on the nature and size of social classes.

The provision of educational facilities for all is a comparatively recent innovation in this country. The Education Act, 1870, effectively began the system, but it was not until the twentieth century that free and compulsory education came fully into being, and even in the first two decades of this century it could hardly be claimed that we had a coherent and completely effective system.[2] The establishment of State-aided Elementary Schools did not bring about very great changes in

[1] See, for example, the belief of the people of Derby as revealed by Cauter and Downham, op. cit.

[2] For an admirably brief account of the development of the statutory system of education from 1900 to 1950 see the *Annual Report of the Ministry of Education for 1950* which surveys the period as a whole in addition to being the report for the year. See, too, the *Report of the Central Advisory Council for Education (England) 15 to 18* (the Crowther Report) H.M.S.O., 1959; and *Half Our Future* (the Newsom Report), H.M.S.O. 1963.

the educational opportunities which are deemed to be essential to a change in social status; the fact that everyone had to go to school at the age of five and stay there for seven or nine years was valuable from many points of view, but it probably had little effect on the future prospects of the few who would in any case have obtained formal education from tutors or at Private and Public Schools before entering the Universities and/or the professions. Even at the turn of the century the chances of a boy proceeding from a State Elementary School to a Grammar School and then on to a University were extremely small,[1] but at least compulsory and free schooling did make it possible for everyone to place their feet on the bottom rung of the educational ladder, and to this extent educational opportunities were increased.

The proportion of the school-age population who would in any case have been educated in the nineteenth century whether there were State schools or not is difficult to determine, and even in the 1950's we could not measure accurately the number and proportion of boys and girls who were at Private and Public Schools. We do know the number and the proportion of the school-age population who attend State-aided Elementary and Secondary Schools, and since 1921 about 90 per cent of the population aged 5 to 14 years have attended schools of this kind.[2] Of the remaining 10 per cent of the school-age population a part would be incapable of receiving normal education because of physical and mental defects of one kind or another, but the majority would be in attendance at Private and Public (non-grant-aided) Schools, or receiving education at home.

Until the Education Act, 1944, came into force the vast majority of children were restricted to public Elementary-School education, and Carr-Saunders and Caradog Jones have

---

[1] There were, of course, exceptions and some who were later to become famous did proceed in this way. See Sir Ernest Barker: *Age and Youth* (Oxford University Press, 1953) for an autobiographical study of one who did succeed in progressing from elementary school to higher education.

[2] For details of the numbers at the various kinds of schools see the Annual Reports of the Ministry of Education, or for summaries see the Annual Abstract of Statistics. In 1961, a new and more detailed series of Educational Statistics were published by the Ministry. See *Statistics of Education*, Parts 1 and 2 published by H.M.S.O. and henceforth to be published annually.

shown that even in 1931 of the population aged 11–12, 12–13 and 13–14 years in England and Wales, the proportions per 1,000 of each age-group in attendance (or not) at educational institutions were as follows: at Public Elementary Schools 853, 824, and 795 per 1,000 of each age-group respectively; at other schools or at home 134, 170, and 182; not attending an educational institution 13, 6, and 23.[1] So that as late as 1931 less than 20 per cent of the population aged between 11 and 14 succeeded in obtaining a Secondary School education. If we go further back in time the proportion would be smaller, and it has been estimated that in 1895 out of every 1,000 children at an Elementary School only four or five succeeded in passing on to a Grammar School. Obviously in the past education, for the great majority of persons, meant elementary schooling and no more.

Since 1947 the school-leaving age has been 15 years and as a result of the Education Act, 1944, all children over the age of 11 have become entitled to some form of secondary education. For those parents who prefer to 'buy' secondary education for their children the position is much as it was in the past except (if the correspondence columns of the newspapers are to be believed) that it is becoming increasingly difficult for parents, who would normally send their children to 'fee-paying schools', to do so because of the burdens of taxation.[2] For the rest (i.e. the majority) of the school-age population there is available, in varying quantities in different local education authority areas, a choice of four main kinds of secondary education, in either a Grammar School, or a Secondary Modern School, or a Secondary Technical School or a Comprehensive School.[3] In January, 1951 and 1961 the numbers of young persons aged 12–14 years (inclusive) in England and Wales was (approximately) 1,727,000 and 2,329,000 respectively and they were distributed among the varieties of schools as follows:

[1] A. M. Carr-Saunders and D. C. Jones: *Survey of the Social Structure of England and Wales*, see Chapter XI on 'Education' for an excellent summary of the position in 1931.

[2] Yet the waiting-lists at fee-paying schools are reported to be longer than ever.

[3] Any reader who is not familiar with the system of education in England and Wales should read, e.g. W. O. Lester Smith: *Education in Great Britain* (Oxford, 1958) or H. C. Dent: *British Education* (published by Longmans, for the British Council, 1946).

Social Classes and Educational Opportunities

Grant-aided schools maintained by Local Education Authorities:	Number (in 000's) of pupils on the register	
	1951	1961
Junior ..	1	0·8
All-age primary Schools	239	73
Secondary Modern ..	912	1,373
„ Grammar..	284	385
„ Technical..	49	61
Bilateral, Multilateral, Comprehensive and Special	41	233
	1,526	2,126
Direct Grant schools ..	40	51
Other schools recognized as efficient	73	100
	1,639	2,277
In other schools or not attending an educational institution ..	88	45
	1,727	2,322[1]

[1] The discrepancy between this total and that of the total number of boys and girls in the age-group may be due to the fact that the estimate of the Registrar-General of the total age-group related to December 1960. Or the difference may represent the numbers of ineducable boys and girls at home or in institutions.

In broad terms, about 88 per cent in 1951 and 91 per cent in 1961 of the 12–14 year-olds were in 'State' schools; in both years about 2 per cent were in 'Direct Grant' schools, and about 4 per cent were in schools recognized as efficient by the Ministry of Education; and about 5 per cent in 1951 and 2 per cent in 1961 were in non-recognized schools or were being educated at home or were not attending an educational institution.[1] The pattern in 1951 and 1961 was therefore very different from that of even 1931,[2] and the main change is that a second rung has been added to the educational ladder on which by now nearly all children can place their feet. The result is that by the middle of the twentieth century the degree of educational inequality is much less than it was in the past, nevertheless recent studies have shown that even in the 1950's educational opportunities were still distributed unevenly among the various social classes (see J. Floud, A. H. Halsey and F. M. Martin, *Social Class and Educational Opportunities*, 1957, and the Crowther and Newsom Reports).[3] There is now, however, an expressed aim of 'second-

[1] See the *Annual Report of the Ministry of Education for the year 1951–52*, Part II, 'Statistics of Public Education'; and *Statistics of Education, 1961*, Part I, for full details.

[2] See Carr-Saunders and D. C. Jones, op. cit.

[3] See, too, J. W. B. Douglas: *The Home and the School*, Mackibbon & Kee, 1964.

ary education for all' according to age, aptitude and ability, but what about the third rung of the ladder which provides full-time education for those beyond the compulsory school-leaving age, and is in essence the step towards higher occupational status?

In 1951 and 1961 the population of England and Wales aged 15–18 years (inclusive) was (approximately) 2,214,000 and 2,565,000 respectively and the numbers on the regsters of grant-aided and other schools recognized as efficient were as follows:

Grant-aided schools maintained by Local Education Authorities:		Numbers (in ooo's) of pupils on the register	
		1951	1961
Secondary Modern		20	67
„ Grammar..		160	243
„ Technical..		22	30
Other L.E.A.		10	37
		212	377
Direct Grant schools		26	37
Others recognized as efficient		51	66
		289	480

In addition to the 289,000 pupils shown above for 1951 there were the young persons in completely independent schools whose numbers were difficult to estimate. The most commonly suggested figure was that in the 1950's there were about 500,000 pupils of all ages in these schools and if we assume that at most one-fifth were 15 years of age and over, then of the population aged 15–18 years in 1951 only 17 per cent were receiving full-time education, the great majority left school at 15 years of age. By 1961 in addition to the 480,000 shown above there were a further 22,000 young people aged 15–18 receiving education in special schools and other independent schools, so that of the age-group approximately 20 per cent were receiving full-time education. Even in 1961, however, the great majority of boys and girls had finished their full-time education by 16 years of age, but many who had left school to take up jobs were released by their employers during working hours to take part-time day courses at educational establishments. For example in the academic year 1960–1 approximately 346,000 young persons aged 15–18 were engaged in 'day-release' education.

P

Social Classes and Educational Opportunities

This dominant pattern of the vast majority of youngsters leaving at age 15 and 16 schools which provide courses beyond the minimum school-leaving age was the subject of a special inquiry (in 1952–3) by the Central Advisory Council for Education in England, and their conclusions and recommendations were published in a report on *Early Leaving*, and then, of course, the whole problem of the educational needs of the 15 to 18-year-olds was examined and reported on in 1959 in the Crowther Report. We cannot be concerned with why such a small proportion continued in full-time education beyond the school-leaving age, but what does concern us is the destination of the Secondary school-leavers. The Ministry of Education provides useful statistics annually on those who leave Secondary Schools and in Table 48 the destinations of pupils who left Secondary Schools in England and in Wales during 1951–2 and 1960–1 are shown.

Table 48 shows some interesting differences between the destinations of school-leavers in England and those in Wales, but more fundamental are the differences arising out of the various kinds of schools. There were, even in 1961, considerable variations in the proportions of Grammar School places in each Local Education Authority area (see the Ministry's List 69 *Secondary Education in each Local Education Authority Area* for 1960) and coupled with the fact that the Grammar School (and the Independent School) is the main avenue of entry to higher education then obviously there must be considerable variations in the opportunity to proceed to higher education. The position can be seen more clearly if the data given in Table 48 is summarized opposite:

TABLE 48

Destination of school-leavers aged 14 and over in England and in Wales during the year ended 31st July, 1952 and aged 15 and over 1960–1.

ENGLAND – BOYS

Destinations:

Type of School	Total Leaving		University		Training College		Other Educ. Inst.		Paid Employment*	
	1952	1961	1952	1961	1952	1961	1952	1961	1952	1961
A. Sec. Modern and all age	172,289	195,205	14	13	7	53	1,830	9,443	170,438	185,696
B. Grammar	38,887	52,713	4,784	9,643	528	1,974	1,476	4,149	32,099	36,947
C. Technical	14,857	11,912	17	235	11	155	688	925	14,141	10,597
D. Bilateral, Multilateral, Comprehensive and other Secondary	4,032	30,952	46	328	5	196	87	1,084	3,894	29,344
All 'State' schools	230,065	290,782	4,861	10,219	551	2,378	4,081	15,601	220,572	262,584
Direct Grant Grammar	4,953	7,040	983	2,308	86	169	375	854	3,509	3,709

ENGLAND – GIRLS

Type of School	Total Leaving		University		Training College		Other Educ. Inst.		Paid Employment*	
	1952	1961	1952	1961	1952	1961	1952	1961	1952	1961
A. Sec. Modern and all age	169,578	187,797	7	3	45	116	4,668	12,699	164,858	174,979
B. Grammar	39,030	54,505	2,061	4,645	3,808	7,036	4,601	8,576	28,650	34,248
C. Technical	8,092	6,857	Nil	27	68	259	484	501	7,540	6,070
D. Bilateral, Multilateral, Comprehensive and other Secondary	3,287	31,228	15	182	49	577	90	1,545	3,133	28,924
All 'State' schools	219,987	280,387	2,083	4,857	3,970	7,988	9,843	23,321	204,091	244,221
Direct Grant Grammar	5,146	6,751	473	1,203	564	962	1,161	1,494	2,948	3,092

TABLE 48 – continued

WALES – BOYS

Destinations:

Type of School	Total Leaving		University		Training College		Other Educ. Inst.		Paid Employment*	
	1952	1961	1952	1961	1952	1961	1952	1961	1952	1961
A. Sec. Modern and all age ..	9,385	10,579	Nil	Nil	Nil	5	57	577	9,328	9,997
B. Grammar	4,251	4,783	804	970	60	311	129	348	3,258	3,154
C. Technical	998	370	3	5	1	6	30	23	964	336
D. Bilateral, Multilateral, Comprehensive and other Secondary	692	2,194	47	101	6	72	15	96	624	1,925
All 'State' schools ..	15,326	17,926	854	1,076	67	394	231	1,044	14,174	15,412
Direct Grant Grammar	49	64	10	20	6	1	5	4	28	39

WALES – GIRLS

Type of School	Total Leaving		University		Training College		Other Educ. Inst.		Paid Employment*	
	1952	1961	1952	1961	1952	1961	1952	1961	1952	1961
A. Sec. Modern and all age ..	9,373	10,020	1	Nil	2	1	381	945	8,989	9,074
B. Grammar	4,213	4,495	384	478	571	716	481	575	2,777	2,726
C. Technical	125	188	Nil	1	3	11	Nil	7	122	169
D. Bilateral, Multilateral, Comprehensive and other Secondary	568	2,168	26	77	45	167	22	158	475	1766
All 'State' schools ..	14,279	16,871	411	556	621	895	884	1,685	12,363	13,735
Direct Grant Grammar	126	200	16	39	16	27	36	77	58	57

* Includes paid employment and other reasons.

Social Classes and Educational Opportunities

	Percentage who left in order to:							
In 1951–2 and 1960–61 of the boys and girls leaving:	Attend University, Training College, or other Further Education				Take up paid Employment or for other reasons			
	Boys		Girls		Boys		Girls	
	1951	1961	1951	1961	1951	1961	1951	1961
L.E.A. Grammar schools:								
England	17	30	27	37	83	70	73	63
Wales	23	34	34	39	77	66	66	61
Direct Grant Grammar schools:								
England	30	47	42	54	70	53	58	46
Wales	43	40	54	70	57	60	46	30
Other L.E.A. Secondary:								
England	3	5	3	7	97	95	97	93
Wales	1	7	5	11	99	93	95	89
All L.E.A. and Direct Grant Grammar schools:								
England	4	10	8	13	96	90	92	87
Wales	8	22	14	19	92	78	86	81

It was not possible to obtain comparable data in 1951 for the Independent Schools recognized as efficient, but in 1960–1 the Statistics of the Ministry of Education show that in England and Wales the destinations of Independent School leavers were as follows:

Boys	Total leaving	Destinations			
		University	Trn. College	Other Educ. Inst.	Paid Employment
England ..	14,326	4,068	192	2,732	7,334
Wales ..	355	30	3	40	282
Girls					
England	13,431	1,254	1,134	5,932	5,111
Wales ..	509	47	54	220	188

Expressed as a percentage 48 per cent of Independent School boys in England and 68 per cent of the girls went on to higher education, and it is therefore abundantly clear that the main avenue to the University is the Direct Grant and the Independent School.

Obviously even in 1961 as compared with 1951 considerable changes have occurred in the Secondary School population;

Social Classes and Educational Opportunities

the numbers of pupils in the late 1950's and early 1960's is greater than ever before in our history; a greater proportion is staying on at school after the statutory leaving age; and secondary education of some kind for all seems to have become an accomplished fact, but what change has there been (and will there be) in the proportion of the population who continue beyond the secondary stage?

Those who wish to continue in full-time education after the age of 17 or 18 years must attend either Universities or Training Colleges or Institutes of Technology or Technical Colleges or some other kind of institution, and already remarkable changes have taken place in the numbers of students attending. To some extent the number of persons who can attend higher educational institutions is dependent on the availability of 'student places' and this is particularly true of the Universities. At the end of the eighteenth century there were only two Universities in England and none in Wales; in the second half of the nineteenth century a number of University Colleges were established and two Universities (London and Durham) which had been founded in the 1830's were enlarged.[1] It was, however, between 1900 and 1957 that the system of 15 Provincial (or Red Brick) Universities,[2] together with the Universities of Oxford, Cambridge and London in England, and the four University Colleges and the Welsh National School of Medicine of the University of Wales was most fully developed. In the middle 1950's vociferous plans were made for an expansion of the University system, and in 1958 the University Grants Committee advised the Government to approve the establishment of the University of Sussex, and in the years immediately following six more Universities at Norwich, York, Canterbury, Colchester, Coventry and Lancaster were established. The Robbins Committee which sat from 1961–3, reported in October 1963 and

[1] For short histories of British Universities see Sir Ernest Barker: *British Universities* (Published by Longmans for the British Council), or Sir Charles Grant Robertson: *The British Universities* (Methuen, 1944) and for the history and a controversial discussion of the aims and purposes of the modern Universities see Bruce Truscott: *Red Brick University* (Pelican Books, 1951). For the most recent analysis of the whole field of higher education see the Report of the Robbins Committee, Cmd. 2154, H.M.S.O., 1963.

[2] The last of the University Colleges in England to be granted full University status was the University College of Leicester in 1957.

recommended a still greater expansion of the system of higher education. It is therefore since the end of the Second World War that the numbers of University students have increased appreciably.

Every University in this country in the middle of the twentieth century admits students irrespective of race, creed and nationality, and the fact that students may (and do) come from all sorts of countries creates difficulties for measuring that part of the University population which is specifically English or Welsh.[1] In the past it was not always possible to distinguish the nationality of the students in British Universities, but in recent years the Annual Reports of the University Grants Committee have provided a useful analysis of the 'home residence' of full-time students. This analysis shows the number of students whose home residence is within 30 miles of the University they are attending, those from other parts of the United Kingdom, those from outside the United Kingdom but within the British Commonwealth, and those from Foreign countries. In 1961–2 the 'Home Residences' of full time students at Universities in England, Wales and Scotland were broadly as follows:

Universities	Home Residence			
	Within 30 miles	Other parts of U.K.	Outside U.K. but in Commonwealth	Foreign Countries
	Per Cent			
In England ..	22	65	7	6
In Wales ..	25	69	4	2
In Scotland ..	52	37	7	4

There are considerable variations in the proportions of each of these groups at the different Universities, but in Great Britain as a whole about 10 per cent of the students attending full-time are from abroad. The precise proportion of English and Welsh students in the Universities of England and Wales are not recorded, and the numbers of students from England and Wales in Universities elsewhere in Britain or abroad are unknown. At best we can make only approximate measurements of national university populations, but they are probably sufficiently useful for our purpose. We need go back no farther than

[1] Religious tests were applied in the past for entry to the ancient Universities.

Social Classes and Educational Opportunities

TABLE 49

University students in Great Britain, 1921–62

Year	Number of new full-time students admitted		Number taking courses full- and part-time		Full-time	
	Men	Women	Men	Women	Men	Women
1921–2	5,828	3,421	37,921	14,221	25,894	10,889
1931–2	10,423	3,879	46,820	15,707	35,741	12,759
1938–9	11,220	3,933	49,220	14,218	36,368	11,634
1946–7	16,791	5,754	63,785	22,551	49,764	18,688
1951–2	16,733	5,681	77,934	22,582	63,970	19,488
1961–2	22,964	9,196	100,330	31,592	84,425	28,718

1921 to see the changes which have taken place in the number of students admitted to and studying at Universities in Great Britain and in Table 49 the changes are shown.

With the publication of the *Report of the Committee on Higher Education* (the Robbins Report) in 1963 and its Appendices we are now able to see more clearly the way in which University education has been extended in the twentieth century. Thus at the beginning of this century less than 1 per cent of 'the age-group'[1] entered Universities in Great Britain, by the 1920's it was about 1½ per cent and in 1961 just over 4 per cent. In part this reflects the enormous change which has taken place in the opportunities for secondary education in modern times, and again the Robbins Report shows clearly the extent of change since 1870 in Great Britain by calculating the percentage of young people of various ages receiving full-time education as follows:

Percentage of young people of various ages receiving full-time education in Great Britain, 1870–1962

	Per cent						Per cent			
	1870	1902	1938	1962			1870	1902	1938	1962
10 year-olds	40	100	100	100		17 year-olds	1	2	4	15
14 year-olds	2	9	38	100		19 year-olds	1	1	2	7

[1] The Robbins Committee defined the concept of 'the percentage of the age-group' as follows: 'The entrants in any year are of various ages. Those of each age are expressed as a percentage of their own age-group, and these separate percentages are then summed. This gives a percentage of a composite age group, suitably weighted to allow for the numbers of each age entering and the size of the age-groups from which they come'.

Social Classes and Educational Opportunities

The extension of secondary education and in recent years of University places has resulted in a change in the proportion of University students coming from different types of Schools. Thus in the 1930's Carr-Saunders and D. C. Jones (op. cit.) calculated that only approximately one third of University entrants came from 'Grant-aided' Schools and the other two thirds were from Independent Schools. By 1952, however, it would seem that about two thirds of the University entrants were from L.E.A. and Grant-aided Schools and only one third from Independent Schools.[1] By 1961–2 the Robbins Committee calculated that of the Undergraduates in British Universities whose homes were in Britain 63 per cent come from L.E.A. Schools, 15 per cent were from Direct-grant Schools and 22 per cent from Independent Schools. Obviously therefore the Independent Schools no longer provide the majority of University students.

Yet despite the changing proportions of University students from different types of schools the Robbins Committee showed clearly (as did earlier studies)[2] that very little change had occurred in the social class background of students entering Universities. For example, in Appendix Two (B) 'students and their education' of the Robbins Report it is shown that the percentage of Home Undergraduates coming from 'working-class homes' (i.e. where the father is in a manual occupation) was 23 in 1928–47, and 25 in 1955 and 1961. Indeed even in 1961–2, the Occupations of the Fathers' of the Undergraduates in British Universities were grouped as follows:

Non-Manual
- 18 per cent were Higher Professional
- 41 ,, ,, ,, Other Professional
- 12 ,, ,, ,, Clerical

Manual
- 18 per cent were Skilled
- 6 ,, ,, ,, Semi-Skilled
- 1 ,, ,, ,, Unskilled

and 4 per cent were 'Not Known'.

---

[1] See the first edition of this book viz. *The Changing Social Structure of England and Wales, 1871–1951.*

[2] For example Carr-Saunders and D. C. Jones, op cit.; Floud, Halsey and Martin, op. cit.; and the Crowther Report, op. cit.

Social Classes and Educational Opportunities

Obviously even in the 1960's University students are pre-dominantly from non-manual worker homes, and if a University education is a determinant of social class then it is only a small proportion of the population as a whole who qualify on this basis despite the extension of secondary education to all young people and the rapid increase in the number of full time University students in recent years.[1]

It is unfortunate that so little use was made in the past of the Census to provide us with a clearer picture of the kinds of education received by the people of this country. At the Censuses of 1851, 1861, 1871, 1881, 1911 and 1921 questions were asked about attendance at school, but the results show little more than the numbers receiving full or part-time education. In 1951, however, new questions were asked which throw some light on the extent to which the population was receiving or had obtained formal education. The results (based on the One Per Cent Sample) showed that in England and Wales 3,300,000 males and 3,160,000 females were in full-time attendance at educational establishments, but of these persons about 3 million males and 2·9 million females were aged 5–14 years. Of the population aged 15–19 years only about 15 per cent of the males and females were in full-time attendance at educational establishments, and a further 6 per cent of the males and 2 per cent of the females were attending part-time. In broad terms, out of every 100 males and females aged 15–19 years in 1951 there were:

Males	Females	
15	15	attending full-time at educational establishments.
6	2	attending part-time.
79	83	were not receiving formal education.

This pattern is similar to that derived from the education statistics, but where the Census of 1951 broke new ground was in showing the terminal education ages (i.e. the age at which formal education ceased) of the occupied population. The results confirm that most of the occupied population in 1951 (76 per cent of the males and 67 per cent of the females) had completed their formal education at age 14 or under, and over

---

[1] A new source of data on the number and types of University students became available in 1965 with the publication of the first *Annual Report of the Universities Central Council on Admissions*. It will be published annually henceforth.

86 per cent of the males and 82 per cent of the females at age 15 or under. Of the occupied males only 2 per cent and of the occupied females only 3 per cent had a terminal education age of 20 years or over, so that in the population as a whole the proportion which had received formal education up to and beyond 20 years of age was minute.

By 1961 the over-all pattern of educational attainment for the population as a whole could not have been expected to have changed significantly, but there were signs of a change in the age-groups 15–19 years. Thus it would seem that in 1961 of young men and women aged 15–19 years about 25 per cent of the males and about 24 per cent of the females were 'students in educational establishments' (compared with 15 per cent for both sexes in 1951). The pattern of terminal education age for this age-group in 1961 in England and Wales was as follows:

	Per cent of 15 19 year olds	
	M.	F.
Students in educational establishments	25	24
Had completed their education at Terminal Education age:		
14 years or under	2	2
15 ,, ,,	56	56
16 ,, ,,	12	12
17 ,, ,,	3·5	4
18 ,, ,,	1·3	1 (just over)
19 ,, ,,	·2	1 (less than)
	100·0	100

Unfortunately out of the total population aged 15–19 in 1961 viz about 1,636,000 males and 1,596,000 females who were asked questions about education as part of the 10 per cent sample, about 76,000 males and 71,000 females did not state their terminal education age, nevertheless there was, by 1961, a clearly established trend towards staying on at school to a later age than in the past. If this trend continues then perhaps at future censuses we shall see a larger number and higher proportion of the population with scientific and technological qualifications than was the case in 1961.

For the first time questions were asked of 10 per cent of the population in 1961[1] for 'additional particulars to be stated in

[1] See the report *Census 1961 – Great Britain, Scientific and Technological Qualifications*, H.M.S.O., 1962. This report also has an interesting description of the method of choosing the 10 per cent sample.

selected returns' to include, *inter alia*, 'in respect of persons with qualifications in science and technology, the qualifications held and the main branch of science and technology in which the qualifications were obtained'.[1] The trend clearly is for a higher proportion of the younger age-groups to obtain qualifications and for men 'each generation is more qualified than its predecessor'.[2] As the opportunities for higher education for all become more widespread so shall we have a much larger proportion of the population with higher terminal education ages and scientific and technological qualifications.

The extent to which education is a determinant of social class is not easily calculated. There is obviously a relationship since certain occupations which acquire 'higher' social class rating also demand particular kinds of specialized education. However, in our existing state of knowledge we are entitled to say no more than that in our society there are social classes which cannot be measured with any degree of accuracy, but that in the past sixty years there have in all probability been changes in their nature and size. On the other hand, we can affirm that during those years there have been dramatic changes in the provision of educational opportunities, particularly in the 'lower rungs of the educational ladder', and that even on the 'top rungs' there are opportunities for persons who in the not so distant past would have been denied the chance of even a secondary education. A change of this magnitude in such a short period could justifiably be termed a 'social revolution' and its impact on the social structure is obviously momentous, but has it altered the fundamental class structure of our society?

[1] ibid.
[2] ibid.

CHAPTER VIII

THE CHANGING PATTERNS OF SOCIAL PROBLEMS

IN less than 100 years, we have moved away from a society in which gross inequalities in opportunity and 'the grinding of the faces of the masses' were acceptable principles to a society in which every individual counts and is at least entitled to the chance of raising his living standards. Exploitation of human labour, all too common in the early years of the first great industrial revolution, which was at the root of so much inequality of opportunity in the past has gradually been removed and to a considerable degree the means of eliminating the inhumanity of the few towards the many has been the development of social and economic policies designed to raise the living standards of the majority of the members of the population. The forces and movements which were responsible for the initiation and implementation of these new policies need not concern us, but if we are to understand the changed attitude towards and the methods of dealing with social problems then we must recognize the principal measures of social action which have contributed to the growth and development of the so-called 'Welfare State'.[1]

The standards of living and the abilities to overcome the ailments and the problems which beset most of us in an industrialized society are determined very largely by the results of our own employment or the employment of the chief wage-earner in the case of non-employed members of a family. In the

[1] For a discussion of the concept of the Welfare State, its growth and development up to the 1960's see David C. Marsh: *The Future of the Welfare State* (Penguin Books, 1964) and David C. Marsh (Ed.): *An Introduction to the Study of Social Administration* (Routledge, 1965.)

nineteenth century and even in the first thirty years of the twentieth century low wages, irregularity and insecurity of employment were all too often the main cause of the poverty of a not inconsiderable proportion of the population of England and Wales, and it may well be that of all the factors which have contributed to the improvements in the standard of living and to the amelioration and even abolition of many of our social problems in modern times the most powerful has been the transformation of conditions of employment.

The control by the State of working conditions through Factory Acts, Shops Acts, Mines Acts and the like, and the gradual acceptance of reasonable levels of minimum wages either through legislation (for example, Trade Boards Acts) or more commonly through agreements negotiated by the Trade Unions with employers have, particularly since the end of the First World War, so transformed conditions of employment that 'the working man' of, say, 1901 would find it difficult to believe that the conditions in 1961 were real. There are, of course, still, unhealthy factories, dangerous mines and uncongenial employments, but there is by now little (if any) sweated labour, or grossly inhuman conditions of work. Whilst in employment therefore the contrast between working conditions in 1871 and 1961 is so great as to be almost beyond measurement.

For most of the occupied population security of employment was, in the past, probably a greater problem than that of working conditions. The weekly wage earner in the factory, the shop, the mine or on the land was always haunted by the fear of losing his job, and on more than one occasion in the past ninety years the worst fears of many hard-working men and women were realized. In the 1930's we even experienced 'mass unemployment' in which not only a considerable proportion of the workers in certain industries were out of work but millions of men and women were rendered job-less in some cases for years on end.[1] The spectre of unemployment and its dreadful consequences seem to have been accepted in the past almost as an act of God and it was not until the twentieth century that serious attempts were made to study the causes and to provide the means of at least ameliorating the effects of interruption of earnings due to

[1] The highest figure of unemployment ever recorded in Great Britain was 2,903,000 on the 23rd January, 1933.

unemployment.[1] In this century the establishment of Labour Exchanges (in 1909) and of a State system of unemployment insurance (in 1911) substantially reduced (though they by no means completely removed) the fear of unemployment, and since 1944 even more positive measures have been adopted to prevent mass unemployment. In that year the Government accepted the maintenance of full employment as a principle of social policy[2] and the system of compulsory national insurance against interruption of earnings due to unemployment was extended by the National Insurance Act, 1946. It may well be that even now the menace of mass unemployment cannot be completely eliminated, but at least there are a variety of methods of aiding the unemployed and, above all, the evils of unemployment are recognized.

The improvements in working conditions, the raising of levels of income from employment, and the maintenance of income (even at much lower levels) during periods of unemployment have obviously contributed substantially to the raising of the standards of living of the majority of the members of the population of this country, and taken in conjunction with other measures designed to provide equality of opportunity for all they constitute in effect a social revolution. The development of a variety of educational and health services, the building of houses to let at reasonable rents, the enforcement of housing standards and the like are examples of the measures which provide greater equality of opportunity and since the Second World War there have been remarkable extensions of all these services. The speed of development and the expansion of the range of social services has been so great that it may well be that by now we have an unnecessarily complex and elaborate system of methods of raising or maintaining standards of living and providing equality of opportunity, but what is certain is that because of these measures the contributory factors giving rise to social problems have been considerably diminished.

[1] A landmark in the recognition of unemployment as an industrial problem was the publication in 1909 of *Unemployment, a Problem of Industry* by W. H. Beveridge.

[2] See the White Paper on employment policy (Cmd. 6527, H.M.S.O., 1944) and, also W. H. Beveridge: *Full Employment in a Free Society* (Allen & Unwin, 1944). On the Social Services designed to deal with unemployment and other industrial problems see *An Introduction to the Study of Social Administration.*

The Changing Patterns of Social Problems

Social problems are, presumably,[1] those problems which affect man in society, and in the main they are problems of the relationship of man to his fellows and to society as a whole. In the nineteenth century the obvious and all too common social problem was poverty and apart from being in itself *the* social problem it was at the root of many others which most people would accept as being social problems. The incidence of poverty arising out of grossly inadequate income in the nineteenth century need not concern us; the evidence of social surveys, of various Commissions of Inquiry and a host of other statutory and voluntary bodies is sufficient proof of the existence of poverty among considerable numbers of the population, and though it would be unwise to claim that poverty has been eliminated by the middle of the twentieth century there can be no doubt that poverty of the kind experienced by the unemployed, the aged, the physically handicapped and even the employed in the past has been drastically reduced. The diminution of the numbers of the poor is, undoubtedly, one of the outstanding features of the changing social structure in modern times, but other social problems remain (though often in a different form) and of these crime and ill-health are the two outstanding examples.

The relationship between poverty and ill-health and poverty and crime was not clearly recognized until late in the nineteenth century, but having accepted the fact that poverty may give rise to ill-health and crime it was all too often assumed that if poverty were abolished then crime would diminish and the incidence of ill-health would be greatly reduced. The causes of crime and to a great extent the causes of ill-health are still by no means fully known and an examination of the incidence of crime and ill-health in modern times shows that the virtual abolition of the worst forms of poverty has certainly not eliminated crime or ill-health. The measurement of the incidence of ill-health is not as simple an exercise as would at first sight appear, and comparisons over time present innumerable difficulties. The initial problem is, of course, that of definition, what

[1] It is extremely difficult to define satisfactorily the term 'social problems' and though many books have been written about and around what are assumed to be 'social problems' there is certainly no universal agreement either as to the nature or the type of problems which can be labelled 'social'.

is ill-health? No precise definition can be given and, at best, we can do no more than accept the fact that varying degrees of unsoundness of mind or body or both are deemed to be forms of ill-health. In modern times advances in medical science have made possible the identification and classification of a wide range of diseases and ailments and therefore we now have more precise forms of measurement of ill-health than we had in the past, but unless a disease is notifiable to the public health authorities there is still no way of determining accurately the number of people suffering from all the non-notifiable diseases. The most commonly accepted measurement of the state of ill-health of the community is the death-rate which despite its inadequacies is at least an indication of changing trends in health standards.[1]

We have seen already that during the nineteenth century and up to the 1920's the death-rate fell almost continuously, and that for the last thirty years it has remained fairly steady, but are we to conclude that there is therefore far less ill-health in England and Wales in, say, 1961 than there was in 1901 or in 1871? Not necessarily, but it is clear that there have been significant changes in the causes of death and these in turn may indicate a marked change in the patterns of ill-health from time to time.

It is only relatively recently that we have learned to distinguish the great variety of causes of death, for example, in 1837 there were less than 100 identifiable distinct causes of death, and they included some very primitive designations such as 'privation', 'mortification' and 'old age', nowadays there are well over 200 more precise and major classified groups with many hundreds of sub-divisions, the result is that comparison with the past is rendered difficult. However, the Registrar-General in his Annual Review for 1937 made an interesting study of some of the changes in the causes of death in England and Wales for the 100 years following the compulsory registration of deaths in 1837 which shows clearly the major trends and these are summarized in Table 50. In this table the actual

[1] In recent years the increase in the number of deaths caused by accidents at work, in the home and on the roads makes the death-rate less satisfactory as a guide to the state of ill-health than it was, say, in the nineteenth century. For example, in 1961 of the total deaths from all causes, 551,753, over 7,000 were caused by traffic accidents and over 6,000 by accidents in the home.

number of deaths which occurred from specified causes in 1837 are compared with the number of deaths which would have occurred from the same causes in a population of the same size in 1937, and it is apparent that there has been a marked decline in deaths from infective diseases like smallpox, measles, scarlet fever, typhus and tuberculosis. Indeed if comparisons are made between the deaths from diseases which are now regarded as 'childish ailments' such as scarlet fever and measles the change is remarkable, for example, the death-rate in England and Wales per million persons under 15 years of age from scarlet fever in 1861–70 was 2,282 per million whereas in 1951 it was 1 per million, and for measles it was 1,148 per million in 1861–70 as against 30 per million in 1951. In 1961 the total number of deaths from scarlet fever was 3, and from measles 152. Even with the danger of a wide margin of error in comparisons of this kind because of changes in identification and classification of causes of death there can be no doubt that the great epidemic diseases have in the main been conquered and are no longer significant as causes of death.

The virtual elimination of the infectious diseases has brought about a transformation in the distribution of deaths in the population, for example, between 1870–2 the annual average total of male deaths in England and Wales was 262,000 and of this total just over half were of persons aged under 20 years. By 1951, on the other hand, of the 282,000 male deaths occurring in that year only 17,000 (or about 6 per cent) were of persons aged under 20 years and the vast majority of deaths were of persons aged 45 and over, and by 1961 of the 281,000 male deaths in that year less than 15,000 or about 5 per cent were of persons aged under 20 years, and about 90 per cent occurred to persons aged 45 and over. The main causes of death by natural causes in 1951 and 1961 were, as we should expect, cancers and heart diseases, which are the killers of middle-aged and elderly people, so that it seems as though the diseases which killed young and old alike in the nineteenth century have by now been replaced by diseases which attack and kill mainly the middle-aged and the elderly.[1] Whether the increase in the

---

[1] For the causes of death and comments on the changing patterns in recent years see the 'Annual Reports' of the Chief Medical Officer of the Ministry of Health which are published usually as Part II or Part III of the *Report of the Ministry of*

number of deaths from, for example, cancer is as substantial as the figures suggest is open to question because of the great improvements in diagnosis in modern times,[1] but there can be no disputing the fact that in the middle of the twentieth century it is primarily persons aged 45 and over who die from natural causes.

TABLE 50

Deaths in England and Wales (from July to December) 1837, from certain causes compared with corresponding deaths in 1937 (July to December) which would have occurred in the same population (without correction for age distribution)

Causes of death (as described in 1937)	Number of deaths	
	July to Dec., 1837	July to Dec., 1937
All causes	148,701	84,010
Smallpox	5,811	Nil
Measles and scarlet fever	7,252	255
Whooping cough	3,044	209
Typhus, typhoid and paratyphoid	9,047	47
Respiratory and disseminated tuberculosis	27,754	4,188
Pneumonia, pleurisy and congestion of lungs ..	7,055	4,542
Maternal mortality	1,265	339
Violent deaths	4,845	4,206
Other causes	82,416	70,144

The number of deaths from all causes in England and Wales since 1870 has remained fairly stable at about 500,000 every year up to 1951 and then rising slowly to about 552,000 in 1961 and it would therefore be fair to assume that at least that number of persons have suffered ill-health each year, but these probably

[1] For example in England and Wales the number of deaths from cancer of the lung remained fairly constant at about 250 during the period 1911–19, then showed a marked rise to 2,286 in 1931 and to 13,247 in 1951 – see a 'Special Report on Mortality from Cancer of the Lung 1931–1951' in the *Annual Report of the Ministry of Health*, Part III, 1951. Since 1951 the association of lung cancer and cigarette smoking has been a frequent topic of discussion and in the Report of the Ministry of Health for 1961 the Chief Medical Officer shows that as a percentage of all deaths lung cancer as a cause has risen from 2·4 per cent in 1951 to 4·1 per cent in 1961.

Health On the State of the Public Health. See too the Statistical Reviews of the Registrar-General (Annual) – *Text Medical* –, and the occasional special supplements on medical subjects. The *Annual Abstract of Statistics* also gives a brief summary of the main causes of death.

account for only a small proportion of the total numbers who experience varying degrees of ill-health at any one time. The calculation of the prevalence of illnesses of all kinds throughout the population would be a herculean task and even if an ill-health census were possible there would be no certainty that it would provide a complete picture of the state of ill-health of the nation. In the official decennial Census of population attempts were made in 1851 and every succeeding Census up to and including 1911 to measure the numbers of the deaf and dumb and the blind, and from 1871 to 1911 additional questions were asked about persons deemed to be lunatics, imbeciles or idiots. It is believed that the results relating to blindness were reasonably accurate but that the numbers of the deaf and the mentally ill were grossly understated.[1] In any case, the fact that this form of inquiry was abandoned in 1911 renders the Census as a possible source of data of relatively little value for purposes of comparison with the present, but, unfortunately, there is no other continuous and comprehensive survey of ill-health.

Some indication of the prevalence of ill-health can, however, be obtained by examining a number of diverse sources of information, for example, hospital statistics showing the average daily number of occupied beds, the numbers of out-patients and of attendances at casualty departments and the numbers on waiting lists for hospital beds; statistics of notifiable diseases; the numbers of the physically and mentally ill in accommodation provided under Part III of the National Assistance Act;[2] and the numbers on the register of disabled persons kept by the Ministry of Labour since the passing of the Disabled Persons (Employment) Act, 1944. Sources of this kind give an indication of the seriously ill and if an examination is made of any recent years it would be found that, for example, in 1961 the numbers receiving care and attention in one form or another were as follows:[3]

[1] See *Census Reports of Great Britain 1801–1931*, Guides to Official Sources No. 2, for comments on the validity of the results and on the unsuitability of the Census for obtaining information of this kind.

[2] Part III of the National Assistance Act, 1948, requires Local Authorities to provide welfare services for the deaf, dumb, the crippled and the blind, and in recent years well over 50 per cent of the persons in special 'welfare' accommodation have been physically or mentally handicapped.

[3] For details of the numbers in 1951 see the previous edition of this book.

The Changing Patterns of Social Problems

ENGLAND AND WALES, 1961

Hospital services

Numbers in 000's

Average daily occupation of hospital beds (excluding mental hospitals) under the National Health Service 404

Total discharges or deaths of in-patients ... 4,269

Out-patients at consultant and general practitioner clinics and casualty departments – new cases during year 13,346

Attendances in these departments during year 42,398

Number on hospital waiting lists at 31.12.1961 474

The mentally disordered[1]

Patients resident at 30.4.1961 in Psychiatric Hospitals 199

Resident in Part III Accommodation

Persons physically or mentally handicapped or partially sighted, deaf and dumb, epileptics and cripples resident on 31.12.1961.[2] 42

These examples of the numbers cared for in institutions of one kind or another give some indication of the prevalence of ill-health, but, unfortunately we cannot add the constituent items in order to arrive at a total. It would, however, be fair to assume that on any one day in 1961, there were at least 700,000 persons who were sufficiently ill to need care and attention and of course there were nearly a half-million on hospital waiting lists, so that in all probability there were at least 1¼ to 1½ million people suffering some form of ill-health on any one day in 1961.[3]

In 1961 there were about 868,000 notifications of infectious diseases (notably measles, scarlet fever, whooping-cough, dysentery, pneumonia and food poisoning)[4] and about 42,000

---

[1] No real comparison can be made with earlier years because of the new provisions of the Mental Health Act, 1959.

[2] See the *Annual Reports of the Ministry of Health, Part I*, 'The Health and Welfare Services.'

[3] The main source of data for information of the kind given above is the *Annual Report of the Ministry of Health*. See these *Annual Reports* for current statistics.

[4] In 1951 the number of notifications of measles – 616,093 – was the highest since measles became notifiable in 1940, and the number of notifications of whooping cough – 169,347 – and of dysentery – 28,564 – were the highest ever

cases of venereal disease and 99,000 cases of 'other conditions' allied to venereal disease were dealt with for the first time at any centre in England and Wales. In the same year there were 21,747 formal notifications of new cases of tuberculosis (compared with 49,440 in 1951) whilst on the registers of Chest Clinics there were (at 31st December, 1961) 313,240 cases of respiratory and non-respiratory tuberculosis.[1]

Then there are those disabled in other ways, for example, on the 31st December, 1961, there were 96,591 registered blind persons, whilst during the year ended 31st December, 1961, there were 10,824 newly-registered blind persons,[2] and on the disabled persons register maintained by the Ministry of Labour and National Service there were, on the 17th April 1961, 666,454 disabled persons, of whom about 40 per cent were in the surgical group (i.e. those with amputations, or injuries of head, face or limbs or non-respiratory tuberculosis); 40 per cent were in the medical group (i.e. were suffering from diseases such as arthritis, rheumatism, respiratory tuberculosis and disease of the heart); 10 per cent were in the psychiatric group and the remainder were suffering from such disablements as congenital deformities, blindness and deafness.[3] We cannot, unfortunately, add together all these separate statistics because of

[1] The decline in the numbers of cases of tuberculosis in recent years is quite striking, for example, formal notifications of tuberculosis in England and Wales fell from 65,468 in 1931 to 21,747 in 1961. Even more remarkable is the decline in deaths from tuberculosis, for example, the standardized death-rate per million persons fell from 2,882 between 1871–80 to 545 between 1941–50 (see the Appendices to the *Annual Report of the Ministry of Health*, Part III, 1951). On the other hand the number of cases of venereal disease is increasing, e.g. the number of cases of gonorrhoea dealt with for the first time rose from about 18,000 in 1951 to about 37,000 in 1961.

[2] On blindness in recent years see Arnold Sorsby: *Blindness in England – 1951–54*, published by the Ministry of Health in 1956, which shows how the incidence of blindness is extremely heavy in persons aged 70 and over.

[3] Registration under the Disabled Persons (Employment) Act, 1944, is voluntary and may be for a period of from one to five years. See the Annual Reports of the Ministry of Labour and National Service, section on 'Resettlement of Disabled Persons'. The last Annual Report was for 1960 and the figures above were obtained from the *Ministry of Labour Gazette*, May 1961).

recorded up to 1951. In 1961, however, there were 763,465 cases of measles, but only 24,469 of whooping cough, and 20,412 of dysentery. Comparisons with past years are not always easy because new diseases become notifiable, e.g. anthrax became notifiable in 1960.

the danger of double counting, but it would be reasonable to assume that at least 2 million people were ill or disabled at any one time in 1961.

The patients in hospitals, the sufferers from notifiable diseases, and the registered disabled can at least be calculated but they are not the only (or necessarily the main) body of persons who experience ill-health at any particular time; there are others whose illness is sufficient to keep them at home but not necessarily of the kind to be separately recorded. It is almost impossible to identify these, but we can obtain some idea of the prevalence of incapacity from, for example, the numbers who apply for sickness benefits and the numbers who seek medical attention. Since the 5th July, 1948, the records of persons applying for sickness and injury benefits under the National Insurance Acts are a guide to the numbers who have to stay away from work because of ill-health and in 1961 there were 8,123,000 new claims for sickness benefit and 728,000 for injury benefit whilst on the 18th December 1961, there were 773,100 persons incapacitated owing to sickness and 49,700 owing to industrial accident or prescribed industrial disease in England and Wales.[1] The majority of sickness benefits are payable for periods of sickness lasting not more than 12 to 24 days, but the fact that out of about 25 million insured persons over three-quarters of a million were receiving sickness or injury benefits at any one time in 1961 is indicative of the prevalence of ill-health among the adult working population.

In the elderly (i.e. persons aged 65 and over) population recent evidence suggests that about 50 per cent suffer from some form of ill-health.[2] Many of the illnesses of the elderly are accepted as part of the natural order of life at advanced ages, but the effects of ill-health among the retired population are, from the point of view of the community, just as serious as those in other age-groups. With an increasing proportion of the

[1] See the Annual Reports of the Ministry of Pensions and National Insurance for detailed statistics relating to the numbers receiving sickness benefits and types of illness for which claims to benefit are made.

[2] See, for example, J. H. Sheldon: *The Social Medicine of Old Age.* In 1955 a survey undertaken by the Department of Social Science, the University of Nottingham, showed that 51 per cent of all elderly persons had suffered at least one ailment in a period of six months prior to the survey.

population living through to old age we cannot expect any great change in the incidence of ill-health among the elderly unless medical science succeeds in dealing as effectively with the diseases of old age as with the diseases of childhood.

The health of schoolchildren has become, particularly in the twentieth century, subject to continuous supervision by statutory authorities and the Annual Reports of the Chief Medical Officer of the Ministry of Education give an indication of the incidence of ill-health in this section of the population.[1] In 1951, for example, about one-third of the pupils on the registers of maintained Primary and Secondary Schools in England and Wales were inspected by School Medical Officers, and of these about 3 per cent were classed as of such 'poor' general condition that they required supervision by school doctors and nurses or other forms of special medical care; about 13 per cent were found to be in need of treatment for such things as defective vision, skin diseases and ear, nose and throat defects; and 6 per cent of the school population were found to be infested with head-lice. In 1961, however, it was reported that only 0·68 per cent of school children were considered by the examining doctors to be of unsatisfactory physical condition. There has been over the years a considerable improvement in the physical health of schoolchildren, in particular certain skin diseases, such as scabies, impetigo and ringworm of the scalp, are now less prevalent, as of course are diseases like diphtheria, acute rheumatism and tuberculosis, yet even in 1961 over three quarters of a million schoolchildren in England and Wales contracted one or other of the notifiable diseases.[2] In addition to the children in ordinary schools who experienced some kind of physical ill-health there were, in 1961, about 46,350 who were known to have received treatment in Child Guidance Centres and about 59,000 received 'Speech Therapy', and there are the children in 'Special Schools' (for the blind, partially sighted,

[1] See the Annual Reports of the Chief Medical Officer of the Ministry of Education.

[2] It is significant that the biggest single cause of deaths in children aged up to 15 years in the 1960's are accidents (notably accidents in the home, which cause more deaths than road accidents) and not diseases. See the Registrar-General's Statistical Reviews – *Text Medical* – from 1948 onwards and the Reports of the Chief Medical Officer of the Ministry of Education.

the deaf, physically handicapped, educationally sub-normal and the like) who, in 1961, numbered about 67,000. The exact number of schoolchildren experiencing some form of physical or mental illness in 1961 cannot be determined, but, it would seem that despite the extraordinary advances which have been made in recent years in the treatment and prevention of disease that large numbers of the school-age population suffer ill-health in various forms.

These separate sources of data on various aspects of the health of the nation are at best a guide to the incidence of ill-health, but they do not provide an answer to the question 'how much ill-health is there in England and Wales at any one time?'. An attempt to answer broadly this kind of question was made by the Social Survey Unit of the Central Office of Information when it began, in 1944, to conduct a regular survey of sickness, but, unfortunately, as an economy measure this valuable experiment came to an end in 1952.[1] The Social Survey Unit interviewed at the beginning of every month a sample of the population aged 16 and over[2] in order to obtain information about the illnesses and injuries that had been experienced in the two previous months, and from this data four principal rates were calculated, viz. a sickness rate, i.e. the number of persons reporting some injury or illness in a month per 100 persons interviewed; a prevalence rate, i.e. the number of illnesses and injuries reported in a month per 100 persons interviewed; an incapacity rate, i.e. the number of days away from work, or for persons not going to work, number of days confined to house on account of sickness per 100 persons interviewed; and a medical consultation rate, i.e. number of visits to or by a medically-qualified practitioner per 100 persons interviewed.

These four rates provide a good guide to morbidity and it is clear from the results that the majority of individuals in the population have experienced some form of ill-health or injury in any one month in recent years. For example, the rates in 1951 (for persons aged 21 and over) were as follows:

[1] See the *Annual Report of the Ministry of Health*, Part III, 1951, for a good summary of the results obtained from the Survey of Sickness between 1944 and 1951, and see, too, Percy Stocks: *Sickness in the Population of England and Wales, 1944–47*, published as a special paper by the General Register Office.

[2] From February, 1951, the sample was drawn from persons aged 21 and over.

Average monthly Sickness, Prevalence, Incapacity and Medical Consultation Rate per 100 persons interviewed for each half-year in 1951

	Sickness rate	Prevalence rate	Incapacity rate	Medical Consultation rate
Jan.–June ..	72	153	136	53
July–Dec. ..	70	147	88	44

In earlier years the rates were generally lower, but they were then applicable to the population aged 16 and over, and we should expect the incidence of sickness to be lower when younger age-groups are included. There is a marked variation by age-groups and by sex in these various rates, for example, in 1951 the average monthly sickness rates for men and women by age-groups were as follows:

Average monthly Sickness rates, by sex and age, January–December, 1951

Age-group	Males	Females
21–24	53	62
25–34	60	67
35–44	63	71
45–54	66	75
55–64	72	80
65–74	79	86
75 and over ..	85	91
All ages.. ..	67	75

The female is consistently higher than the male rate and as would be expected the sickness rate increases progressively with advancing age. All four rates are in fact higher for females than for males, and of course for the older age-groups. There are, too, regional and occupational variations,[1] but perhaps of greater importance is the fact that this survey provides data on the kinds

[1] For a very detailed analysis of the survey of sickness from 1947 to 1951 see *The Registrar-General's Statistical Review for England and Wales for the two years 1950–51 – Supplement on General Morbidity, Cancer and Mental Health.* Note that the four rates originally used have in this report been renamed as follows: sickness rate becomes 'Monthly Prevalence Rate (persons)'; Prevalence rate becomes 'Monthly Prevalence Rate (spells)'; Incapacity rate becomes 'Average duration of incapacity per 100 persons'; but Consultation rate remains unchanged.

of illnesses and injuries suffered. The most prevalent group of complaints was (in 1951) 'ill-defined symptoms', such as headaches, coughs, pains in chest, abdomen or back, vomiting, diarrhoea, and the other main groups of causes of sickness were rheumatism, colds and influenza.[1] There have been criticisms of the causes of sickness revealed by the Survey because they are not supported by clinical evidence, thus a person may say to the interviewer that he (or she) suffered rheumatism in the previous month, whereas in fact he may have suffered from something quite different. From the purely medical point of view there may be some validity in this argument, but from the social problem point of view if a person thinks he is suffering from some illness or other then surely that in itself is important.

There is now a growing interest in the measurement of sickness and it may well be that in the not too distant future methods and forms of measurement will be available which will provide accurate information on the extent to which the general population experiences sickness at any one time.[2] It is abundantly clear that there is a great deal of ill-health in the middle of the twentieth century in England and Wales, and that it must create innumerable social and economic problems, but were we any less healthy in 1961 than our ancestors in 1871? This question cannot be answered with certainty; we know that death-rates have fallen substantially, that the incidence of infectious diseases is much less now than in the past, and that methods of prevention and treatment of illness are available today which were unknown in the late nineteenth century, but there is a great deal that we do not know about the past and the present. It would, however, probably be fair to assume that the incidence of sickness from physical disease is less now than in the past, and that in all probability there is now a greater proportion of the population which suffers injuries from accidents. It is probable, too, that the incidence of psychiatric disorders is much

[1] See the Supplement cited above.

[2] See *The Measurement of Morbidity – a Report of the Statistics Sub-Committee of the Registrar-General's Advisory Committee on Medical Nomenclature and Statistics*, published by the General Register Office as report No. 8 in Studies on Medical and Population Subjects, 1954. More recently the Ministry of Health has encouraged far more research then in the past, for example, with the General Register Office it carried out in detail a survey of Hospital In-patients for 1956–7; and there have been surveys of General Practice.

higher now than in the past, but again it would be almost impossible to make comparisons because of the tremendous advances which have been made in psychology and psychiatry in recent years. The line between physical and mental illness is becoming exceedingly blurred and there is a growing body of opinion which supports the view that psychosomatic illnesses now greatly exceed purely physical illnesses. There can be no doubt of the increase in mental, psychoneurotic and personality disorders in modern times and it may well be that the history of ill-health in the general population in the past 100 years can be summarized by stating that due to improvements in the physical environment (especially in living conditions and working conditions) and to advances in medical science (and of course its application in public health) many of the physical diseases which affect man have been conquered or brought under control, but they have been replaced by illnesses which attack the mind. We may be healthier in body than we were, but the whole man is not necessarily healthier now than he was in the past.

The fact that in this country in modern times we have been prepared to use a considerable proportion of our national resources in an all-out fight to reduce the incidence and prevalence of ill-health is indicative of the way in which the social problems of ill-health have come to be recognized as of fundamental importance to the life of the community,[1] but another social problem, crime, which could well be injurious to the well-being of the nation as a whole has received relatively little attention.

THE CHANGING PATTERNS OF CRIME

The measurement of the incidence and prevalence of crime presents as many difficulties as the measurement of ill-health and there are certainly very great obstacles to comparisons over time. The initial and fundamental difficulty is that of definition; what is crime? In the widest sense any infringement of the law

---

[1] Yet, to quote the Chief Medical Officer of the Ministry of Health, it is surely 'paradoxical that records of sickness and death should be our main index of the state of the public health . . . and that preventive medicine is the Cinderella of the Health Services' – *Annual Report*, Part II, 1952.

which is punishable by the State is a crime, therefore, for example, failure to take out a wireless licence is just as much a crime as murder.[1] It is in this wide sense that we shall use the term because the main sources of data for the measurement of crime are the criminal statistics (published annually by the Home Office) which relate to all offences against the law punishable by the Courts. Very broadly, all offences may be grouped into indictable and summary and the main distinction between them is that an indictable offence is one which is primarily triable by jury, whereas a summary offence is usually tried by a magistrate.[2] In general, the indictable offences are looked upon as serious crimes, whereas summary offences are of a less serious nature, but we cannot be concerned with matters of this kind which are essentially problems for lawyers and criminologists, except in so far as this system of classification of offences into groups facilitates the measurement of the incidence of crime.

The range of offences capable of being committed has been greatly extended (particularly in modern times) and therefore any comparison of the incidence of crime now and, say, eighty or even fifty years ago must take account of this fact. For example, before 1911 it was not possible to commit the offence of failure to pay National Insurance contributions, before 1870 there were no offences against the Education Acts, and prior to 1948 there were no offences against the National Health Service Acts. Obvious as these examples may be it is essential to recognize that many of our present-day offences are of very recent origin and that one result at least of the spate of legislation in modern times is that it is now possible to commit many more offences than in the past. Similarly, modern inventions have given us means of committing offences which were not available to our ancestors; the obvious example is the mechanically propelled vehicle, and the extent to which the volume of offences has been swollen by the use of the motor-car alone may be gauged from the fact that the annual average number of non-indictable offences under the Highway Acts between

[1] For an interesting discussion on the meaning of crime see H. Mannheim: *Criminal Justice and Social Reconstruction* (Routledge, 1946).

[2] There are certain summary offences which carry the right of trial by jury. For a good account of the intricacies of the law on points of this kind see R. M. Jackson: *The Machinery of Justice in England* (Cambridge University Press 1942).

1899–1903 directly connected with motoring was about 1,600, whereas even in 1925 there were about 151,000, and by 1961 over 700,000 traffic offences which accounted for more than 60 per cent of all persons found guilty of offences of all kinds.[1] Allowing for changes of this magnitude how can one measure the incidence of crime at different periods?

The incidence of crime may be measured in three main ways; first by compiling a record of all offences, second by recording all offenders and, thirdly, by taking into account both offences and offenders. Whichever unit of measurement is chosen it will be found that difficulties arise when we try to translate total offences, or total offenders, or both, into the incidence of crime as a whole. But let us examine the existing sources of data in order to see the problems involved in making an assessment of crime as a social problem.

From the criminal statistics we can get information dating back to the nineteenth century on the indictable offences known to the police, but for our purpose and in view of the changes in the law and social conditions we need go back no further than the beginning of the twentieth century. In the criminal statistics the indictable offences are classified into six main groups: Class I covers offences against the person and includes murder, manslaughter, infanticide, unnatural offences, rape, indecency with males, bigamy and incest; Class II covers offences against property with violence and includes burglary, housebreaking and robbery; Class III covers offences against property without violence and includes embezzlement, false pretences, larceny of various kinds and receiving stolen goods; Class IV comprises malicious injuries to property, viz. arson and other malicious injuries; Class V covers forgery and offences against the currency; and Class VI 'Other Offences', includes High Treason, perjury, attempting to commit suicide and other misdemeanours.[2] This method of grouping is by no means completely acceptable, but at least it enables us to see the main fields of indictable offences known to the police and in Table

---

[1] See Table 57 for number of persons found guilty of traffic offences in 1938, 1951 and 1961.

[2] See the *Criminal Statistics for England and Wales* for details of the offences in each class. From the 3rd August 1961 when the Suicide Act, 1961, came into force, suicide has ceased to be a criminal offence.

51 some indication is given of the changing pattern in this century.

Before we jump to any conclusions about (what appears to be) the remarkable increase in indictable offences it is essential to remember that Table 51 refers to offences known to the police and not necessarily to actual offences which have been committed. This is to say, these figures show no more than the fact that on reports which the police have received they have decided that an offence has been committed and hence a record is made. It does not follow that an offence has in fact been committed, for example, a person may think that his watch has been stolen, he reports 'the theft' to the police, who on the available evidence decide that an offence has been committed, but the offence may never be proved and one can only conclude that it may or may not have been committed.[1] These problems of accurate reporting, of interpretation of the reports and the like are serious and it is perhaps significant that of the offences known to the police in any year in modern times not more than 50 per cent have been 'cleared up' during the year.[1]

Apart from the problem of reporting and interpretation there is a further difficulty in making comparisons over time and that arises out of the changes which have occurred in the attitude of society as expressed by the law, the police and the public at large towards certain offences. For example, an offence such as 'indecency between males', may nowadays be reported and action may more often be taken by the police than would have been the case in the past and this may account for the apparent increase from 103 such offences known to the police on the average between 1900–04 to 1,152 in 1951 and 1,653 in 1961. It may well be that there is now a greater readiness on the part of the public to report what appear to be offences and an equally more active response on the part of the police in accepting such reports. If, however, we accept that there are valid objections

---

[1] On the difficult question of assessing the validity of the statistics relating to offences known to the police see H. Mannheim: *Social Aspects of Crime in England between the Wars* (Allen & Unwin, 1940) and on the problem of measuring the incidence of sexual offences see *Sexual Offences: a Report of the Cambridge Department of Criminal Science*, published in 1957.

[2] 'Cleared-up' means, for example, that a person has been arrested or summoned for the offence, or a person is known or suspected to be guilty but cannot be prosecuted (e.g. because he has died). The fact that only about half the offences are cleared-up should not be taken to mean that the police are inefficient.

TABLE 51

Indictable offences known to the police in England and Wales, 1900–61

Offences	Annual average number						No. for year			
	1900–04	% of total	1925–29	% of total	1935–39	% of total	1951	% of total	1961	% of total
1. Offences against the person	3,522	4	5,181	4	7,238	3	21,149	4	38,005	5
2. Offences against property with violence	9,277	11	20,505	16	44,569	17	96,820	18	167,540	21
3. Offences against property without violence	67,732	80	97,823	77	209,328	78	392,538	75	584,858	72
4. Malicious injuries to property	485	1	306	0·2	549	0·2	4,993	1	5,606	0·7
5. Forgery and offences against the currency	536	1	904	0·7	1,680	0·6	3,378	1	6,924	0·8
6. Other offences	2,695	3	2,921	2	3,922	1	5,628	1	3,967	0·5
Total	84,247	100	127,640	100	267,286	100	524,506	100	806,900	100

to these statistics it still would appear that there must have been a real increase in indictable offences in this century, but the increase has not been evenly distributed over all kinds of offences.

Of all indictable offences known to the police in England and Wales in the twentieth century never less than 90 per cent have been offences against property with and without violence, but (as shown in Table 51) offences against property with violence have increased at a faster rate than any other single group of offences. Within this group it is housebreaking, shop-breaking and entering with intent to commit a felony which have increased most markedly in number, though not necessarily as a proportion of all offences against property with violence, as shown in Table 52.

There is no clearly apparent pattern of change, shop-breaking and attempts to break in have increased absolutely and proportionately, but housebreaking and burglary have declined relatively to all offences against property with violence.[1] The term 'violence' is perhaps misleading and it certainly should not be interpreted as indicating that in recent years there has been an orgy of physical violence, for example, the offence of burglary may involve no more violence than cutting neatly a pane of glass in a window in order to gain entry to a dwelling-house at night or indeed 'the violence' may consist of nothing more than opening a door! The legal meaning of violence is highly complex and technical and the problem of classification of offences against property with violence is therefore difficult.

Offences against property without violence still remain the major group of indictable offences known to the police in any one year, though in recent years they have declined as a proportion of all such offences. Some of this group, for example, embezzlement, remained relatively stable until the middle 1950's at about 2,000 per annum, but have since increased and in 1961 there were 4,115 such offences known to the police. Others like larceny of horses and cattle have declined in number, and some such as larceny in house have increased appreciably from about 1,000 at the turn of the century to nearly 20,000 in 1951 and

---

[1] The offence of sacrilege, not shown in Table 52, seems to be out of place as an offence against property with violence. The number known to the police between 1900–04 was 153, in 1951 and 1961 there were 353 and 477 respectively.

TABLE 52

The most common offences against property with violence known to the police in England and Wales, 1900–61.

	Annual average			For year		
	1900–04	1925–29	1935–39	1949	1951	1961
All offences against property with violence	9,277	20,505	44,569	92,578	96,820	167,540
Shopbreaking	3,415	9,533	18,292	41,656	44,873	73,474
Per cent of group total	37	46	41	45	46	44
Housebreaking	3,393	7,613	16,257	26,980	26,292	47,728
Per cent of group total	37	37	36	29	27	28
Attempts to break into houses, shops, etc., and entering with intent to commit a felony*	676	1,603	7,749	18,281	20,142	37,375
Per cent of group total	7	8	17	20	21	22
Burglary	1,314	1,260	1,399	3,741	3,729	5,211
Per cent of group total	14	6	3	4	4	4

* Note the offences shown above as one group in fact comprise two separate groups in the Criminal Statistics.

30,558 in 1961. Within this group of offences there are a number concerned with vehicles, e.g. larceny from unattended vehicles and thefts of motor-vehicles, including motor-cycles; obviously the opportunities for committing offences connected with vehicles are very much greater now than they were fifty years ago. Unfortunately offences such as larceny from unattended vehicles were re-grouped in the criminal statistics in 1934 and therefore comparisons cannot satisfactorily be made with the past. However, the number of offences of larceny from unattended vehicles has increased markedly from, for example, 17,548 in 1935 to 43,127 in 1951, and 112,671 in 1961, and it may be presumed that at the beginning of this century they were negligible in number. It is perhaps the increase in the opportunities for committing offences against property such as larceny from unattended vehicles, unauthorized takings and thefts of motor-vehicles, stealing electricity, and larceny from automatic machines and meters, which makes it so difficult to compare even 1901 with 1961 and therefore dangerous to jump to conclusions about the real increase in criminality.

The kinds of offences which may be committed against the person have remained largely unchanged, but the numbers known to the police have increased markedly though they have remained-stable as a proportion of all indictable offences in the past 60 years. Within this group of offences, murder of persons aged one year and over has remained relatively stable, for example, the number known to the police in England and Wales was:

1900–04 annual average...	...	99
1925–29 annual average...	...	108
1935–39 annual average...	...	107
1945 number for year ...	...	173
1949 number for year ...	...	119
1951 number for year ...	...	123
1961 number for year ...	...	136[1]

With the exception of 1945 the annual number of murders (of persons aged one year and over) since 1901 has declined relative to total population, and the murder of infants aged under one

[1] Since the Homicide Act, 1957 the figures for murder are not strictly comparable with those of earlier years. See a report of the Home Office Research Unit on *Murder*, Studies in the Cause of Delinquency and the Treatment of Offenders, No. 4, H.M.S.O., 1961.

The Changing Patterns of Social Problems

year has declined absolutely from fifty-six on the average between 1900 and 1904 to nine in 1951 and eleven in 1961.[1] On the other hand, some other offences against the person have increased appreciably and they are shown in Table 53.

Of the offences against the person it is the so-called sexual offences which have increased most. Whether the increase is as marked as the figures in Table 53 suggest has recently been the subject of intensive study by the members of the Department of Criminal Science, the University of Cambridge, and from their report it is clear that whilst 'it would be an idle speculation to attempt to assess in statistical terms the real extent to which crime has increased' there can be no doubt of the fact 'that the number of persons brought before the courts on sexual charges has reached proportions hitherto unknown in the criminal records of this country'. On the other hand, the incidence of undetected and indeed unreported sexual offences is acknowledged to be very great and it has been suggested that the amount of illegal sexual misconduct revealed to the police may amount to no more than 5 per cent of the actual crime committed.[2] If this is true, then clearly comparison with the past becomes difficult because the amount of undetected sexual crime may, for example, have been very much greater in 1901 than in 1961. Nevertheless the fact that between 1951 and 1961 the offence of defilement (i.e. unlawful sexual intercourse with girls under 16) increased from just under 2,000 to just under 4,000 is obviously not without significance, and in view of the absolute increase in offences of all kinds against the person it is not surprising that there should be sustained public interest in these types of offences in recent years. The setting up of a Royal Commission on Capital Punishment which sat from 1949–53[3] and a departmental Committee of Inquiry into Homosexual Offences and Prostitution in 1954[4] is evidence of the degree of concern on the part of the State. The urgent need now is for

[1] Since the Homicide Act, 1957 the figures for murder are not strictly comparable with those of earlier years. See a report of the Home Office Research Unit on *Murder*, Studies in the Cause of Delinquency and the Treatment of Offenders, No. 4, H.M.S.O., 1961.
[2] L. Radzinowicz in the preface to the Cambridge Study.
[3] See the Report, Cmd. 8932, H.M.S.O., 1953.
[4] The *Report of the Committee on Homosexual Offences and Prostitution*, Cmd. 247, was published on the 4th September, 1957.

TABLE 53

The most common offences against the person known to the police in England and Wales 1900–61

	Annual average			For year		
	1900–04	1925–9	1935–9	1949	1951	1961
All offences against the person	3,522	5,181	7,238	17,250	21,149	38,005
Malicious wounding	930	938	1,639	3,705	4,445	13,972
Per cent of group total	26	18	23	21	21	37
Felonious wounding	260	152	286	625	1,078	1,913
Per cent of group total	7	3	4	4	5	5
Attempts to commit unnatural offences	53	331	703	2,409	3,272	3,224
Per cent of group total	2	6	10	14	15	9
Indecent assaults on females	695	1,844	2,347	6,191	7,287	9,386
Per cent of group total	20	36	32	36	34	24
Defilement of girls under 16	130	269	468	838	1,199	3,923
Per cent of group total	4	5	6	5	6	10
Indency with males	103	170	299	852	1,152	1,653
Per cent of group total	3	3	4	5	5	4
Procuring abortion..	12	82	156	228	237	245
Per cent of group total	0·3	2	2	1	1	1
Incest	*	101	91	161	209	335
Per cent of group total		2	1	1	1	1

* This offence was created by the Punishment of Incest Act, 1908.

even more intensive research into the incidence and causes of sexual offences.[1]

The increase in the number of sexual offences known to the police is far greater than the increase in population from 1901 to 1961, and if the increase in offences is real then a radical change has occurred in the social structure of modern England. Until, however, it can be proved that the volume of sexual offences has actually grown and that the greater numbers reveal a greater incidence of criminality and not merely greater efficiency on the part of the police or greater readiness in reporting offences of this kind on the part of the public, too much should not be read into the criminal statistics. In any case it should be remembered that the sexual offences represented even in 1961 a very small proportion (less than 3 per cent) of all indictable offences known to the police.

The remaining indictable offences known to the police in England and Wales have (as shown in Table 51) increased substantially in the twentieth century, especially the group of malicious injuries to property. This group includes a variety of offences of a destructive nature,[2] but there is no readily obvious reason for the increase in the number of offences recorded.

The broad pattern of change in the indictable offences known to the police in this century is that up to the end of the First World War there were less than 100,000 such offences recorded annually, from the early 1920's to the mid-1930's the number more than doubled, from 1935 to 1945 they increased again by about 100 per cent, and from 1945 to 1950 they remained at about the half-million mark and reached a peak of 524,506 in 1951. At the end of the first half of the twentieth century there were, therefore, about six times as many indictable offences known to the police in England and Wales as there were at the beginning of the century. In that time the total population had grown by about one-third, so that the growth of indictable offences was very much greater than the growth of population. Between 1951 and 1956 the number dropped slightly remaining

[1] In 1957 the Home Secretary announced that a small research unit was to be set up in the Home Office in order to prosecute research into the problems of crime. Since that time the Research Unit has either carried out itself or encouraged research in a variety of fields. See *Penal Practice in a Changing Society*, Cmd. 645, H.M.S.O., 1959.

[2] See the list in the *Criminal Statistics*.

at less than 500,000 in those years, from 1956, however, the indictable offences known to the Police have increased substantially and a new peak was reached in 1961 when there were 806,900 such offences. Whether the differences in the rates of increase provide evidence of a substantial change in lawlessness or criminality in the community is an open question which certainly cannot be answered by an examination of the criminal statistics partly because of defects in the statistics themselves and of course because the number of offences may bear little or no relation to the number of offenders.[1]

The main guide to the number of offenders is provided by the statistics of persons tried and persons found guilty by the Courts. Until about 1925 the number of persons tried for indictable offences was on the average about 60,000 a year and the majority were found guilty, but because of the growth of population the number tried and found guilty gradually declined as a proportion of the total population. Since the mid-1930's, however, the pattern has changed appreciably, as shown in Table 54. It is perhaps the number found guilty which can be taken as the minimum of indictable offenders in any one year and it can be seen (Table 54) that the proportion of the population found guilty has increased appreciably in recent years. No real relationship between offences and offenders can be established because of the fact that one offender may have committed numerous offences, but it is clear that of the offenders found guilty the vast majority are males.

Of all persons found guilty of indictable offences since 1938 the majority have been under 30 years of age, as shown in Table 55.

It would seem that the commission of indictable offences is primarily a pastime of younger persons and there is a fairly clear pattern of relationship between age and type of offence. For example, in 1951 and 1961 of the males in age-group 8–14 years found guilty about 90 per cent were concerned in the offences of larceny and breaking and entering, and presumably young persons of this age are relatively easily detected when commit-

[1] In June, 1963, the Home Secretary appointed a Committee 'to consider and report what changes, if any, are desirable in existing arrangements in England and Wales for the recording and reporting for statistical purposes of information about criminal offences and proceedings . . . and in the collection and presentation of statistics relating to these matters'.

ting offences of this kind.[1] Nevertheless the fact remains that young persons (between 8 and 17 years of age) constitute about one-third of indictable offenders and these of course are the detected and proved who may in fact represent only a small proportion of offenders as a whole.

TABLE 54

Indictable offences and offenders in England and Wales in selected years

Years	No. of indict-able offences known to the Police	No. of persons tried	No. found guilty		Persons found guilty per 100,000 of population*	
			M.	F.	M.	F.
1938 ..	283,220	85,405	68,679	9,784	393	51
1948 ..	522,684	139,391	112,181	17,203	612	87
1951 ..	524,506	142,168	117,004	15,813	645	79
1961 ..	806,900	192,983	158,717	23,500	818	111

* The male and female population aged 8 and over because persons under the age of 8 cannot be guilty of any offence. As from 1963 the age of criminal responsibility will be 10 years.

TABLE 55

Percentage of persons found guilty of indictable offences in England and Wales by age and sex, 1938, 1951 and 1961

Age-group	Males			Females		
	1938	1951	1961	1938	1951	1961
8 and under 14 years	19	20	16	1	2	2
14 ,, ,, 17 ,,	15	13	16	1	1	2
17 ,, ,, 21 ,,	13	9	15	2	1	2
21 ,, ,, 30 ,,	18	19	20	2	2	2
30 and over	23	27	20	6	6	5
All ages	88	88	87	12	12	13

Indictable offenders form a small proportion of the total number of offenders found guilty in any one year, but we cannot be certain of the ratio of indictable offences to other offences. The reason is that whilst the criminal statistics provide infor-

[1] See the *Criminal Statistics* for full analyses of age and sex distribution and pattern of offences. Furthermore the Home Office is prepared to make available *Supplementary Statistics* giving even greater detail to persons especially interested in criminal statistics.

mation on indictable offences and to some extent offenders there is no comparable data for non-indictable offences. The available data on non-indictable offences is limited to persons found guilty. It may well be that the number of persons found guilty is equal to the number of non-indictable offences committed, but until information is available on the number of 'offences known' we cannot be certain that there is in fact equality between offences and offenders.

The range of non-indictable offences which it is possible to commit is extremely wide and it has increased appreciably in modern times with the passing of legislation of various kinds. However, by grouping offences it is possible to discern the major changes which have occurred in the pattern of non-indictable offenders in this country. Between 1899 and 1903 the annual average number of persons found guilty in England and Wales was about 730,000; from 1904 to 1913 the number fell to an annual average of about 650,000; from the end of the First World War to 1925 the number fell again to an annual average of about 540,000, and then they rose from 1925 to the outbreak of the Second World War to between 600,000 and 700,000. After the Second World War the numbers decreased appreciably until 1949 and then began to rise slowly, until in 1957 a new peak for the twentieth century was established by the fact that 733,270 persons were found guilty of non-indictable offences. This upward trend continued and in 1961 the number had risen to 970,180 as shown in Tables 56 and 57.

As with indictable offences so, too, for non-indictable offences it is primarily males who are found guilty, but there is perhaps some consolation in the fact that whilst the number of males found guilty of non-indictable offences between 1938 and 1951 fell by about 18 per cent, the number of females fell by only about 12 per cent, and that in relation to the growth of population there was a distinct decline in the proportion of the population as a whole found guilty of non-indictable offences. However, in the decade 1951–61 a new pattern was established and the number of males found guilty of non-indictable offences increased by nearly 70 per cent and females by just over 10 per cent, so that relative to the rate of growth of population there has been a substantial increase in the proportion of males committing offences. Before jumping to conclusions about a remark-

TABLE 56

Persons found guilty of non-indictable offences in England and
Wales, 1938–61, by age and sex

(000's)

Year	Males				Females				Males and females all ages
	Under 17	17–21	21 and over	Total all ages	Under 17	17–21	21 and over	Total all age	
1938 ..	26·3	51·5	570·0	647·7	1·1	3·0	57·1	61·3	709
1946 ..	23·3	27·6	310·6	361·5	1·7	4·1	46·9	52·7	414
1949 ..	23·8	31·3	415·8	470·9	1·4	3·4	47·8	52·6	524
1951 ..	26·9	36·9	467·1	530·9	1·4	3·2	49·0	53·6	585
1961 ..	53·6	126·0	731·1	910·7	2·2	4·5	52·6	59·3	970

able increase in crime we must examine the types of crime for which these greater numbers of persons have been found guilty.

Some significant changes have occurred in the kinds of offences for which persons have been found guilty which reflect to some extent changes in social conditions, for example, at the end of the nineteenth and the beginning of the twentieth centuries the largest single group of non-indictable offences for which persons were found guilty was drunkenness, but by the middle of the twentieth century it has lost its pride of place to traffic offences. Between 1899 and 1903 the annual average number of persons found guilty of drunkenness in England and Wales was 213,083, whereas in 1951 the number was only 51,239 and in 1961 it was 71,614. Doubtless changes in the licensing laws, in the strength and type of alcoholic beverages, in their retail price and in standards of living generally have been contributory factors in this remarkable decrease, and the result is that by now the vast majority of non-indictable offenders are guilty essentially of offences against statutory regulations as shown in Table 57.

Each of these groups of offences includes a variety of forms of illegal actions; many are relatively trivial such as failure to take out dog licences (included in Revenue Offences in Table 57) whilst others such as dangerous driving may be quite as serious as many indictable offences. It is of course traffic offences which account for the remarkable increase between 1951 and 1961 when the number of traffic offenders increased by just over 90 per cent, and of all persons found guilty of non-indictable offences nearly three-quarters committed traffic offences. In view of the extraordinary increase in car-ownership, the congestion on the roads, and the ever-growing parking problems in towns it is hardly surprising that traffic offences now constitute a major activity for the police and traffic wardens, and affect a greater number and proportion of the population than ever before.

More recent changes between 1951 and 1961 in the numbers of persons found guilty of non-indictable offences are due essentially to changes in legislation, for example, the numbers found guilty of betting and gaming offences and of offences of prostitution dropped substantially (see Table 57) as a result of the changes brought about by the Betting and Gaming Act, 1960, and the Street Offences Act, 1957. It is factors of these kinds which make it difficult to measure accurately the changing pattern of crime.

Whether the number of persons found guilty of offences of all kinds can be taken as a measure of the incidence of crime in the community as a whole is by no means certain, and even if it could it would be extremely difficult to discern any clearly defined changes in the pattern of crime. Does the fact that 717,271 persons were found guilty of offences of all kinds (other than offences against Defence Regulations) in 1951 as compared with 787,472 persons in 1938 mean that there was less crime in 1951 than in 1938[1] or that because 1,152,397 persons were found guilty in 1961 as compared with 717,271 in 1951 therefore there has been a substantial increase in crime in that period? Not necessarily, and if comparisons are made with still earlier years it would be extremely dangerous to draw any conclusions at all. Until a great deal more is known about the incidence and pattern of crime in the community it would be unwise to suggest that there has been any marked increase or decrease in modern times.

Another possible guide to a change in the incidence of crime may be provided by comparing the number of persons receiving sentences in penal institutions at different times, but again there

[1] As offences against Defence Regulations are in essence purely technical offences arising out of war-time conditions they have been ignored. In any case the numbers have allen appreciably in recent years, for example, 6,049 persons were found guilty of such offences in 1951 and only 642 in 1954. See the *Criminal Statistics* for details.

TABLE 57

Numbers of persons found guilty of non-indictable offences in England
and Wales, 1938, 1951 and 1961 by type of offence

Offences	Numbers found guilty			Percentage of all persons found guilty of non-indictable offences		
	1938	1951	1961	1938	1951	1961
Traffic offences	475,124	370,912	712,584	67	64	73
Drunkenness	52,661	51,239	71,614	7	9	7
Revenue offences	33,516	29,657	29,286	5	4	3
Railway offences	8,627	19,321	20,757	3	4	2
Breach of local or other regulations	17,877	12,008	9,788		2	1
Disorderly behaviour	17,379	13,255	15,974	6	2	1·5
Betting and gaming	18,504	13,285	4,901		2	0·5
Assaults	10,699	11,847	11,937	2	2	1
Education Act offences	*	8,937	5,280		1	0·5
Malicious damage	9,621	9,374	15,123	2	1	1·5
Offences of prostitution	3,192	7,872	2,259			
Vagrancy Acts offences	6,326	4,998	6,324			
Wireless Telegraphy Acts offences	6,266	2,691	9,516	2	1	2
Cruelty to or neglect of children	932	1,046	772			
Others	48,295	37,013	54,965	7	7	7
Total	709,019	584,454	970,180	100	100	100

* No comparable figure available for 1938.

have been so many changes in methods of punishment that it is difficult to make valid comparisons.[1]

The total annual receptions on conviction into penal institutions in England and Wales fell from about 155,000 in 1900 to just over 40,000 in the mid 1920's, to about 35,000 in 1950 and about 46,000 in 1960, and the daily average population in penal institutions varied from about 17,500 in 1900, to about 11,000 in the mid-1920's and then rose sharply after the Second World War to just over 20,000 in 1950 and to about 27,000 in 1960.[1] Statistics of this kind tell us little about the incidence of crime because persons are sent to prison for non-criminal acts such as failure to comply with orders for payment of money, for example, of the 46,000 receptions on conviction in 1960 about 8,000 were civil prisoners the majority of whom were imprisoned for failure to comply with orders for payment of monies. If length of sentence is any indication of the severity of the crime then only a small proportion of the persons imprisoned in the twentieth century may be said to have committed serious offences. For example, in 1913, 1950 and 1960 the following were the proportions of all prisoners serving varying sentences of imprisonment in England and Wales:

| Length of sentence | Percentage of total receptions on conviction with sentences of imprisonment | | | | | |
| | Males | | | Females | | |
	1913	1950	1960	1913	1950	1960
Not exceeding 5 weeks	78·2	27·4	20·8	87·7	40·2	39·2
Over 5 weeks but not more than 3 months	13·3	24·9	24·8	8·8	29·0	33·6
Over 3 months but not more than 6 months	4·0	18·4	21·4	2·6	17·4	13·9
Over 6 months but not more than 12 months	2·5	14·2	15·4	0·7	7·9	8·1
Over 12 months and not more than 2 years	1·2	9·4	11·4	0·1	4·1	3·5
Over 2 years	0·8	5·7	6·2	0·1	1·4	1·7
	100	100	100	100	100	100

[1] On the penal system of England and Wales see L. W. Fox: *The English Prison and Borstal System* (Routledge, 1952); and Winifred A. Elkin: *The English Penal System* (Penguin Books, 1957).

[2] See the Annual Reports of the Commissioners of Prisons for details of the prison and Borstal populations and particularly the Report for the year 1951 (Cmd. 8692) for an interesting graph of receptions on conviction and daily average population of prisons and Borstals from 1890–1950.

The Changing Patterns of Social Problems

During the past fifty years there have been significant changes in the law relating to imprisonment especially by the Criminal Justice Act, 1948, and above all the system of probation has been very fully developed as a means of dealing with offenders against the law other than by fines or imprisonment.[1] Probation was firmly established in this country by the Probation of Offenders Act, 1907, but it is only since the end of the First World War that the Courts have used probation orders to any great extent, for example, in 1921 the number of offenders placed on probation in England and Wales was 10,293 (7,810 males and 2,483 females) but by 1938 the number had grown to 29,301 (25,252 males and 4,049 females) and in 1951 probation orders were made in respect of 33,941 persons (28,544 males and 5,397 females). In 1961 the number of persons placed on probation had increased to 45,062 of whom 37,971 were males and 7,091 were females. It may well be that had there been no system of probation a large proportion of 'the probationers' would in fact have been sentenced to imprisonment and it is significant that of the persons placed on probation in 1921 no less than 7,478 had committed indictable offences and in succeeding years this pattern was maintained. For example in 1951 and 1961 no less than just over 30,000 and nearly 40,000 respectively of persons placed on probation had committed indictable offences.

At best the prison and probation statistics are a pointer to the incidence of crime and not a good measuring-rod, and in view of all the changes which have occurred in the attitudes towards and the treatment of offenders it would be unwise to make comparisons over time from such information as is available. There is, however, one aspect of crime which has aroused considerable discussion and been the subject of extensive research in modern times and that of course relates to the incidence of crime among juveniles.

It is customary in the middle of the twentieth century to regard juvenile delinquency as being distinct from adult crime and this separation of the youthful from the adult offender is indicative of a considerable change in the attitude of society

[1] For an interesting survey of the methods of probation see *Probation and Related Measures* (1951) and *Practical Results and Financial Aspects of Adult Probation in Selected Countries* (1954) published by the United Nations Department of Social Affairs.

towards the young offender. This changed attitude dates from the middle of the nineteenth century when, for example, the subject of juvenile crime was a topic of discussion by such bodies as the National Association for the Promotion of Social Science,[1] and the State recognized the need for distinctive treatment of juvenile offenders by the provision of Industrial and Reformatory Schools. It was not, however, until the twentieth century that more extensive provisions were made by, for example, the establishment of Borstals and by special legislation such as the Children Act, 1908, and the Children and Young Persons Act, 1933. At the same time the scientific study of juvenile delinquency was being advanced by among others William Heeley, Augusta Bronner and S. and E. Glueck in America and Cyril Burt in England, with the result that after the end of the Second World War there was a revolution in our thinking about the causes and patterns of juvenile crime and certainly there has been a great increase in the published information on juvenile delinquency. Yet there are still enormous difficulties involved in measuring the change in the incidence of juvenile delinquency over time though it is possible to see broad trends.[2]

We have seen already that since 1938 young persons aged 8 and under 17 constitute a significant proportion of all persons found guilty of indictable and non-indictable offences,[3] and it is this fact which has given rise to the alarm which has been publicly expressed about juvenile delinquency in modern times.[4] Yet this is no few feature of our social structure. From the end of the First World War to the outbreak of the Second, there was certainly a steady increase in the number of persons (mainly

[1] The National Association for the Promotion of Social Science was founded in 1857 and met annually in succeeding years. See an interesting comment on its formation in the *Manchester Guardian* of 29th August, 1857.

[2] For a good account of the difficulties see A. Carr-Saunders, H. Mannheim and E. C. Rhodes: *Young Offenders* (Cambridge University Press, 1942). For an interesting analysis of the effect of war-time conditions on juvenile delinquency see *Delinquent Generations*, Home Office Research Unit Report, published by H.M.S.O. 1960.

[3] See Tables 55 and 56 above.

[4] For a good account of the changes in the pattern of, the growth of interest in and the measures taken to deal with the increase in juvenile delinquency since 1938 see *The Sixth Report on the Work of the Children's Department of the Home Office*, H.M.S.O., May 1951, and the *Report on the Work of the Children's Department 1961–3*, published by the Home Office jn 1964.

males) under the age of 17 found guilty of indictable offences,[1] but it is the increase since 1938 which has caused so much alarm and despondency. The absolute increase is shown in Table 58, and the significant feature is the marked rise in the number of boys and girls under the age of 14 found guilty of indictable offences. As a proportion of all persons found guilty of indictable offences young persons under 17 years of age accounted for 37 per cent in 1938, 36 per cent in 1951, and 35 per cent in 1961 so that though the absolute numbers have increased markedly the proportion has in fact fallen, but, of all boys and girls in the age-groups 8–14 and 14–17, the proportion found guilty of indictable offences has obviously increased substantially. Of every 100,000 boys and girls in England and Wales in each age-group the numbers found guilty of indictable offences in 1938, 1951 and 1961 were as shown in Table 59.

TABLE 58

Number of young persons found guilty of indictable offences in England and Wales – All Courts – 1938, 1948, 1951, and 1961

Age	Boys		Girls		Total
	8–14	14–17	8–14	14–17	
1938 ..	14,724	11,645	835	912	28,116
1948 ..	24,684	15,980	2,043	1,727	44,434
1951 ..	26,561	17,274	2,017	1,621	47,473
1961 ..	29,890	28,244	2,845	3,305	64,284

TABLE 59

Number found guilty per 100,000 by sex and age-group

	Age 8–14		Age 14–17	
	Boys	Girls	Boys	Girls
1938 ..	798	46	1,131	90
1951 ..	1,503	119	2,044	195
1961 ..	1,425	142	2,535	310

[1] See Cart-Saunders and Caradog Jones: *Survey of the Social Structure of England and Wales*, Chapter 18, for the position up to 1937.

The Changing Patterns of Social Problems

The fact that, in 1961, one out of about every forty boys aged 14–17 in England and Wales was found guilty of an indictable offence as compared with one out of about every 100 in 1938 clearly cannot be ignored, but hasty conclusions should not be drawn about what appears to be a dramatic increase in lawlessness among the youths of this country. It may well be that the intense public interest in 'juvenile delinquency' during and after the Second World War was in part responsible for more sustained efforts to detect and prosecute young offenders who in earlier years might have been subject to no more than a serious talking-to by the local constable and would not therefore have been shown in the criminal statistics.[1] It is by no means safe to draw too many conclusions from the figures alone and certainly unwise to make comparisons from one period to another. At least it may be said with certainty that more young persons were prosecuted and found guilty in 1961 than in earlier years, but that does not necessarily mean that there were more offenders.

The number of juveniles found guilty of non-indictable offences remained relatively stable until 1956, for example, in 1938 the number of persons under 17 years of age found guilty of non-indictable offences in England and Wales was 27,395, in 1948 it was 27,435, in 1951 the number had increased slightly to 28,331, and in 1956 to 28,909. From 1957 however the numbers increased substantially and by 1961 there were 55,914 young persons under 17 years of age found guilty of non-indictable offences. The offences for which they were found guilty in 1938, 1951 and 1961 were as follows:

---

[1] As examples of the public interest shown in juvenile delinquency note a conference at the Home Office in 1941 to consider the problems of juvenile delinquency in war-time; June 1941, a memorandum issued by the Secretary of State and the President of the Board of Education entitled *Juvenile Offences*; November 1948, a debate in the House of Lords on juvenile delinquency; March, 1949, a central conference in Westminster called by the Secretary of State and the Minister of Education to discuss measures for dealing with juvenile delinquency; in addition there were innumerable articles, reports and books on the subject and finally there were conferences to discuss possible lines of research into the causation and prevention of juvenile delinquency. See the *Sixth Report of the Children's Department of the Home Office*, for good summaries of the interest shown during the years 1941–51. Since 1951 there has been continuing interest and in 1963 the Government appointed an advisory committee on Juvenile Delinquency, see the *Report on the Work of the Children's Department 1961–1963*.

The Changing Patterns of Social Problems

The non-indictable offences for which persons under 17 were found guilty in England and Wales in 1938, 1951 and 1961

Offences	Numbers found Guilty		
	1938	1951	1961
Traffic offences:			
Obstruction and nuisance other than by vehicles	1,672	2,202	2,235
Offences with pedal cycles	8,927	7,218	8,600
Other traffic offences	1,473	1,601	19,305
Malicious damage	5,515	5,750	7,121
Railway offences	2,611	4,736	6,076
Stealing and receiving	1,062	1,751	745
Playing games in street	1,306	726	131
Gaming..	809	317	6
Others	4,020	4,030	11,695
	27,395	28,331	55,914

If indictable and non-indictable offences are taken together then in 1938, 1951 and 1961 the number of young persons under 17 years of age found guilty was approximately 55,000, 75,000 and 120,000 respectively so that of all persons found guilty of offences in England and Wales, young persons accounted for about 7 per cent in 1938, 10 per cent in 1951 and 1961 of all offenders found guilty, and of all young persons under 17 years of age just under 1 per cent in 1938 and just under 2 per cent in 1961 were guilty of some act of lawlessness.

It could be argued that the picture is by no means as sombre as that shown by the criminal statistics because of all boys and girls aged over 8 and under 17 years of age, about 99 in 1938 and about 98 in 1961 out of every 100 were not found guilty of offences of any kind. Indeed in the population as a whole aged 8 and over only 2 per cent in 1938 and just over 2½ per cent in 1961 were gound guilty of offences. If therefore the criminal statistics are regarded as a guide to criminality then clearly the vast majority of the citizens of England and Wales are law-abiding, but recent researches have shown that the volume of undetected crime is considerable and it may well be that the incidence of crime is very much greater than the imperfect data available (even in the middle of the twentieth century) would lead us to expect.

Despite the inadequate knowledge which still exists concerning the incidence and patterns of ill-health and crime in the community and the insuperable difficulties which prevent comparisons over time it would probably be fair to assume that during the last quarter of the nineteenth and the first half of the twentieth centuries, considerable changes have occurred in both these features of our social structure. Whether we are healthier in mind and body and less prone to commit offences than our forefathers cannot easily be determined, though it could be argued that with all the advances in medical science, with improvements in the physical conditions of the majority of the population, and the myriad services available to us today we ought to be considerably healthier and have less need to commit offences than our Victorian forebears. The fact is, however, that there are still dark areas of ignorance about the causes and incidence of ill-health and crime in our society, and until a great deal more is known than we know now it would be unwise to suggest that physical and mental ill-health and criminal behaviour are of greater or less significance in our social structure than they were in the past.

CONCLUSION

I N the relatively short period of history covered by this study the social structure of England and Wales has undergone changes of a kind which even the most Utopian of writers in the middle of the nineteenth century would not have dared to predict. We cannot, convenient though it would be, demarcate set periods within which changes of a specific kind occurred and indeed it is often difficult even to mark the beginning of a particular process of change. Men, in developed societies, continually modify the resources which nature provides in order to vary their way of life and institutions are devised or adapted to bring about social change, and in the years since 1870 the rate and manner of change has been particularly rapid and complex.

The conventional historical approach of dealing with 'periods' of history in terms of the duration of the reign of a King or Queen or some other arbitrary allocation of years cannot easily be applied to modern England and Wales.[1] It has been said, for example, that the death of Queen Victoria 'marked the close not only of a reign but of an epoch',[2] 'revolutions' in political, economic and social conditions thought to be 'epoch-making' during that reign are by now looked upon as relatively unimportant or are still in the process of fulfilment. There is undoubtedly a great deal of truth in the view expressed by G. M. Trevelyan in his *English Social History* that 'In everything the old overlaps the new – in religion, in thought, in family custom. There is never any clear cut; there is no single moment when all Englishmen adopt new ways of life and thought.' How then should we look at the years since 1870 to determine what patterns

[1] See G. M. Trevelyan *English Social History* for a good discussion of the problems of dividing up periods of social history.

[2] Quoted in *Social Policy* by T. H. Marshall, Hutchinson, 1965. This is an extremely interesting study of the growth and development of social policy from the end of the nineteenth century to the early 1960's.

of change have affected significantly the social structure of England and Wales?

In the earlier chapters of this book an attempt has been made to trace the development of those aspects of social life associated with the composition, distribution and divisions of the population in a chronological sequence, but not in such a way as to suggest a beginning and an end. The period 1871–1961 is in some ways irrelevant, what is important is that we should be able to identify and analyse the factors producing or contributing to change in the context of the past and the present so that we may be able to predict for the future. Obviously it is convenient, and in many ways inevitable, for a period of time to be used, but this must not be taken as a restrictive frame of reference, it is only a convenient method of channelling one's thoughts and encompassing the area studied. In human affairs continuity is fundamental, generation succeeds generation not at one point in time but continuously; the customs, traditions and the whole cultural heritage of a society are handed down from one generation to another in a continuous process, therefore any particular facets of social change identified in a given period of time must always be looked at in the context of continuity.[1]

Continuity is not necessarily synonymous with consistency. Thus one of the outstanding features of change in the late nineteenth century was that the consistent pattern of rapid increase in population growth which had persisted for at least a century was not maintained. Nevertheless the process of continuous growth was maintained, though of course at a slower rate. However, it is when changes within the continuous pattern are examined in isolation and not within the context of the continuous process that problems arise for predicting future patterns. If, for example, the rate of population growth in England and Wales in, say, the years 1871–1901 was examined in detail without reference to earlier years then the prediction as to future rates of growth would be based on very insecure foundations. Equally if the trends from, say, 1901 to 1931 were to be used for predicting the total population in later years then what in fact happened was quite different from what many people predicted.

[1] For an introduction to the study of social change see Wilbert E. Moore *Social Change*, Prentice-Hall, 1963.

Indeed even as late as 1946 many experts were predicting that the population would be smaller in 1951 than it was twenty years earlier. For example, Cole and Postgate in their revised version of *The Common People, 1746–1946*, argued that 'there were few things more certain in 1946 than that in a short time the population of Great Britain would become static, and thereafter would, for some time at least, decline. . . . It was almost certain that by 1951 the population would be something like two million less than it was twenty years before'. In fact there were just over 4 million more people in Britain in 1951 than there were in 1931! Why were the predictions in the 1930's about the future size of population so very wide of the mark?

In part because the analytical tools necessary for the measurement of population were not sufficiently refined, but there is of course always an element of chance in population forecasting. Indeed even over relatively short periods of time dramatic changes may occur in the desires of married couples to have more or fewer children, in mortality at all ages, and in the balance of migration each of which could upset the most systematically calculated predictions of demographers. In the last quarter of the nineteenth century the trend towards a slowing down in the rate of population growth was firmly established, by the 1930's the fact of a radical decrease in the rate of growth was plain for all to see, but by the late 1950's we see a reversal of the trend. How far are we justified in predicting that in the second half of the twentieth century the tendency to increase the rate of growth will be maintained or perhaps even accelerated?

We have become accustomed to the idea that we are, in the 1960's, witnessing a 'population explosion' in the world as a whole, and within our own country fears are being expressed that our population is growing too rapidly to be properly accommodated in our already overcrowded towns. We have now reached the stage where we are attempting to slow down the rate of growth by controlling immigration, yet with all our more elaborate sources of demographic data than in the past and refinements in statistical techniques of measurement we are not in a position to make positive predictions for the future. Undoubtedly our predictions ought to be less inaccurate than those made in the thirties, but there are so many factors involved

Conclusion

in accelerating or diminishing the rate of growth which cannot easily be measured accurately.

What effects, for example, are the advances which have been made in the production and effectiveness of new techniques of contraception going to have on the birth-rate? If 'the pill' or some other relatively simple method of contraception became universally acceptable will the number of babies born radically decline in the future? What are likely to be the consequences of changes in economic and social conditions on the number of children which women will want to bear? Will the spread of higher education and the emancipation of women have any noticeable effect on the number of women who marry and on the number of children they would like to have? No positive answers can be given but at least we can analyse some of the factors which seem to have operated in the past and make an assessment to the extent to which they may again play a part.

There can be no doubt that in the latter part of the nineteenth century industrialization and urbanization contributed substantially to the changing pattern of population growth. The exact manner in which industrialization and technological advance affected the desire of married couples to have fewer children cannot easily be determined, but there is at least strong circumstantial evidence which lends support to the view that as a society becomes more highly industrialized and urbanized so its rate of population growth decreases.[1]

By the end of the nineteenth century the process of industrialization, which had of course been going on for centuries, had made us not only 'a nation of shopkeepers' (as had been said of us at the beginning of the century) but also 'the workshop of the world'. We had become a highly industrialized society and surely it is more than a coincidence that our pattern of population growth was to exhibit changes just as marked as those occurring in the economic system. Our experience is paralleled by other societies in Europe and North America which showed a slowing down in the rate of population growth as they became industrialized, but even so the precise relationship between

[1] For interesting discussions of 'The impact of Technological Change on Demographic patterns' and 'Industrialization and Family Change' see *Industrialization and Society* edited by Bert F. Hoselitz and Wilbert E. Moore, UNESCO, 1963.

industrialization and population growth has not yet been firmly established.

The difficulties involved in establishing the precise relationship are very great, though not insuperable.[1] As more systematic studies are made on a comparative basis between societies so may we be in a position to establish causal relationships between changes in the economic system and demographic patterns. It will be especially valuable to study the changes as they occur in the 'developing countries' which have by now obtained political independence and are desperately attempting to achieve economic standards of the kind attained by most European and North American countries at the turn of the century.

One of the most difficult problems in unravelling cause and effect is that the changes in the economic system were in our own case accompanied by 'social revolutions' which in part sprang out of and in part contributed to economic progress. For example, the growth and development of a national system of education produced a literate population whose attitudes towards family size are presumably very different from those of an illiterate population. It is surely fair to assume that the spread of education has contributed substantially to the acceptance of the idea and the practice of planned parenthood, and of course to a range of values about family relationships, aspirations for standards of living and so on very different from those of our illiterate ancestors. The chain reaction effects of education on the economic system, of economic development on the education system, of both on family relationships and the functions of the family, on the nature and structure of society and on the development of social policy are not easy to disentangle. Education was of course not the only aspect of social life to be changed in the years from 1870, our whole system of public control through the system of government was to be dramatically altered and a whole host of new concepts concerning the rights of the individual and of the relationship of the individual to society were to be developed.[2]

[1] See Hoselitz and Moore op. cit. on the ways in which experimental methods could be applied to establishing the relationship. On the problems of making scientific studies in the 'developing countries' which are attempting to become industrialized see the Appendices to their report.

[2] See T. H. Marshall *Social Policy* and *An introduction to the study of Social Administration* ed. David C. Marsh, Routledge and Kegan Paul, 1965.

Conclusion

It used to be thought that the years from 1870 to the outbreak of the First World War in 1914 were 'years of transition', in which we moved from the relatively static conditions of earlier centuries to a dynamic phase of rapid change in social and economic conditions. Undoubtedly this was a period of dynamism economically and politically and it was, too, a period of acute questioning about the nature of society and perhaps even more significantly of revelation. The revelation that despite the rapid progress made in making ours one of the richest countries in the world there was nevertheless a great deal of poverty in the midst of plenty. The first decade of the twentieth century was to witness the first real attempts made by governmental action to remedy the evils of poverty which were to lead to the concept of the Welfare State and to the transformation of our society in ways which could not have been even imagined in the nineteenth century.

The years from the First to the Second World War were marked by economic depression of a kind unknown in the past and by a relatively slow rate of change in social conditions, and of course by a serious decline in the rate of population growth. Nevertheless the processes of change continued and we were to see especially a revolution in the growth of knowledge particularly in the fields of natural and physical science.

The Second World War was to have an impact on our ideas about the nature of society and of social relationships of a kind which only the most far sighted of social reformers could have envisaged even as late as the 1930's. Despite the fact that the war imposed crushing burdens upon our economic system and that we paid a heavy price for victory we were to move in the post-war years into an era of Welfare policies and economic innovations of a radically different pattern of those of the past. We were to enter upon what many people believed to be the third industrial revolution, the first had been based on steam, the second on electrical power and the third was to utilize and harness atomic energy, and we were to become accustomed to material standards of living of such a high order as to justify the use of the label 'The affluent society'. An affluent society protected by the Welfare State. Whether these descriptive labels accurately describe the Britain of the 1960's is open to question,[1]

[1] See for example *The Future of the Welfare State*, David C. Marsh, Penguin Books, 1964.

267

nevertheless they are indicative of the changes which have occurred in our social and economic systems and in our patterns of living.

There are by now positive measurable indicators of the changes which have occurred in modern times. We have a wealth of data on the population, its size, and age and sex structure; on occupational patterns; on education; on economic conditions; on membership of associations and the like which when examined over time enable us to assess the degree of change. But all too often we cannot easily establish causal relationships or even associational effects, and there are still many aspects of the social structure about which we are woefully ignorant. However, there are encouraging signs of a marked resurgence of interest in the analysis of society and its problems. Indeed in the 1950's 'the social sciences' became firmly established as disciplines of study and social research began to be undertaken on a greater scale than ever before.[1] Yet by the early 1960's it had become apparent that far more research was necessary if we were to understand the complex nature of our society and attempt to solve the myriad varieties of economic and social problems.

In June 1963 the Government set up a Committee, under the Chairmanship of Lord Heyworth, 'to review the research at present being done in the field of social studies in Government departments, universities and other institutions and to advise whether changes are needed in the arrangements for supporting and co-ordinating this research'. The 'Report of the Committee on Social Studies' (Cmnd 2660) was published in June 1965 and recommends the establishment of a Social Science Research Council and the expenditure of greatly increased Government funds to stimulate and support social research.

If these recommendations are implemented and if research on a scale greater than ever before is carried out then many of the areas of ignorance which now abound may be removed. We may then be in a better position than we are now to evaluate the changes which have occurred and are taking place continuously in the social structure of England and Wales, and, perhaps, we

---

[1] For a brief account of the subject matter of the social sciences and their development as disciplines of study see *The Social Sciences, an outline for the intending student*, ed. David C. Marsh, Routledge and Kegan Paul, 1965.

may be able more successfully to predict the kinds of changes likely to occur in the future. We may, too, be in a better position to decide whether our society is better or worse now than it was in the past, and whether as individuals we are fundamentally different from our ancestors.

INDEX

Abrams, M., 205
Age, distribution, 22–26
  groups, balance of, 25–28
Agriculture – *see* Occupations
Areas, administrative, 64–65
  geographical, 65
Associations – *see* Employers,
  Trade Unions, Religious

Barlow, Report, 111
Besant, Annie, 17, 47
Beveridge Report, 26
Birth control, 35, 46
  rates, 8, 63
Births, illegitimate, 8–9, 63
Booth, Charles, 196
Bradlaugh, Charles, 17, 47
Butler, D. E., 180 n., 191

Carr-Saunders, A., 146 n., 187 n,
  202 n., 208, 209 n., 218
Census, the, 5–6, 33, 38, 41, 47–
  49, 52, 65, 88, 95, 100, 107,
  112, 116, 154, 163, 165,
  196–8, 201, 220, 230
Cole, G. D. H., 171 n., 178 n.,
  196 n., 198 n., 264
Communist party, 183
Conservative party, 179–81
Conurbation, definition of, 102
  population changes in, 101–5
Co-operative societies, 175–8
Counties, areas of, 76–77, 82
  administrative, 76
  population changes in, 76–101
County Boroughs, 76
Crime, definition of, 238
  measurement and incidence of
  239–60

Criminal Statistics, 239 et seq
Crowther Report, 207

Death rates, 9–10, 237
Deaths, causes of, 227–9
  numbers of, 10–11, 227–9
Delinquency – *see* Juvenile
Development areas, 84
Disabled Persons (Employment)
  Act, 230
  numbers of, 232
Divorce, 32–33, 36–38
  Royal Commission on – *see*
  Marriage
Divorced persons, age of, 37
  numbers of, 34, 36

Education Acts, 128, 207, 208
  Central Advisory Council for,
  207, 212
  Numbers attending educa-
  tional establishments, 207
  et seq.
  terminal age of, 220
Educational opportunities, 210
Elections, results of, 182
Employers' associations, 172–5
Employment status, 162–3
Expectation of life, 28–29

Family – Census 41
  functions of, 55
  limitation, 16, 46–47
  size, 41–45
Fertility census, 1911, 41
  definition of, 11
Finer, H., 179 n., 181 n.

271

Friendly Societies, Chief Registrar of, 168, 179
membership of, 183–4

Glass, D. V., 16 n., 196 n., 201 n

Highet, J., 188
Households, composite, 49, 51
primary family unit, 48, 51–52
private, 47–50, 52–53
size of, 48–54

Ill-health, definition of, 227
incidence of, 230–38
Immigration Act 1962, 14
Imprisonment, numbers of prisoners, 255–6
Industrial, classification, 112–14
distribution 111 et seq.
population, Royal Commission on the Distribution of (Barlow Report),111
status, 151–162
Industry, Distribution of Industry Act, 84
Infant mortality, 10, 63
Infectious diseases, 231

Jones, D. C. – see Carr-Saunders
Juvenile delinquency, 256–60

Labour party, 178, 179, 180, 183
Liberal party, 179, 180, 181
Local Government Acts, 64, 76, 107
Authorities, 76, 107
Boundaries, 76, 107

Malthus, Rev. T. R. 16, 47
Marital distribution, 32–35, 63
status, 32
Market research surveys 203–206

Marriage, Age of, 35
Age of Marriage Act, 32
Breakdown, 37
Restrictions on, 32
Royal Commission on Marriage and Divorce, 36–37
Marriages, numbers of, 35
Marshall, T. H., 196 n., 262 n., 266 n.
McKenzie, R. T., 179 n., 180 n., 181
Mentally ill – see Ill-health
Migration, balance of, 7, 12–14
Monopoly and Restrictive Practices Commission, 173

National Assistance Act, 55, 230
Insurance, 152, 225, 233
Nationalised industries, 174
Natural increase, 7, 11, 14
Newsom Report, 207
Northcote – Trevelyan report, 121

Occupational distribution, 112 et seq.
Occupations, classification of, 112, 116–19, 130–2 197
numbers engaged in, 118 et seq.
Offences, classification and measurement of, 238–260
indictable, definition of, 239
range of, 240
summary, definition of, 239
Old Age Pensions Acts, 23
Old People, 23, 26–28

Parkinsons Law, 140
Paul, Leslie, 191
Pensions, old age, 23
widows', 23
Phillips Committee, 27, 29
Political parties, 179–83

Poor Law, 55
Population census, see Census
    county born, 88–95
    density, 12, 64, 69
    growth, 5 et seq.
    industrial – see Industrial
    occupied – see Occupations
    Royal Commission on, 6, 17, 41–43, 31 n., 46, 56–57
    Rural, 105–10
    Urban, 105–10
Probation, 256
Professions, 121, 138–41
Psephology, 183 n.

Readership Surveys, 203–5
Registrar-General, 3, 35 n., 37, 187
Religious associations, membership of, 186–92
    Buildings, 188
Retirement, patterns of, 133
    ages, 23
Robbins Report, 216–19
Rowntree, Seebohm, 53 n., 143, 190 n.
Rural – see Population

Schools – see Education
School leavers, destination of, 212–16
Servants, domestic, 54, 125–6
Sex distribution, 19–22, 60–63
    ratios, 19–22, 60–63
Sickness survey, 235–7

Social class, 50, 195–8
    change, 263
    problems, definition of, 226
    science, 268
    „ National Association for the promotion of, 257
    „ Research Council, 268
    services, voluntary, 193
    structure, definition of, 1
Survey Unit, 235
    surveys, 196
Socio-economic groups, 199–203

Town, definition of, 66
    Populations and densities, 66–76
    New Towns Act, 74–75
Trade Union Acts, 166, 179
    definition of, 167
    membership, 167–72
Trades Union Congress, 170

Unemployment, 224
    Insurance, 229
Universities, 216
    numbers of students in, 218
Urban – see Population

Welfare State, 223, 267
Widowhood – incidence of, 38
Women, married, employment of, 128–9, 134, 155
    married, with gainful occupations, 128, 134, 155
    numbers of in occupations, 128–9, 144–7, 159–61

Routledge Social Science Series

Routledge & Kegan Paul   London, Henley and Boston

39 Store Street, London WC1E 7DD
Broadway House, Newtown Road, Henley-on-Thames,
Oxon RG9 1EN
9 Park Street, Boston, Mass. 02108

Contents

International Library of Sociology 3
General Sociology 3
Foreign Classics of Sociology 4
Social Structure 4
Sociology and Politics 5
Criminology 5
Social Psychology 6
Sociology of the Family 6
Social Services 7
Sociology of Education 8
Sociology of Culture 8
Sociology of Religion 9
Sociology of Art and Literature 9
Sociology of Knowledge 9
Urban Sociology 10
Rural Sociology 10
Sociology of Industry and Distribution 10
Anthropology 11
Sociology and Philosophy 12
International Library of Anthropology 12
International Library of Social Policy 13
International Library of Welfare and Philosophy 13
Primary Socialization, Language and Education 14
Reports of the Institute of Community Studies 14
Reports of the Institute for Social Studies in Medical Care 15
Medicine, Illness and Society 15
Monographs in Social Theory 15
Routledge Social Science Journals 16
Social and Psychological Aspects of Medical Practice 16

*Authors wishing to submit manuscripts for any series in
this catalogue should send them to the Social Science Editor,
Routledge & Kegan Paul Ltd, 39 Store Street,
London WC1E 7DD*

●*Books so marked are available in paperback
All books are in Metric Demy 8vo format (216 × 138mm approx.)*

International Library of Sociology

General Editor John Rex

GENERAL SOCIOLOGY

Barnsley, J. H. The Social Reality of Ethics. *464 pp.*
Belshaw, Cyril. The Conditions of Social Performance. *An Exploratory Theory. 144 pp.*
Brown, Robert. Explanation in Social Science. *208 pp.*
● Rules and Laws in Sociology. *192 pp.*
Bruford, W. H. Chekhov and His Russia. *A Sociological Study. 244 pp.*
Cain, Maureen E. Society and the Policeman's Role. *326 pp.*
●**Fletcher, Colin.** Beneath the Surface. *An Account of Three Styles of Sociological Research. 221 pp.*
Gibson, Quentin. The Logic of Social Enquiry. *240 pp.*
Glucksmann, M. Structuralist Analysis in Contemporary Social Thought. *212 pp.*
Gurvitch, Georges. Sociology of Law. *Preface by Roscoe Pound. 264 pp.*
Hodge, H. A. Wilhelm Dilthey. *An Introduction. 184 pp.*
Homans, George C. Sentiments and Activities. *336 pp.*
Johnson, Harry M. Sociology: *a Systematic Introduction. Foreword by Robert K. Merton. 710 pp.*
●**Keat, Russell, and Urry, John.** Social Theory as Science. *278 pp.*
Mannheim, Karl. Essays on Sociology and Social Psychology. *Edited by Paul Keckskemeti. With Editorial Note by Adolph Lowe. 344 pp.*
Systematic Sociology: *An Introduction to the Study of Society. Edited by J. S. Erös and Professor W. A. C. Stewart. 220 pp.*
Martindale, Don. The Nature and Types of Sociological Theory. *292 pp.*
●**Maus, Heinz.** A Short History of Sociology. *234 pp.*
Mey, Harald. Field-Theory. *A Study of its Application in the Social Sciences. 352 pp.*
Myrdal, Gunnar. Value in Social Theory: *A Collection of Essays on Methodology. Edited by Paul Streeten. 332 pp.*
Ogburn, William F., and Nimkoff, Meyer F. A Handbook of Sociology. *Preface by Karl Mannheim. 656 pp. 46 figures. 35 tables.*
Parsons, Talcott, and Smelser, Neil J. Economy and Society: *A Study in the Integration of Economic and Social Theory. 362 pp.*
Podgórecki, Adam. Practical Social Sciences. *About 200 pp.*
●**Rex, John.** Key Problems of Sociological Theory. *220 pp.*
Sociology and the Demystification of the Modern World. *282 pp.*
●**Rex, John** (Ed.) Approaches to Sociology. *Contributions by Peter Abell, Frank Bechhofer, Basil Bernstein, Ronald Fletcher, David Frisby, Miriam Glucksmann, Peter Lassman, Herminio Martins, John Rex, Roland Robertson, John Westergaard and Jock Young. 302 pp.*
Rigby, A. Alternative Realities. *352 pp.*
Roche, M. Phenomenology, Language and the Social Sciences. *374 pp.*

Sahay, A. Sociological Analysis. *220 pp.*
Simirenko, Alex (Ed.) Soviet Sociology. *Historical Antecedents and Current Appraisals. Introduction by Alex Simirenko. 376 pp.*
Strasser, Hermann. The Normative Structure of Sociology. *Conservative and Emancipatory Themes in Social Thought. About 340 pp.*
Urry, John. Reference Groups and the Theory of Revolution. *244 pp.*
Weinberg, E. Development of Sociology in the Soviet Union. *173 pp.*

FOREIGN CLASSICS OF SOCIOLOGY

●**Durkheim, Emile.** Suicide. *A Study in Sociology. Edited and with an Introduction by George Simpson. 404 pp.*
●**Gerth, H. H.,** and **Mills, C. Wright.** From Max Weber: *Essays in Sociology. 502 pp.*
●**Tönnies, Ferdinand.** Community and Association. (*Gemeinschaft und Gesellschaft.) Translated and Supplemented by Charles P. Loomis. Foreword by Pitirim A. Sorokin. 334 pp.*

SOCIAL STRUCTURE

Andreski, Stanislav. Military Organization and Society. *Foreword by Professor A. R. Radcliffe-Brown. 226 pp. 1 folder.*
Carlton, Eric. Ideology and Social Order. *Preface by Professor Philip Abrahams. About 320 pp.*
Coontz, Sydney H. Population Theories and the Economic Interpretation. *202 pp.*
Coser, Lewis. The Functions of Social Conflict. *204 pp.*
Dickie-Clark, H. F. Marginal Situation: *A Sociological Study of a Coloured Group. 240 pp. 11 tables.*
Glaser, Barney, and **Strauss, Anselm L.** Status Passage. *A Formal Theory. 208 pp.*
Glass, D. V. (Ed.) Social Mobility in Britain. *Contributions by J. Berent, T. Bottomore, R. C. Chambers, J. Floud, D. V. Glass, J. R. Hall, H. T. Himmelweit, R. K. Kelsall, F. M. Martin, C. A. Moser, R. Mukherjee, and W. Ziegel. 420 pp.*
Johnstone, Frederick A. Class, Race and Gold. *A Study of Class Relations and Racial Discrimination in South Africa. 312 pp.*
Jones, Garth N. Planned Organizational Change: *An Exploratory Study Using an Empirical Approach. 268 pp.*
Kelsall, R. K. Higher Civil Servants in Britain: *From 1870 to the Present Day. 268 pp. 31 tables.*
König, René. The Community. *232 pp. Illustrated.*
●**Lawton, Denis.** Social Class, Language and Education. *192 pp.*
McLeish, John. The Theory of Social Change: *Four Views Considered. 128 pp.*
Marsh, David C. The Changing Social Structure of England and Wales, 1871-1961. *288 pp.*
Menzies, Ken. Talcott Parsons and the Social Image of Man. *About 208 pp.*

●**Mouzelis, Nicos.** Organization and Bureaucracy. *An Analysis of Modern Theories. 240 pp.*

Mulkay, M. J. Functionalism, Exchange and Theoretical Strategy. *272 pp.*

Ossowski, Stanislaw. Class Structure in the Social Consciousness. *210 pp.*

●**Podgórecki, Adam.** Law and Society. *302 pp.*

Renner, Karl. Institutions of Private Law and Their Social Functions. *Edited, with an Introduction and Notes, by O. Kahn-Freud. Translated by Agnes Schwarzschild. 316 pp.*

SOCIOLOGY AND POLITICS

Acton, T. A. Gypsy Politics and Social Change. *316 pp.*

Clegg, Stuart. Power, Rule and Domination. *A Critical and Empirical Understanding of Power in Sociological Theory and Organisational Life. About 300 pp.*

Hechter, Michael. Internal Colonialism. *The Celtic Fringe in British National Development, 1536–1966. 361 pp.*

Hertz, Frederick. Nationality in History and Politics: *A Psychology and Sociology of National Sentiment and Nationalism. 432 pp.*

Kornhauser, William. The Politics of Mass Society. *272 pp. 20 tables.*

●**Kroes, R.** Soldiers and Students. *A Study of Right- and Left-wing Students. 174 pp.*

Laidler, Harry W. History of Socialism. *Social-Economic Movements: An Historical and Comparative Survey of Socialism, Communism, Co-operation, Utopianism; and other Systems of Reform and Reconstruction. 992 pp.*

Lasswell, H. D. Analysis of Political Behaviour. *324 pp.*

Martin, David A. Pacifism: *an Historical and Sociological Study. 262 pp.*

Martin, Roderick. Sociology of Power. *About 272 pp.*

Myrdal, Gunnar. The Political Element in the Development of Economic Theory. *Translated from the German by Paul Streeten. 282 pp.*

Wilson, H. T. The American Ideology. *Science, Technology and Organization of Modes of Rationality. About 280 pp.*

Wootton, Graham. Workers, Unions and the State. *188 pp.*

CRIMINOLOGY

Ancel, Marc. Social Defence: *A Modern Approach to Criminal Problems. Foreword by Leon Radzinowicz. 240 pp.*

Cain, Maureen E. Society and the Policeman's Role. *326 pp.*

Cloward, Richard A., and **Ohlin, Lloyd E.** Delinquency and Opportunity: *A Theory of Delinquent Gangs. 248 pp.*

Downes, David M. The Delinquent Solution. *A Study in Subcultural Theory. 296 pp.*

Dunlop, A. B., and **McCabe, S.** Young Men in Detention Centres. *192 pp.*

Friedlander, Kate. The Psycho-Analytical Approach to Juvenile Delinquency: *Theory, Case Studies, Treatment. 320 pp.*

Glueck, Sheldon, and **Eleanor.** Family Environment and Delinquency. *With the statistical assistance of Rose W. Kneznek. 340 pp.*

Lopez-Rey, Manuel. Crime. *An Analytical Appraisal. 288 pp.*
Mannheim, Hermann. Comparative Criminology: *a Text Book. Two volumes. 442 pp. and 380 pp.*
Morris, Terence. The Criminal Area: *A Study in Social Ecology. Foreword by Hermann Mannheim. 232 pp. 25 tables. 4 maps.*
Rock, Paul. Making People Pay. *338 pp.*
●Taylor, Ian, Walton, Paul, and Young, Jock. The New Criminology. *For a Social Theory of Deviance. 325 pp.*
●Taylor, Ian, Walton, Paul, and Young, Jock (Eds). Critical Criminology. *268 pp.*

SOCIAL PSYCHOLOGY

Bagley, Christopher. The Social Psychology of the Epileptic Child. *320 pp.*
Barbu, Zevedei. Problems of Historical Psychology. *248 pp.*
Blackburn, Julian. Psychology and the Social Pattern. *184 pp.*
●Brittan, Arthur. Meanings and Situations. *224 pp.*
Carroll, J. Break-Out from the Crystal Palace. *200 pp.*
●Fleming, C. M. Adolescence: Its Social Psychology. *With an Introduction to recent findings from the fields of Anthropology, Physiology, Medicine, Psychometrics and Sociometry. 288 pp.*
● The Social Psychology of Education: *An Introduction and Guide to Its Study. 136 pp.*
●Homans, George C. The Human Group. *Foreword by Bernard DeVoto. Introduction by Robert K. Merton. 526 pp.*
● Social Behaviour: *its Elementary Forms. 416 pp.*
●Klein, Josephine. The Study of Groups. *226 pp. 31 figures. 5 tables.*
Linton, Ralph. The Cultural Background of Personality. *132 pp.*
●Mayo, Elton. The Social Problems of an Industrial Civilization. *With an appendix on the Political Problem. 180 pp.*
Ottaway, A. K. C. Learning Through Group Experience. *176 pp.*
Plummer, Ken. Sexual Stigma. *An Interactionist Account. 254 pp.*
●Rose, Arnold M. (Ed.) Human Behaviour and Social Processes: *an Interactionist Approach. Contributions by Arnold M. Rose, Ralph H. Turner, Anselm Strauss, Everett C. Hughes, E. Franklin Frazier, Howard S. Becker, et al. 696 pp.*
Smelser, Neil J. Theory of Collective Behaviour. *448 pp.*
Stephenson, Geoffrey M. The Development of Conscience. *128 pp.*
Young, Kimball. Handbook of Social Psychology. *658 pp. 16 figures. 10 tables.*

SOCIOLOGY OF THE FAMILY

Banks, J. A. Prosperity and Parenthood: *A Study of Family Planning among The Victorian Middle Classes. 262 pp.*
Bell, Colin R. Middle Class Families: *Social and Geographical Mobility. 224 pp.*

Burton, Lindy. Vulnerable Children. *272 pp.*
Gavron, Hannah. The Captive Wife: *Conflicts of Household Mothers.* *190 pp.*
George, Victor, and **Wilding, Paul.** Motherless Families. *248 pp.*
Klein, Josephine. Samples from English Cultures.
  1. Three Preliminary Studies and Aspects of Adult Life in England. *447 pp.*
  2. Child-Rearing Practices and Index. *247 pp.*
Klein, Viola. The Feminine Character. *History of an Ideology. 244 pp.*
McWhinnie, Alexina M. Adopted Children. *How They Grow Up. 304 pp.*
● **Morgan, D. H. J.** Social Theory and the Family. *About 320 pp.*
● **Myrdal, Alva,** and **Klein, Viola.** Women's Two Roles: *Home and Work.* *238 pp. 27 tables.*
Parsons, Talcott, and **Bales, Robert F.** Family: Socialization and Inter-action Process. *In collaboration with James Olds, Morris Zelditch and Philip E. Slater. 456 pp. 50 figures and tables.*

SOCIAL SERVICES

Bastide, Roger. The Sociology of Mental Disorder. *Translated from the French by Jean McNeil. 260 pp.*
Carlebach, Julius. Caring For Children in Trouble. *266 pp.*
George, Victor. Foster Care. *Theory and Practice. 234 pp.*
  Social Security: *Beveridge and After. 258 pp.*
George, V., and **Wilding, P.** Motherless Families. *248 pp.*
●**Goetschius, George W.** Working with Community Groups. *256 pp.*
Goetschius, George W., and **Tash, Joan.** Working with Unattached Youth. *416 pp.*
Hall, M. P., and **Howes, I. V.** The Church in Social Work. *A Study of Moral Welfare Work undertaken by the Church of England. 320 pp.*
Heywood, Jean S. Children in Care: *the Development of the Service for the Deprived Child. 264 pp.*
Hoenig, J., and **Hamilton, Marian W.** The De-Segregation of the Mentally Ill. *284 pp.*
Jones, Kathleen. Mental Health and Social Policy, 1845-1959. *264 pp.*
King, Roy D., Raynes, Norma V., and **Tizard, Jack.** Patterns of Residential Care. *356 pp.*
Leigh, John. Young People and Leisure. *256 pp.*
●**Mays, John.** (Ed.) Penelope Hall's Social Services of England and Wales. *About 324 pp.*
Morris, Mary. Voluntary Work and the Welfare State. *300 pp.*
Nokes, P. L. The Professional Task in Welfare Practice. *152 pp.*
Timms, Noel. Psychiatric Social Work in Great Britain (1939-1962). *280 pp.*
● Social Casework: *Principles and Practice. 256 pp.*
Young, A. F. Social Services in British Industry. *272 pp.*

SOCIOLOGY OF EDUCATION

Banks, Olive. Parity and Prestige in English Secondary Education: a Study in Educational Sociology. *272 pp.*

Bentwich, Joseph. Education in Israel. *224 pp. 8 pp. plates.*

●**Blyth, W. A. L.** English Primary Education. *A Sociological Description.*
   1. Schools. *232 pp.*
   2. Background. *168 pp.*

Collier, K. G. The Social Purposes of Education: *Personal and Social Values in Education. 268 pp.*

Dale, R. R., and **Griffith, S.** Down Stream: *Failure in the Grammar School. 108 pp.*

Evans, K. M. Sociometry and Education. *158 pp.*

●**Ford, Julienne.** Social Class and the Comprehensive School. *192 pp.*

Foster, P. J. Education and Social Change in Ghana. *336 pp. 3 maps.*

Fraser, W. R. Education and Society in Modern France. *150 pp.*

Grace, Gerald R. Role Conflict and the Teacher. *150 pp.*

Hans, Nicholas. New Trends in Education in the Eighteenth Century. *278 pp. 19 tables.*

● Comparative Education: *A Study of Educational Factors and Traditions. 360 pp.*

●**Hargreaves, David.** Interpersonal Relations and Education. *432 pp.*

● Social Relations in a Secondary School. *240 pp.*

Holmes, Brian. Problems in Education. *A Comparative Approach. 336 pp.*

King, Ronald. Values and Involvement in a Grammar School. *164 pp.*
   School Organization and Pupil Involvement. *A Study of Secondary Schools.*

●**Mannheim, Karl,** and **Stewart, W. A. C.** An Introduction to the Sociology of Education. *206 pp.*

Morris, Raymond N. The Sixth Form and College Entrance. *231 pp.*

●**Musgrove, F.** Youth and the Social Order. *176 pp.*

●**Ottaway, A. K. C.** Education and Society: An Introduction to the Sociology of Education. *With an Introduction by W. O. Lester Smith. 212 pp.*

Peers, Robert. Adult Education: *A Comparative Study. 398 pp.*

Pritchard, D. G. Education and the Handicapped: *1760 to 1960. 258 pp.*

Stratta, Erica. The Education of Borstal Boys. *A Study of their Educational Experiences prior to, and during, Borstal Training. 256 pp.*

Taylor, P. H., Reid, W. A., and **Holley, B. J.** The English Sixth Form. *A Case Study in Curriculum Research. 200 pp.*

SOCIOLOGY OF CULTURE

Eppel, E. M., and **M.** Adolescents and Morality: *A Study of some Moral Values and Dilemmas of Working Adolescents in the Context of a changing Climate of Opinion. Foreword by W. J. H. Sprott. 268 pp. 39 tables.*

●**Fromm, Erich.** The Fear of Freedom. *286 pp.*

● The Sane Society. *400 pp.*

Mannheim, Karl. Essays on the Sociology of Culture. *Edited by Ernst Mannheim in co-operation with Paul Kecskemeti. Editorial Note by Adolph Lowe. 280 pp.*
Weber, Alfred. Farewell to European History: *or The Conquest of Nihilism. Translated from the German by R. F. C. Hull. 224 pp.*

SOCIOLOGY OF RELIGION

Argyle, Michael and **Beit-Hallahmi, Benjamin.** The Social Psychology of Religion. *About 256 pp.*
Glasner, Peter E. The Sociology of Secularisation. *A Critique of a Concept. About 180 pp.*
Nelson, G. K. Spiritualism and Society. *313 pp.*
Stark, Werner. The Sociology of Religion. *A Study of Christendom.*
Volume I. *Established Religion. 248 pp.*
Volume II. *Sectarian Religion. 368 pp.*
Volume III. *The Universal Church. 464 pp.*
Volume IV. *Types of Religious Man. 352 pp.*
Volume V. *Types of Religious Culture. 464 pp.*
Turner, B. S. Weber and Islam. *216 pp.*
Watt, W. Montgomery. Islam and the Integration of Society. *320 pp.*

SOCIOLOGY OF ART AND LITERATURE

Jarvie, Ian C. Towards a Sociology of the Cinema. *A Comparative Essay on the Structure and Functioning of a Major Entertainment Industry. 405 pp.*
Rust, Frances S. Dance in Society. *An Analysis of the Relationships between the Social Dance and Society in England from the Middle Ages to the Present Day. 256 pp. 8 pp. of plates.*
Schücking, L. L. The Sociology of Literary Taste. *112 pp.*
Wolff, Janet. Hermeneutic Philosophy and the Sociology of Art. *150 pp.*

SOCIOLOGY OF KNOWLEDGE

Diesing, P. Patterns of Discovery in the Social Sciences. *262 pp.*
●**Douglas, J. D.** (Ed.) Understanding Everyday Life. *370 pp.*
●**Hamilton, P.** Knowledge and Social Structure. *174 pp.*
Jarvie, I. C. Concepts and Society. *232 pp.*
Mannheim, Karl. Essays on the Sociology of Knowledge. *Edited by Paul Kecskemeti. Editorial Note by Adolph Lowe. 353 pp.*
Remmling, Gunter W. The Sociology cf Karl Mannheim. *With a Bibliographical Guide to the Sociology of Knowledge, Ideological Analysis, and Social Planning. 255 pp.*

Remmling, Gunter W. (Ed.) Towards the Sociology of Knowledge. *Origin and Development of a Sociological Thought Style. 463 pp.*

Stark, Werner. The Sociology of Knowledge: *An Essay in Aid of a Deeper Understanding of the History of Ideas. 384 pp.*

URBAN SOCIOLOGY

Ashworth, William. The Genesis of Modern British Town Planning: *A Study in Economic and Social History of the Nineteenth and Twentieth Centuries. 288 pp.*

Cullingworth, J. B. Housing Needs and Planning Policy: *A Restatement of the Problems of Housing Need and 'Overspill' in England and Wales. 232 pp. 44 tables. 8 maps.*

Dickinson, Robert E. City and Region: *A Geographical Interpretation 608 pp. 125 figures.*

The West European City: *A Geographical Ínterpretation. 600 pp. 129 maps. 29 plates.*

● The City Region in Western Europe. *320 pp. Maps.*

Humphreys, Alexander J. New Dubliners: *Urbanization and the Irish Family. Foreword by George C. Homans. 304 pp.*

Jackson, Brian. Working Class Community: *Some General Notions raised by a Series of Studies in Northern England. 192 pp.*

Jennings, Hilda. Societies in the Making: *a Study of Development and Re-development within a County Borough. Foreword by D. A. Clark. 286 pp.*

●**Mann, P. H.** An Approach to Urban Sociology. *240 pp.*

Morris, R. N., and **Mogey, J.** The Sociology of Housing. *Studies at Berinsfield. 232 pp. 4 pp. plates.*

Rosser, C., and **Harris, C.** The Family and Social Change. *A Study of Family and Kinship in a South Wales Town. 352 pp. 8 maps.*

●**Stacey, Margaret, Batsone, Eric, Bell, Colin,** and **Thurcott, Anne.** Power, Persistence and Change. *A Second Study of Banbury. 196 pp.*

RURAL SOCIOLOGY

Haswell, M. R. The Economics of Development in Village India. *120 pp.*

Littlejohn, James. Westrigg: *the Sociology of a Cheviot Parish. 172 pp. 5 figures.*

Mayer, Adrian C. Peasants in the Pacific. *A Study of Fiji Indian Rural Society. 248 pp. 20 plates.*

Williams, W. M. The Sociology of an English Village: *Gosforth. 272 pp. 12 figures. 13 tables.*

SOCIOLOGY OF INDUSTRY AND DISTRIBUTION

Anderson, Nels. Work and Leisure. *280 pp.*

●**Blau, Peter M.,** and **Scott, W. Richard.** Formal Organizations: *a Comparative approach. Introduction and Additional Bibliography by J. H. Smith. 326 pp.*

Dunkerley, David. The Foreman. *Aspects of Task and Structure. 192 pp.*

Eldridge, J. E. T. Industrial Disputes. *Essays in the Sociology of Industrial Relations. 288 pp.*

Hetzler, Stanley. Applied Measures for Promoting Technological Growth. *352 pp.*

Technological Growth and Social Change. *Achieving Modernization. 269 pp.*

Hollowell, Peter G. The Lorry Driver. *272 pp.*

●**Oxaal, I., Barnett, T.,** and **Booth, D.** (Eds). Beyond the Sociology of Development. *Economy and Society in Latin America and Africa. 295 pp.*

Smelser, Neil J. Social Change in the Industrial Revolution: *An Application of Theory to the Lancashire Cotton Industry, 1770–1840. 468 pp. 12 figures. 14 tables.*

ANTHROPOLOGY

Ammar, Hamed. Growing up in an Egyptian Village: *Silwa, Province of Aswan. 336 pp.*

Brandel-Syrier, Mia. Reeftown Elite. *A Study of Social Mobility in a Modern African Community on the Reef. 376 pp.*

Dickie-Clark, H. F. The Marginal Situation. *A Sociological Study of a Coloured Group. 236 pp.*

Dube, S. C. Indian Village. *Foreword by Morris Edward Opler. 276 pp. 4 plates.*

India's Changing Villages: *Human Factors in Community Development. 260 pp. 8 plates. 1 map.*

Firth, Raymond. Malay Fishermen. *Their Peasant Economy. 420 pp. 17 pp. plates.*

Gulliver, P. H. Social Control in an African Society: a Study of the Arusha, Agricultural Masai of Northern Tanganyika. *320 pp. 8 plates. 10 figures.*

Family Herds. *288 pp.*

Ishwaran, K. Tradition and Economy in Village India: *An Interactionist Approach.*
Foreword by Conrad Arensburg. 176 pp.

Jarvie, Ian C. The Revolution in Anthropology. *268 pp.*

Little, Kenneth L. Mende of Sierra Leone. *308 pp. and folder.*

Negroes in Britain. *With a New Introduction and Contemporary Study by Leonard Bloom. 320 pp.*

Lowie, Robert H. Social Organization. *494 pp.*

Mayer, A. C. Peasants in the Pacific. *A Study of Fiji Indian Rural Society. 248 pp.*

Meer, Fatima. Race and Suicide in South Africa. *325 pp.*

Smith, Raymond T. The Negro Family in British Guiana: *Family Structure and Social Status in the Villages. With a Foreword by Meyer Fortes. 314 pp. 8 plates. 1 figure. 4 maps.*

Smooha, Sammy. Israel: Pluralism and Conflict. *About 320 pp.*

SOCIOLOGY AND PHILOSOPHY

Barnsley, John H. The Social Reality of Ethics. *A Comparative Analysis of Moral Codes. 448 pp.*

Diesing, Paul. Patterns of Discovery in the Social Sciences. *362 pp.*

●**Douglas, Jack D.** (Ed.) Understanding Everyday Life. *Toward the Reconstruction of Sociological Knowledge. Contributions by Alan F. Blum. Aaron W. Cicourel, Norman K. Denzin, Jack D. Douglas, John Heeren, Peter McHugh, Peter K. Manning, Melvin Power, Matthew Speier, Roy Turner, D. Lawrence Wieder, Thomas P. Wilson and Don H. Zimmerman. 370 pp.*

Gorman, Robert A. The Dual Vision. *Alfred Schutz and the Myth of Phenomenological Social Science. About 300 pp.*

Jarvie, Ian C. Concepts and Society. *216 pp.*

●**Pelz, Werner.** The Scope of Understanding in Sociology. *Towards a more radical reorientation in the social humanistic sciences. 283 pp.*

Roche, Maurice. Phenomenology, Language and the Social Sciences. *371 pp.*

Sahay, Arun. Sociological Analysis. *212 pp.*

Sklair, Leslie. The Sociology of Progress. *320 pp.*

Slater, P. Origin and Significance of the Frankfurt School. *A Marxist Perspective. About 192 pp.*

Smart, Barry. Sociology, Phenomenology and Marxian Analysis. *A Critical Discussion of the Theory and Practice of a Science of Society. 220 pp.*

International Library of Anthropology

General Editor Adam Kuper

Ahmed, A. S. Millenium and Charisma Among Pathans. *A Critical Essay in Social Anthropology. 192 pp.*

Brown, Paula. The Chimbu. *A Study of Change in the New Guinea Highlands. 151 pp.*

Gudeman, Stephen. Relationships, Residence and the Individual. *A Rural Panamanian Community. 288 pp. 11 Plates, 5 Figures, 2 Maps, 10 Tables.*

Hamnett, Ian. Chieftainship and Legitimacy. *An Anthropological Study of Executive Law in Lesotho. 163 pp.*

Hanson, F. Allan. Meaning in Culture. *127 pp.*

Lloyd, P. C. Power and Independence. *Urban Africans' Perception of Social Inequality. 264 pp.*

Pettigrew, Joyce. Robber Noblemen. *A Study of the Political System of the Sikh Jats. 284 pp.*
Street, Brian V. The Savage in Literature. *Representations of 'Primitive' Society in English Fiction, 1858–1920. 207 pp.*
Van Den Berghe, Pierre L. Power and Privilege at an African University. *278 pp.*

International Library of Social Policy

General Editor Kathleen Jones

Bayley, M. Mental Handicap and Community Care. *426 pp.*
Bottoms, A. E., and **McClean, J. D.** Defendants in the Criminal Process. *284 pp.*
Butler, J. R. Family Doctors and Public Policy. *208 pp.*
Davies, Martin. Prisoners of Society. *Attitudes and Aftercare. 204 pp.*
Gittus, Elizabeth. Flats, Families and the Under-Fives. *285 pp.*
Holman, Robert. Trading in Children. *A Study of Private Fostering. 355 pp.*
Jones, Howard, and **Cornes, Paul.** Open Prisons. *About 248 pp.*
Jones, Kathleen. History of the Mental Health Service. *428 pp.*
Jones, Kathleen, with **Brown, John, Cunningham, W. J., Roberts, Julian,** and **Williams, Peter.** Opening the Door. *A Study of New Policies for the Mentally Handicapped. 278 pp.*
Karn, Valerie. Retiring to the Seaside. *About 280 pp. 2 maps. Numerous tables.*
Thomas, J. E. The English Prison Officer since 1850: *A Study in Conflict. 258 pp.*
Walton, R. G. Women in Social Work. *303 pp.*
Woodward, J. To Do the Sick No Harm. *A Study of the British Voluntary Hospital System to 1875. 221 pp.*

International Library of Welfare and Philosophy

General Editors Noel Timms and David Watson

● **Plant, Raymond.** Community and Ideology. *104 pp.*

● **McDermott, F. E.** (Ed.) Self-Determination in Social Work. *A Collection of Essays on Self-determination and Related Concepts by Philosophers and Social Work Theorists. Contributors: F. P. Biestek, S. Bernstein, A. Keith-Lucas, D. Sayer, H. H. Perelman, C. Whittington, R. F. Stalley, F. E. McDermott, I. Berlin, H. J. McCloskey, H. L. A. Hart, J. Wilson, A. I. Melden, S. I. Benn. 254 pp.*
Ragg, Nicholas M. People Not Cases. *A Philosophical Approach to Social Work. About 250 pp.*

● **Timms, Noel,** and **Watson, David** (Eds). Talking About Welfare. *Readings in Philosophy and Social Policy. Contributors: T. H. Marshall, R. B. Brandt, G. H. von Wright, K. Nielsen, M. Cranston, R. M. Titmuss, R. S. Downie, E. Telfer, D. Donnison, J. Benson, P. Leonard, A. Keith-Lucas, D. Walsh, I. T. Ramsey. 320 pp.*

Primary Socialization, Language and Education

General Editor Basil Bernstein

Adlam, Diana S., *with the assistance of Geoffrey Turner and Lesley Lineker.* Code in Context. *About 272 pp.*

Bernstein, Basil. Class, Codes and Control. *3 volumes.*
   1. *Theoretical Studies Towards a Sociology of Language. 254 pp.*
   2. *Applied Studies Towards a Sociology of Language. 377 pp.*
● 3. *Towards a Theory of Educatiomal Transmission. 167 pp.*

Brandis, W., and **Bernstein, B.** Selection and Control. *176 pp.*

Brandis, Walter, and **Henderson, Dorothy.** Social Class, Language and Communication. *288 pp.*

Cook-Gumperz, Jenny. Social Control and Socialization. *A Study of Class Differences in the Language of Maternal Control. 290 pp.*

● **Gahagan, D. M.,** and **G. A.** Talk Reform. *Exploration in Language for Infant School Children. 160 pp.*

Hawkins, P. R. Social Class, the Nominal Group and Verbal Strategies. *About 220 pp.*

Robinson, W. P., and **Rackstraw, Susan D. A.** A Question of Answers. *2 volumes. 192 pp. and 180 pp.*

Turner, Geoffrey J., and **Mohan, Bernard A.** A Linguistic Description and Computer Programme for Children's Speech. *208 pp.*

Reports of the Institute of Community Studies

● **Cartwright, Ann.** Parents and Family Planning Services. *306 pp.*
   Patients and their Doctors. *A Study of General Practice. 304 pp.*

Dench, Geoff. Maltese in London. *A Case-study in the Erosion of Ethnic Consciousness. 302 pp.*

● **Jackson, Brian.** Streaming: *an Education System in Miniature. 168 pp.*

Jackson, Brian, and **Marsden, Dennis.** Education and the Working Class: *Some General Themes raised by a Study of 88 Working-class Children in a Northern Industrial City. 268 pp. 2 folders.*

Marris, Peter. The Experience of Higher Education. *232 pp. 27 tables.*
   Loss and Change. *192 pp.*

Marris, Peter, and **Rein, Martin.** Dilemmas of Social Reform. *Poverty and Community Action in the United States. 256 pp.*

Marris, Peter, and Somerset, Anthony. African Businessmen. *A Study of Entrepreneurship and Development in Kenya. 256 pp.*
Mills, Richard. Young Outsiders: *a Study in Alternative Communities. 216 pp.*
Runciman, W. G. Relative Deprivation and Social Justice. *A Study of Attitudes to Social Inequality in Twentieth-Century England. 352 pp.*
Willmott, Peter. Adolescent Boys in East London. *230 pp.*
Willmott, Peter, and Young, Michael. Family and Class in a London Suburb. *202 pp. 47 tables.*
Young, Michael. Innovation and Research in Education. *192 pp.*
●Young, Michael, and McGeeney, Patrick. Learning Begins at Home. *A Study of a Junior School and its Parents. 128 pp.*
Young, Michael, and Willmott, Peter. Family and Kinship in East London. *Foreword by Richard M. Titmuss. 252 pp. 39 tables.*
The Symmetrical Family. *410 pp.*

Reports of the Institute for Social Studies in Medical Care

Cartwright, Ann, Hockey, Lisbeth, and Anderson, John L. Life Before Death. *310 pp.*
Dunnell, Karen, and Cartwright, Ann. Medicine Takers, Prescribers and Hoarders. *190 pp.*

Medicine, Illness and Society

General Editor W. M. Williams

Robinson, David. The Process of Becoming Ill. *142 pp.*
Stacey, Margaret, *et al.* Hospitals, Children and Their Families. *The Report of a Pilot Study. 202 pp.*
Stimson, G. V., and Webb, B. Going to See the Doctor. *The Consultation Process in General Practice. 155 pp.*

Monographs in Social Theory

General Editor Arthur Brittan

●Barnes, B. Scientific Knowledge and Sociological Theory. *192 pp.*
Bauman, Zygmunt. Culture as Praxis. *204 pp.*
●Dixon, Keith. Sociological Theory. *Pretence and Possibility. 142 pp.*
Meltzer, B. N., Petras, J. W., and Reynolds, L. T. Symbolic Interactionism. *Genesis, Varieties and Criticisms. 144 pp.*
●Smith, Anthony D. The Concept of Social Change. *A Critique of the Functionalist Theory of Social Change. 208 pp.*

Routledge Social Science Journals

The British Journal of Sociology. *Editor – Angus Stewart; Associate Editor – Leslie Sklair. Vol. 1, No. 1 – March 1950 and Quarterly. Roy. 8vo. All back issues available. An international journal publishing original papers in the field of sociology and related areas.*

Community Work. *Edited by David Jones and Marjorie Mayo. 1973. Published annually.*

Economy and Society. *Vol. 1, No. 1. February 1972 and Quarterly. Metric Roy. 8vo. A journal for all social scientists covering sociology, philosophy, anthropology, economics and history. All back numbers available.*

Religion. Journal of Religion and Religions. *Chairman of Editorial Board, Ninian Smart. Vol. 1, No. 1, Spring 1971. A journal with an inter-disciplinary approach to the study of the phenomena of religion. All back numbers available.*

Year Book of Social Policy in Britain, The. *Edited by Kathleen Jones. 1971. Published annually.*

Social and Psychological Aspects of Medical Practice

Editor   Trevor Silverstone

Lader, Malcolm. Psychophysiology of Mental Illness. *280 pp.*

● **Silverstone, Trevor,** and **Turner, Paul.** Drug Treatment in Psychiatry. *232 pp.*

Printed in Great Britain by Unwin Brothers Limited
The Gresham Press Old Woking Surrey
A member of the Staples Printing Group